THE CODES OF THE CONSTITUTION

This book describes an astounding feat of constitutional writing and publication. For a number of decades, officials working across different branches of the United Kingdom (UK) constitution have been engaged in a series of separate projects. Taken in their totality they amount to a vast enterprise. Yet, until now, no one has fully recognised or critically analysed what has taken place. There has been a proliferation in the UK of publicly available codes, normally lacking a basis in statute, providing official accounts of a variety of different features of UK constitutional rules and principles. They cover institutions ranging from the Cabinet to the Civil Service to the judiciary, and relationships between entities such as central government and the devolved executives; and between the UK executive and the Westminster Parliament. Among them are prominent texts such as the *Ministerial Code*, *The Cabinet Manual* and the devolution *Memorandum of Understanding*—as well as more obscure documents that nonetheless contain important stipulations regarding the operation of the system. Similar developments have taken place in countries including Australia, Canada and New Zealand. The author explores the history of this phenomenon in the UK, how it functions today here and elsewhere in the Commonwealth, and its implications for the UK constitution.

Volume 6 in the series Hart Studies in Constitutional Law

Hart Studies in Constitutional Law

Volume 1 The House of Lords 1911–2011: A Century of Non-Reform
Chris Ballinger

Volume 2 Parliament and the Law
Edited by Alexander Horne, Gavin Drewry and Dawn Oliver

Volume 3 Law in Politics, Politics in Law
Edited by David Feldman

Volume 4 Parliamentary Sovereignty in the UK Constitution
Michael Gordon

Volume 5 Parliament: Legislation and Accountability
Edited by Alexander Horne and Andrew Le Sueur

The Codes of the Constitution

Andrew Blick

• H A R T •
OXFORD • LONDON • NEW YORK • NEW DELHI • SYDNEY

HART PUBLISHING
Bloomsbury Publishing Plc
Kemp House, Chawley Park, Cumnor Hill, Oxford, OX2 9PH, UK

HART PUBLISHING, the Hart/Stag logo, BLOOMSBURY and the Diana logo are trademarks of Bloomsbury Publishing Plc
First published in Great Britain 2016

First published in hardback, 2016
Paperback edition, 2019

A catalogue record for this book is available from the British Library.

Library of Congress Cataloging-in-Publication Data

Names: Blick, Andrew, author.

Title: The codes of the constitution / Andrew Blick.

Description: Oxford ; Portland, OR : Hart Publishing, 2016. | Series: Hart studies in constitutional law ; volume 6 | Includes bibliographical references and index.

Identifiers: LCCN 2016019862 (print) | LCCN 2016020003 (ebook) | ISBN 9781849466813 (hardback : alk. paper) | ISBN 9781509904105 (Epub)

Subjects: LCSH: Constitutional law—Great Britain—Codification. | Constitutional history—Great Britain. | Great Britain—Politics and government.

Classification: LCC KD3989 .B553 2016 (print) | LCC KD3989 (ebook) | DDC 342.41—dc23

LC record available at https://lccn.loc.gov/2016019862

ISBN: HB: 978-1-84946-681-3
PB: 978-1-50992-681-7
ePDF: 978-1-50990-409-9
ePub: 978-1-50990-410-5

Typeset by Compuscript Ltd, Shannon

To find out more about our authors and books visit www.hartpublishing.co.uk. Here you will find extracts, author information, details of forthcoming events and the option to sign up for our newsletters.

For Frederick, George and Nicola

Acknowledgements

As always, this book owes much to others. While all of the following must share in the credit for any of its strengths, blame for its defects rests with myself. Professor Peter Hennessy, now Lord Hennessy of Nympsfield, first ignited my interest in the codes of the constitution during my time as an MA and then PhD student in contemporary history at Queen Mary, University of London, during the late 1990s and early 2000s. I was also fortunate enough to write a pamphlet with him for the Institute of Public Policy Research in 2011, about *The Cabinet Manual* when it was in draft form, commissioned by Guy Lodge. At King's College London, Professor Robert Blackburn and I were the recipients of a grant from the Nuffield Foundation that made possible extended study of the *Manual* and other documents. Anthony Tomei, then Director of the Foundation, was particularly helpful. This book is an output of that project.

Others who have helped me during the conception and execution of this work include my colleagues at the Institute of Contemporary British History, King's College London; History & Policy; Professor George Jones; Professor Vernon Bogdanor; Graham Allen; Giles Radice; Nat le Roux and The Constitution Society; Brendan Donnelly and the Federal Trust for Education and Research; and Sean Kippin and Democratic Audit. My family members—Frederick Blick, George Blick, Nicola Blick, Karen Blick, Katharine Blick and Robin Blick—each contributed in their own ways.

Once again the team at Hart Publishing including Mel Hamill, Tom Adams and Emily Braggins, excelled in their support for my efforts, as did Catherine Minahan as copy editor.

Andrew Blick
Acton, London
April 2016

Contents

Part Two: The Content of Codes

Introduction

THIS IS A book about rules, writing and power. It involves an heroic—though not faultless—collective endeavour. For many decades a largely unacknowledged but nonetheless significant constitutional process has been taking place in the United Kingdom (UK). The executive in Whitehall has been the primary participant, but other institutions, including Parliament and the judiciary, have been involved. No entry in the canon they have created is a masterpiece of language, and the style employed is often deliberately flat. But taken as a whole, this body of work amounts to a literary project of breathtaking scale, scope and complexity. It has entailed the writing down in official documents of governmental principles, rules and practices that in many cases were not previously recorded in this way. This tendency matters, because it engages important operational features of our constitutional system and the values underpinning it. The texts in question are likely to have an impact upon the environment in which they operate. It is possible to raise questions about their legitimacy, about their content, and about how they were written and by whom. But it is safe to assume that the drafting and use of these documents is not about to end.

For the purposes of this book, I use the word 'codification' to describe this process. I do so partly because some of the most important of these texts have the word 'code' in their titles—for instance, the *Civil Service Code* and the *Ministerial Code*. However, a careful definition of terms is required—and encourages a useful discussion of the subject matter. Codification as I employ it here differs from the more conventional sense. Jeremy Bentham is credited as coining the word.[1] As a concept it clearly long pre-dates him. In the Ancient world we can look to examples such as the law code of the Babylonian king, Hammurabi, dating to the second millennium BCE, or the 12 tables of Rome from the fifth century BCE. In English history there is a series of Anglo-Saxon law codes, beginning with that of Ethelbert of Kent around the beginning of the seventh century; and in the post-Conquest era more followed, the most famous of which is the text known as *Magna Carta*, first agreed in 1215.[2] Bentham attached the specific term 'codification' to the project he developed from the late eighteenth century onwards for the explicit rationalisation of all law into a single instrument.[3] It became a powerful influence on the

[1] D Alfange Jr ,'Jeremy Bentham and the Codification of Law', *Cornell Law Review*, 55(1), November 1969, 77.

[2] A Blick, *Beyond Magna Carta: a constitution for the United Kingdom* (Oxford, Hart Publishing, 2015), chs 2–3.

[3] Alfange Jr, above n 1.

Victorian practice of consolidation acts, supplanting a mass of earlier law deemed to have become inefficient and anachronistic. We can interpret codification in this form as relating to 'hard' law, enacted by legislatures and enforceable by the courts, with the possibility of material penalties for non-compliance.

However, I use the term differently here. Many of the most important constitutional stipulations contained in the texts with which this book is concerned do not have direct legal force, and are known as 'conventions'. Codification of Benthamite derivation is difficult to reconcile with these types of provisions, as the parliamentary Joint Committee on Conventions found in 2006. The Committee was set up to assess 'the practicality of codifying the key conventions on the relationship between' the House of Lords and the House of Commons, while accepting the 'primacy' of the latter chamber over the former. However, it displayed reluctance regarding fulfilment of its own terms of reference. The Committee came to the view that 'the word "codification" is unhelpful' since it was generally interpreted as entailing 'rule-making, with definitions and enforcement mechanisms'. A convention was, conversely, 'unenforceable'. Consequently, the idea that a convention could be codified was 'a contradiction in terms'. An effort to do so would 'raise issues of definition, reduce flexibility and inhibit the capacity to evolve'. Furthermore it could potentially generate a requirement for 'adjudication' through the judiciary or a newly-established entity given this role. Such a practice would not be possible to reconcile with 'parliamentary sovereignty'. It would also create confusion and procrastination in the work of Parliament. For these reasons, the Committee argued, codification might be a source of division between the two Houses of Parliament rather than of more harmonious interaction.[4]

Yet it is possible to discern a variety of codification different from that identified by the Joint Committee in 2006. It has similarities to the first type of codification, in that it involves the compilation in a single text of official status a series of stipulations, often for such purposes as transparency, clarity and rationalisation. But an important difference is that such texts do not possess 'hard' legal force, and are not a definitive source for any kind of obligation or rule, since they purport to describe rather than create (though in practice they may play a part in determining the existence and form of obligations and rules). To suppose that these texts inevitably lack any kind of legal status would be mistaken. It is even plausible that courts may one day come to make regular use of them, and the issues identified by the Joint Committee could come into play. But it is currently possible to apply to these texts the label 'soft law', which differentiates them from the 'hard' variety and suggests we are dealing with two species that—if not entirely removed—are distinct from each other.[5] (I also distinguish codes here from the law and custom of Parliament, rules that are enforceable by parliamentary authorities.)

[4] House of Lords/House of Commons Joint Committee on Conventions, *Conventions of the UK Parliament* (2005–06, HL 265-I, HC 1212-I) 70–71.

[5] For a discussion of codes as a species of 'soft law', see D Oliver, *Constitutional Guardians: the House of Lords* (London, The Constitution Society, 2015) 16–20.

The impact these codes wield is at present primarily one of political influence, rather than 'hard' legal compulsion. Grant Duncan, in an assessment of the New Zealand *Cabinet Manual* that provided proximate inspiration for the equivalent text in the UK (a core document for present purposes), notes that 'In the strictly *legal* sense … the New Zealand Cabinet Manual is not a codification of convention. It is a written description of … the current understanding of constitutional conventions in New Zealand'. Yet—as Grant acknowledges—whatever the exact legal status, the *Manual* is 'a politically *authoritative* description, formally adopted by successive cabinets'.[6]

Most of the texts I encompass within 'codification' as I employ it have no statutory basis. However, some of them—in particular those pertaining to the Civil Service—have lately come to be issued under the authority of a parent Act (namely the Constitutional Reform and Governance Act 2010). But because the documents that now have a grounding in an Act of Parliament previously existed without this connection, I treat them as still within the broad phenomenon I address. Indeed, it could be that statutory foundation will—and perhaps even should—be extended to more codes in future. But we have not yet reached this position. Moreover, there is a difference between a set of rules written into an Act of Parliament and those that an Act simply requires to be issued (or authorises the introduction of), perhaps making some minimum stipulations for their content, as is the case with the Constitutional Reform and Governance Act 2010.

The codes I consider have been issued by constitutional branches including the UK executive, the Westminster Parliament and the judiciary. Some of them involve agreements between different institutions, in particular the UK and the devolved administrations. They engage issues including Cabinet government, the Civil Service, the legislative process, accountability to Parliament, devolution and the judiciary. I have deliberately concentrated on texts that have a UK-wide dimension to them, and have omitted those documents that operate only at sub-UK level, such as ministerial codes applying to devolved administrations. This book also considers texts from other countries, especially Australia, Canada and New Zealand, that are equivalent to those included from the UK. Though the task involves a degree of arbitrary judgement, in all documents analysed here I have set out to consider those portions of them that are of substantial constitutional importance, and to avoid engaging excessively in any less significant detail they may contain. I have also tended to focus less on simple descriptions of statutory regulations, concentrating on accounts of more amorphous arrangements, such as those that are the subject of conventions and other understandings.

Events during the closing months of 2015 provided evidence of the significance of codification as defined in this book. In October, following the General Election in May (won by the Conservative Party), the new edition of the *Ministerial Code* appeared. The opening passage of the previous edition had referred to 'the

[6] G Duncan, 'New Zealand's Cabinet Manual: How Does It Shape Constitutional Conventions?', *Parliamentary Affairs*, Advance Access published 6 November 2014, 1–20, 4.

overarching duty on Ministers to comply with the law including international law and treaty obligations and to uphold the administration of justice and to protect the integrity of public life'.[7] But this sentence was reworded in 2015 to describe 'the overarching duty on Ministers to comply with the law and to protect the integrity of public life'.[8] The reference to the need to adhere to 'international law and treaty obligations and to uphold the administration of justice' had vanished. Widespread protests followed from the Opposition and within the legal community, with claims made that the change amounted to an attack on the international rule of law. Why had it come about and what did it mean? A Conservative Party policy document of the previous year had stated—in setting out a wider package of proposed alterations to the way in which the UK adhered to the European Convention on Human Rights—that '[w]e will amend the Ministerial Code to remove any ambiguity in the current rules about the duty of Ministers to follow the will of Parliament in the UK'.[9] Perhaps the alteration in the 2015 text was a fulfilment of this pledge. Paul Jenkins, until recently the head of the government legal service, told the press that the previous wording had induced 'intense irritation' on the part of the Prime Minister, who had ultimate responsibility for the content of the *Ministerial Code*.[10] However, a Cabinet Office spokesperson insisted that the wording was merely 'simplified' and that existing obligations remained in force. Nonetheless, a campaign organisation, Rights Watch UK, announced that it was coordinating a legal challenge to the decision.[11] It was not clear how this plan to seek redress through the courts would work in practice.

Another modification in the Code as between the 2010 and 2015 editions did not receive the same level of publicity. In 2010 it had proved necessary—as a consequence of the formation of a Conservative-Liberal Democrat coalition—to include a special stipulation qualifying the longstanding constitutional principle that all Cabinet members maintain a united front in public around collective decisions, whatever their private views expressed in internal discussions might be. Paragraph 1.2a of the 2010 Code read, '[t]he principle of collective responsibility, *save where it is explicitly set aside*, applies to all Government Ministers' (emphasis added). In 2015 paragraph 1.2a stated baldly that '[t]he principle of collective responsibility applies to all Government Ministers'. The return to what might be regarded as the normality of single-party government had facilitated the removal of the specific reference to the possibility of the suspension of the default rule. But simply changing the wording would not prevent pressure from some quarters

[7] Cabinet Office, *Ministerial Code* (Cabinet Office, London, 2010) para 1.2.

[8] Cabinet Office, *Ministerial Code* (Cabinet Office, London, 2015) para 1.2.

[9] Conservative Party, *Protecting Human Rights in the UK: The Conservative Proposals for Changing Britain's Human Rights Law* (Conservative Party, London, 2014) 7.

[10] J Halliday, 'Ministerial code: No 10 "Showing contempt for international law"', *Guardian*, 26 October 2015.

[11] ibid.

for ministers to be allowed to take different public lines regarding a forthcoming event over which there was likely to be significant dissent within the Conservative Party, that is the referendum on membership of the European Union. Early in 2016, the Prime Minister, David Cameron, conceded that he would allow open dissent over this matter.[12]

There was further controversy with a connection to codification. In November 2015, leaked correspondence showed that Cameron had written to councillors from his parliamentary constituency in Witney, offering them the advice of No 10 staff on the implementation of spending retrenchment. The Labour Party wrote to the Cabinet Secretary, Sir Jeremy Heywood, raising the question of whether there had been a violation of the *Ministerial Code*.[13] Labour had in mind the principle stated in paragraph 6.1 that 'Ministers are provided with facilities at Government expense to enable them to carry out their official duties. These facilities should not generally be used for Party or constituency activities.' However, whatever the possible merits of the case, other stipulations contained in the Code surely made it clear that the complaint had no chance of success. Paragraph 1.3 described how '[i]t is not the role of the Cabinet Secretary or other officials to enforce the Code'. In circumstances of 'an allegation about a breach of the Code' it fell to the Prime Minister, 'having consulted the Cabinet Secretary', to decide whether or not to refer the matter on to the 'independent adviser on Ministers' interests'. Moreover, as paragraph 1.5 iterated, it was the premier who was 'the ultimate judge of the standards of behaviour expected of a Minister and the appropriate consequences of a breach of those standards'. Cameron was his own umpire in this instance.

Finally, in December 2015, codification as an historic process proved its significance. After a prolonged legal struggle, the 1992 edition of a document called the *Precedent Book* was released into the public domain under the Freedom of Information Act 2000. Media attention focused on the stipulation it contained that the Prince of Wales, in addition to the Queen, should receive Cabinet papers. But the 200 pages of text provided a far wider range of detail regarding the inner workings of central government in the UK. The release of the text occasioned criticism that it had been held back for so long, and complaints that it was not appropriate for the Prince to have access to the information he was receiving.[14]

Codification has not until now received the full appreciation it warrants. But as the incidents described above demonstrate, it can frequently achieve political piquancy. They raise a number of issues that recur during this work, concerning the significance of these texts in what they say—and *do not* say; their legal status; and the importance of control over their drafting and their enforcement. While for some codification may imply the compilation of rules that already exist, this act is

[12] 'EU Referendum: ministers will be able to campaign for either side', *BBC News* website, 5 January 2016, at <http://www.bbc.co.uk/news/uk-politics-eu-referendum-35230959>.

[13] M Dathan, 'David Cameron accused of breaking ministerial code in row with his local council over cuts to frontline services', *Independent*, 12 November 2015.

[14] R Booth, 'Revealed: Prince Charles has received confidential cabinet papers for decades', *Guardian*, 15 December 2015.

not as easy to separate from the bringing about of change as might be supposed. Whether or not these texts are present in the public domain is also important; and codification is clearly a process with a past, one moreover that can—as in the case of the *Precedent Book*—become live many years after a text was first issued.

These are documents of many layers. At times they can appear superficial. In February 2011, Lord Powell of Bayswater, formerly foreign affairs private secretary at No 10 under Margaret Thatcher, took part in a parliamentary evidence session investigating *The Cabinet Manual*, a code that existed in draft form at the time. Powell described the text as 'a bit of a Janet and John guide to the Queen and so on … it is almost like a guidebook for foreign tourists'.[15] Certainly, the document in its final version[16] contains some statements that seem far from revelatory, or simply bland and unimportant. For instance, paragraph 1.3 tells us that '[a]s Head of State, the Sovereign undertakes and hosts a number of state visits, helping to build relations with other nations'; while paragraph 2.1 states, 'General elections allow voters on the electoral roll to cast their ballot for an MP to represent them in the House of Commons.' Another example of stating the obvious comes in paragraph 3.9: 'The most senior ministers in the Government are the members of Cabinet.' Paragraph 3.20 of the manual reads, 'Where a minister resigns their post by writing to the Prime Minister, it is often the case that the exchange of letters is published.' 'Scrutiny of the Executive', the reader of paragraph 5.11 learns, 'is one of the core functions of Parliament'; while paragraph 5.31 explains that 'The Budget, which sets out the Government's taxation plans, is delivered by the Chancellor of the Exchequer, usually in March.'

But the Janet and John characterisation has its limits. Powell applied this description during an evidence session held by the House of Lords Select Committee on the Constitution, of which he was a member. The former Cabinet Secretary, Lord Wilson of Dinton, subsequently told the Committee that 'The point about Janet and John statements is that quite often, when they really come alive, there's much more to them than appears on the surface. Simple statements can prove to be very pregnant with implications.' It was right that the text of the *Manual*, Wilson felt, should be kept straightforward.[17] In this work, I seek to explore his 'implications'. An excellent example of how codes can act as a trigger for complex constitutional discussions comes with the 16-paragraph 'Introduction' to *The Cabinet Manual*. It provides a sweeping overview of the nature of the UK constitution, beginning by stating in paragraph 1:

> The UK is a Parliamentary democracy which has a constitutional sovereign as Head of State; a sovereign Parliament, which is supreme to all other government institutions,

[15] House of Lords Select Committee on the Constitution, *The Cabinet Manual* (HL 2010–11, 107) 15. The Janet and John books are simple primers, originating in the mid-twentieth century, for teaching English to young children.

[16] Cabinet Office, *The Cabinet Manual: A guide to laws, conventions and rules on the operation of government* (Cabinet Office, London, 2011).

[17] House of Lords Select Committee on the Constitution, above n 15, 17.

> consisting of Sovereign, the House of Commons and the House of Lords; an Executive drawn from and accountable to Parliament; and an independent judiciary.

The *Manual* was, at least in the mind of the Prime Minister who authorised its production, Gordon Brown, a possible first step towards a written constitution for the UK.[18] This passage performs a function we might associate with the preamble to such a document, giving an account of the core values of the text itself and the polity it serves. If the *Manual* were simply a guide for those responsible for operating the system, perhaps it might not require such a statement. Like a preamble, of necessity paragraph 1 is of a general rather than a precise character. A detailed inspection reveals much scope for nuanced consideration. One of its assertions in particular stands out: the reference to the existence of 'a sovereign Parliament, which is supreme to all other government institutions'. The doctrine of parliamentary sovereignty is a subject of controversy.[19] Disputes surround whether it is intellectually viable; whether—even if it has ever applied—it persists today; and whether it is desirable anyway.

Paragraph 3 elaborates on this version of parliamentary authority. It states:

> Parliament is sovereign and it has provided by Acts of Parliament—which by their nature, may be repealed—for certain issues to be considered and determined at different levels: within the European Union (EU); by the Devolved Administrations; and by local government.

This statement raises a number of difficulties. The first involves UK participation in the EU. It is an established proposition in courts at both EU and UK level that it is necessary to disapply Acts of Parliament in as far as they conflict with European law, even if the former post-date the latter (though it might be held that the source of authority for European law in the UK is itself an Act of Parliament, the European Communities Act 1972). Only a UK statute that explicitly stated its intention to apply regardless of European law as incorporated under the 1972 Act could achieve this objective: an implication is not sufficient. This legal rule contradicts a principle traditionally held central to parliamentary sovereignty: that an Act of Parliament overturns all that comes before it with which it conflicts, regardless of whether it does so expressly or only by implication. Simply possessing the ability to amend or repeal the European Communities Act 1972 does not—in some accounts—make Parliament sovereign, though in other versions of the doctrine the retention of this ultimate sanction is sufficient.

Secondly, the idea that the legislation providing for the 'Devolved Administrations' can be repealed surely now requires qualification. In the lead up to the Scottish Independence Referendum of September 2014, the leaders of the three largest parties in the Westminster Parliament signed up to a package of promises that

[18] A Blick and P Hennessy, *The Hidden Wiring Emerges: the Cabinet Manual and the working of the British constitution* (London, Institute for Public Policy Research, 2011) 12.

[19] J Goldsworthy, *Parliamentary Sovereignty: Contemporary Debates* (Cambridge, Cambridge University Press, 2010); V Bogdanor, 'Imprisoned by a doctrine: The modern defence of parliamentary sovereignty' (2012) 32:1 *OJLS* 179.

would apply if Scotland voted 'No'. Known as the 'Vow', it included a statement that the Scottish Parliament was 'permanent'. Following the work of the Smith Commission, the Government introduced the Scotland Bill in May 2015, stating in section 1 that both the Scottish Parliament and Government were 'recognised as a permanent part of the United Kingdom's constitutional arrangements'. In October 2015, the Draft Wales Bill proposed a similar provision for the National Assembly and Government of Wales. Such measures, once enacted, would nonetheless be, in theory, potentially subject to repeal through regular legislative procedures in the Westminster Parliament. Yet if a future edition of the *Manual* were wholly to retain its present wording in this area, and not somehow deal with these developments, it would risk appearing to contradict commitments made regarding devolution, and undermining their credibility.

Thirdly and lastly, the idea that Parliament 'provided' for 'local government' to consider 'certain issues' is historically misleading if perhaps technically correct. The powers, structure and organisation of local government as it exists now have a basis in statute. But beyond these particular and changing qualities, it is a system of self-rule that pre-dates (the English) Parliament, with (English) documentary reference to it extending back as far as the tenth century. To present local government as a creature of the Westminster legislature is to belittle it and deny it its proper place in the UK constitution as it has developed across millenniums, though such an account may be an accurate presentation of its current impoverished (in political as well as financial terms) condition.

The introduction to the *Manual* returns to parliamentary 'sovereignty' again in paragraph 9. It states that 'In the exercise of its legislative powers, Parliament is sovereign.' Yet 'In practice', the *Manual* goes on, 'Parliament has chosen to be constrained in various ways—through its Acts, and by elements of European and other international law.' This statement raises but does not resolve important philosophical questions pertaining to the parliamentary sovereignty doctrine. For instance, we might ask, what form of constraint is it that an institution can 'choose' and then presumably overturn if it wishes? This discussion takes us back to the previous debate about whether or not Parliament is 'sovereign' while its Acts are subject to European law. It would be possible to elaborate in immense detail, if space allowed. It is sufficient to note that one concept employed in the opening passages of a single code has provided ample illustration of the view advanced by Lord Wilson about the contents of these texts being 'pregnant with implications.'

As well as providing a basis for important constitutional discussion, codification has the potential to surprise. The following passage, found in the current edition of the Cabinet Office text *Guide to Making Legislation*,[20] is an explanation of the briefing that officials should provide to ministers taking bills through a Public Bill Committee in the Commons:

> [T]he bill team should clarify in advance what the minister wants: either a series of points set out crisply and clearly, in tolerably short sentences, for the minister to build into a

[20] Cabinet Office, *Guide to Making Legislation* (London, Cabinet Office, 2014).

> speech in their own way; or (as is more usual with any minister unfamiliar with the subject) a speaking note which he or she can simply deliver verbatim, adding only the conventional courtesies (which officials need not draft). There is, of course, a degree of risk with a speaking note drafted in advance: if when the amendment is proposed officials realise that they have missed the point, they will have to warn the minister somehow. (paragraph 30.71)

That the speeches of ministers can in no substantive sense be their own and little more than a script produced by others is not necessarily a revelation. But the public admission of this fact in an official document is startling. Further advice to officials contained in the *Guide* regarding the contribution of ministers to the legislative process is more notable for its substantive content and the insight it provides. The text warns that a court might, in seeking to interpret an Act of Parliament, utilise 'parliamentary material including ministerial speeches (from any stage of debate on the bill in either House, including debate in Committee)'. Consequently, officials must exercise especial caution in the texts that they draft for ministers. Ministers, the *Guide* goes on, should if necessary stall on providing an explanation of a provision when asked for one, offering to 'reflect on a point and reply on a future occasion'. We receive a further glimpse of the inner workings of our governmental system in the requirement that

> [t]he bill team and legal adviser should always review the Hansard record of ministers' contributions to a debate and consider whether there is any inaccuracy or other hostage to fortune. Where it is decided that the record needs to be corrected during the passage of the bill, this should be done at a time and in such a way that it would be clear to the courts in the future that Parliament was aware of the matter before passing the bill, and should be discussed with Parliamentary Counsel and the Government Whips' Offices. (p 171)

This passage suggests insecurity on the part of those working within Whitehall, and that they have a pervasive sense of the fallibility of ministers and of vulnerability to legal intervention. While codification can be an exercise of strength on the part of the UK executive, from this perspective it can also amount to a expression of weakness and of being subject to contingencies and external forces.

It is clear from this introductory discussion that codification provides much to consider. The purpose of this book is two-fold. The focus is on the texts themselves and the words contained within them. But as well as looking *at* codes, I seek to look *behind* them. Without doubt they contain within them valuable information, some of which we might not otherwise be able readily to obtain, about the UK constitution. This contribution is valuable. But they do not have the authority of full constitutional texts—and indeed they tend to deny any such status for themselves. Consequently it is apt to avoid treating them as literal statements of truth, and to assess them as what they are, and what they generally purport to be: attempts to describe what is—or in some cases, what should be—from a particular perspective. It is therefore apt to use the approach of the historian to sources when considering these texts. This methodology suggests a number of questions to pose. Who are the authors of these documents? What was their perspective and their motivation? How accurately does their work represent the reality they addressed?

What impact did these texts have? What do they tell us about the environment in which they appeared?

This is the first work to consider the phenomena it investigates specifically and in full. Some commentaries on the nature of the UK constitution have made reference to the growth of codes. For instance, the former Cabinet Secretary and Head of the Home Civil Service, Lord Wilson of Dinton, referred to it in a 2004 article based on a public lecture, but did not explore it in detail.[21] Peter Hennessy (now Lord Hennessy of Nympsfield) has discussed codification, including the acceleration of this trend during the 1990s, in his work on the office of Prime Minister.[22] Some UK constitutional textbooks include accounts of the contents of certain codes as part of their overall depictions of arrangements.[23] In an article from 2008, Aileen McHarg discussed the general significance of codifying conventions.[24] Nicholas Barber, in a 2010 book, considered the UK *Ministerial Code* in a discussion of the relationship between convention and law, and how a set of rules might transfer from inclusion within the former category to the latter.[25] I have also written an article assessing the implications of codification, taking the UK *Cabinet Manual* as a starting point.[26] Literature exists covering comparable processes in other countries, such as Australia.[27] A volume to which I contributed on conventions in Commonwealth countries contained a number of discussions of the codification trend in different territories.[28]

Authors have carried out studies of particular codes or groups of codes. Amy Baker produced in 2000 an account of the *Ministerial Code*—or as it was known before 1997, *Questions of Procedure for Ministers*.[29] This study focused in particular on the evolution of the text in question over time and its content. Richard Rawlings, in a journal article in 2000, provided a more theoretical focus in relation to the non-legal codification of devolution practices.[30] In an historical study of special advisers to ministers in the UK, I considered the development and importance of a number of codes with relevance to the Civil Service.[31] I have also written, with Peter Hennessy, the fullest assessment to date of the genesis and content

[21] Lord Wilson of Dinton, 'The Robustness of Conventions in a Time of Modernisation and Change' [2004] *Public Law* 207.

[22] P Hennessy, *The Prime Minister: the office and its holders since 1945* (London, Penguin, 2001).

[23] See, eg, AW Bradley, A and KD Ewing, *Constitutional and Administrative Law*, 15th edn (Harlow, Longman, 2011).

[24] A McHarg, 'Reforming the United Kingdom Constitution: Law, Convention, Soft Law' (2008) 71 *MLR* 853.

[25] NW Barber, *The Constitutional State* (Oxford, Oxford University Press, 2010).

[26] A Blick, 'The Cabinet Manual and the Codification of Conventions' (2014) 67(1) *Parliamentary Affairs* 191.

[27] C Sampford, '"Recognize and Declare": An Australian Experiment in Codifying Constitutional Conventions' (1987) 7 *OJLS* 369.

[28] B Galligan and S Brenton (eds), *Constitutional Conventions in Westminster Systems: Controversies, Changes and Challenges* (Cambridge University Press, Cambridge, 2015).

[29] A Baker, *Prime Ministers and the Rule Book* (London, Politico's, 2000).

[30] R Rawlings, 'Concordats of the Constitution' (2000) 116 *LQR* 257.

[31] A Blick, *People Who Live in the Dark: the history of the special adviser in British politics* (London, Methuen, 2004).

of *The Cabinet Manual*.[32] Lastly, a valuable source of information on many of the codes, used extensively here, is provided by briefing papers produced by the House of Commons Library. They are another example of texts initially intended for the internal purposes of an institution that have subsequently become available to the wider public, to great benefit.

Engaging with this literature, Part One of the book considers the phenomenon of codification from a number of perspectives. It begins with two chapters assessing the history of this tendency, and how it came about. There then follows a comparative assessment of codes in other countries, in particular Australia, Canada and New Zealand. The purpose is to establish how far similar trends have taken hold elsewhere, and what they reveal about the constitutions involved. A further chapter discusses the implications of codification for the UK constitution, in particular the role of conventions within it. Part Two is a snapshot of the codes in force at the time the book was being written, divided up according to the aspects of the constitution they address. It assesses the content of codes, their silence and the implications. While this portion of the work will search for wrinkles and assess the underlying philosophy, its central purpose is consider the body of codes as individually and collectively providing a constitutional infrastructure for the UK, and to consider the consequences for our understanding of the UK polity. It draws heavily on *The Cabinet Manual*, the most expansive of the texts to have emerged from codification, but extends substantially beyond it. The 'Conclusion' then makes an assessment of codification in the UK constitution, and discusses possible future developments.

Some qualifications and an acknowledgement are necessary. First, it has not been possible to write about every available code past and present, nor to assess in full all those that I have depicted. But the purpose is to at least give some idea of the body of texts that has appeared. Secondly, inevitably some of the editions I have used were or will be supplanted during the process of writing and producing the book, with newer versions than those referred to available by the time of publication. The importance of carrying out this work is greater than the need to avoid this complication. The central propositions made here hold. Thirdly, I only work with texts that exist in the public domain, either because they have been released as historic documents, or because they were intended for publication. The degree of openness surrounding these codes has expanded over time, sometimes to a surprising extent. Yet I know, partly through deduction, that there are other documents the contents and even the existence of which remain suppressed, some for good reason, others less justifiably. Fourthly, while I treat all the documents as though they matter as constitutional statements, it is not easy to tell how widely

[32] A Blick and P Hennessy, *The Hidden Wiring Emerges: the Cabinet Manual and the working of the British constitution* (London, Institute for Public Policy Research, 2011). For other work on *The Cabinet Manual* see, eg, Political and Constitutional Reform Committee, *Constitutional Implications of the Cabinet Manual*, vol I (London, Stationery Office, 2011). For an international comparison see, eg, from New Zealand, R Kitteridge, 'The Cabinet Manual: Evolution with Time', paper presented to the 8th Annual Public Law Forum, 20–21 March 2006.

read they have been among those to whom they are supposed to apply, or how closely their stipulations are followed. Impact upon the outside world is slightly easier to monitor, for instance through media coverage and parliamentary interest (particularly within select committees); and it is seemingly sometimes the existence—or merely the possibility—of such attention that elevates the importance of a text internally.

Fifthly, some of my criticism of the contents of the codes or the means by which they were produced may at times seem harsh. However, that these texts are able to stimulate discussion is a tribute to their achievement in engaging with serious matters that are core to our system of government. No perfect account would be attainable, and improvement is always possible over subsequent editions, if they are produced. Some of the publications, such as *The Cabinet Manual*, are impressive efforts. They were produced in relatively short periods of time when other issues must often have seemed more important, with the authors obliged to navigate the sensitivities that some of the subject matter must have raised, both within and outside the particular issuing institution. I therefore wish to put on record my gratitude to the largely nameless officials entrusted with producing these documents. Whether or not they knew it, they have contributed to an important constitutional construction. This avid reader of their output hopes to provide it with the recognition it deserves.

Part One

The Codification Phenomenon

1

Historic Origins of Codification

THE CODIFICATION PHENOMENON is historical in nature. It began to come about in the form described in this book from the First World War onwards, arising from a combination of different tendencies, each of which had its own time phase and pattern of development. To consider the historic gestation of the present codification environment, then, is a means of understanding the nature of this process in the contemporary UK. But what are these prerequisites to and drivers of codification we should assess? When did they appear? And how might we detect their impact both in earlier and in more recent times? An effective means of answering these questions is both to assess the tendencies underlying codification and to consider a variety of relevant texts themselves. The latter part of this task can also serve to demonstrate the value of these documents beyond their being manifestations of a particular official literary genre, and as sources providing insight into constitutional perceptions at given points in history.

Fundamental to any project for the writing down of rules is the ability to write. Literacy has existed in UK—or to be precise, English—governmental institutions at least since the early seventh century and the time of the law code of King Ethelbert of Kent. This text represents the first known use—by a considerable margin—of the English language in written form. Indeed it seems likely that more than the ability to write being a precondition for the production of this document, the desire to create the code spurred Ethelbert to bring about the creation of the written English language. After Ethelbert, subsequent Anglo-Saxon rulers continued to produce legal texts.[1] By the post-Conquest era, Latin was the language employed, however.

Describing principles and practices in writing is one feature of codification as defined in this book. Another, developing later, has been that increasingly they are made publicly available. While literacy may have existed among medieval royal officials and the clergy, more widely it was a rare skill. Furthermore the technology for mass dissemination of the written word was not as developed as it would later become. The printing press, for instance, did not appear in Europe until the fifteenth century; while the Internet and World Wide Web were inventions of the

[1] For the history of Anglo-Saxon law making, see P Wormald, *The Making of English Law: King Alfred to the Twelfth Century*, vol 1: *Legislation and Its Limits* (Oxford, Blackwell, 2001).

late twentieth.[2] Nonetheless, it was possible for scribes to produce multiple copies of documents for distribution to key locations such as cathedrals, as happened with the text now known as *Magna Carta*; and they could be read aloud to an illiterate public.

At the time that *Magna Carta* was first agreed, in 1215, Parliament did not exist.[3] Neither, therefore, did Acts of Parliament, let alone secondary legislation deriving its authority from parent Acts or codes issued under the authority of Acts. The differentiations made in this book between the legal status of different documents could not fully apply until the set of categories employed today became more clearly discernible. Only with this means of distinguishing texts could we conceive of official statements of rules that did not have direct legal force, lacking enforcement specifically through an Act of Parliament (though some of the codes considered, such as the *Civil Service Code*, are now issued under statutory authority). Codification should be understand historically in the context of a legal system that has become more sophisticated, within which different categories of instrument or text are possible and can be deployed to suit particular circumstances. However, whether the differentiation that the UK executive today hopes to maintain between texts that are and are not legally enforceable is sustainable remains to be seen, an issue considered more fully in Chapter 4.

I. PRECURSORS TO CODIFICATION

Despite the qualifications set out above, we should avoid imagining that codification as understood today is wholly new. The idea of writing down values, rules and practices is an ancient one. An example of an attempt to codify principles can be found in books of chivalry from medieval Europe. Though they might not be official in the sense that they were issued by a governmental body, they engage with the functions of what could be perceived as public offices. The most famous such text is *A Knight's Own Book of Chivalry*,[4] attributed to Geoffroi de Charney, a French knight who lived from about 1306 to 1356. He participated in the conflict now known as the 'Hundred Years War' (1337–1453), and was the earliest person recorded as in possession of the 'Shroud of Turin'. While his name is attached to the text, how directly involved he was in writing it is not certain—much in the way that in the contemporary era the Prime Minister or the Cabinet may sign off a document that is in practice largely the work of officials. A further similarity with the present codification trend is that the de Charney book reads as an attempt to bring together in a single, written document already existing understandings.

[2] For a work placing the printing press in historical perspective, see E Eisenstein, *The Printing Revolution in Early Modern Europe*, 2nd edn (Cambridge, Cambridge University Press, 2012).

[3] The definitive modern work is D Carpenter, *Magna Carta* (London, Penguin, 2015).

[4] G de Charny, *A Knight's Own Book of Chivalry*, trans E Kennedy (University of Pennsylvania Press, Philadelphia, Pa, 2005), 'Introduction' by RW Kaeuper.

The de Charney book deals with a range of issues, including ethical conduct, general principles of governance, and the characteristics of different groups, such as the knighthood, priesthood and monastic orders. It considers matters such as the types of advice that worthy men should give to others (paragraph 34), and how they should be recruited into particular groups (paragraphs 36–40). The book holds, for instance, that it is possible to join the monastic order at an age

> so young that one has no knowledge of sin nor of the world; those who enter at such an age are brought up in the order and should accept it more willingly; they should, therefore, conduct themselves better and adhere more closely to the rules of the religious order. (paragraph 38)

On the other hand, there are those who have spent time in the outside world and then

> want to enter a religious order, lightly and without being truly devout. Then it is very hard for them to keep to and follow the right paths and the precepts and rules to which religious [*sic*] are required to adhere, and they are very reluctant to do so.(paragraph 38)

These matters—the relationship between recruitment, propriety and the world beyond the institution concerned—remain important subjects in various texts today, such as those that regulate the Civil Service. These later documents might aspire to bring about the highest standards of conduct, and they can in the process become celebrated—as did the de Charney work. Yet how effective they are in practice is a different subject. The extent to which those to whom codes are supposed to apply actually adhere to them is another perennial concern.

Knights are still with us, though the title is honorific and does not denote the specific social role it once did. Some of the precursors to codification offer more direct continuity to the present. The Privy Council was formalised in the fifteenth century out of the inner group of advisers around the monarch. It remains a working body in the twenty-first century. Moreover, membership of the Council in itself has a practical use. All members of the Cabinet are required to take the Oath of a Privy Counsellor (the spelling used in *The Cabinet Manual* and other official present-day texts) to bind them to secrecy. A text of the Oath dating from 1570 (the source uses the spelling 'councillor' rather than 'counsellor') has survived. It stresses, among other stipulations, the importance of loyalty to Elizabeth, the then monarch, and that 'You shall keep secret all matters committed and revealed to you as her Majesty's councillor or that shall be treated of secretly in council.' A further commitment was mirrored consciously in later codes applying to civil servants. The oath taker is bound to 'give true, plain and faithful counsel at all times, with respect either of the cause of the person, laying apart all favour, meed, affection, and partiality'. This service is to be provided to the Queen, as well as to 'her heirs and lawful successors'.[5]

[5] 'The Oath of a Privy Councillor [*sic*], 1570', reproduced in JR Tanner, *Tudor Constitutional Documents: AD 1485–1603, with an historical commentary* (Cambridge at the University Press, 1930) 225. For the Tudor influence on Civil Service codification, see P Hennessy, *Whitehall* (London, Phoenix, 2001) 345.

For comparative purposes, the current version of *The Oath of a Privy Counsellor* reads as follows:

> You do swear by Almighty God to be a true and faithful Servant unto The Queen's Majesty as one of Her Majesty's Privy Council. You will not know or understand of any manner of thing to be attempted, done or spoken against Her Majesty's Person, Honour, Crown or Dignity Royal, but you will lett and withstand the same to the uttermost of your power, and either cause it to be revealed to Her Majesty Herself, or to such of Her Privy Council as shall advertise Her Majesty of the same. You will in all things to be moved, treated and debated in Council, faithfully and truly declare your Mind and Opinion, according to your Heart and Conscience; and will keep secret all matters committed and revealed unto you, or that shall be treated of secretly in Council. And if any of the said Treaties or Counsels shall touch any of the Counsellors you will not reveal it unto him but will keep the same until such time as, by the consent of Her Majesty or of the Council, Publication shall be made thereof. You will to your uttermost bear Faith and Allegiance to the Queen's Majesty; and will assist and defend all civil and temporal Jurisdictions, Pre-eminences, and Authorities, granted to Her Majesty and annexed to the Crown by Acts of Parliament, or otherwise, against all Foreign Princes, Persons, Prelates, States, or Potentates. And generally in all things you will do as a faithful and true Servant ought to do to Her Majesty.
>
> SO HELP YOU GOD

The linkages between the historic Privy Council and the current Cabinet extend beyond the use of an Oath. Part of the function of the Privy Council was as an executive decision-taking body, and it was in this sense a precursor to the Cabinet, an entity that developed from the late seventeenth century onwards and that is frequently described as a sub-committee of the Privy Council. Paragraph 1.14 of *The Cabinet Manual*,[6] for instance, states that 'Cabinet is the executive committee of the Privy Council'. Efforts to codify the practices and principles of Cabinet have their precursors in attempts to do the same for the Council. In 1553, Edward VI issued *A Method for the Proceedings in the Councils*, part of which he wrote out himself.[7] It listed the members of the Council, and then set out a series of subject-specific committees, and who would serve on them. A document issued in the same year sought to ensure that the Council functioned more effectively. It required members to seek permission before leaving court for more than two days (paragraph 9); it set a quorum of four (paragraph 10), with special procedural requirements to follow if there were fewer than six in attendance (paragraph 11). Paragraph 12 required that 'if there rise such matter of weight as it shall please the King's Majesty himself to be at the debating of, then warning shall be given, whereby the more may be at the debating of it'. A need to provide due notice to ensure meaningful discussion remains a concern for Cabinet and its committees.

[6] Cabinet Office, *The Cabinet Manual: A guide to the laws, conventions and rules on the operation of government* (Cabinet Office, London, 2011).

[7] 'A Method for the Proceedings in the Councils, 1553', reproduced in Tanner, above n 5, 221–23.

And recognising a reality that no doubt persists in Cabinet today, since the conduct of government relies on fallible human beings, the 1553 articles sought to deal with the limited attention span of Council members. They required:

> In matters that be long, tedious, and busy there may be appointed or chosen two or three, more or less as the case shall seem to require, to prepare, set forth, and make plain the things being less cumbrous and diffuse may the easilier be dispatcht. (paragraph 15)[8]

Though it has now been supplanted in importance by its supposed executive committee, the Cabinet, the Privy Council remains a subject of codification today. *The Cabinet Manual* describes how the Privy Council—convened under the ancient monarchical authority known as the Royal Prerogative—'advises' the head of state on the deployment of 'prerogative powers' and 'certain functions assigned' to the head of state and the Privy Council by Acts of Parliament. According to the *Manual* the Council is the means of achieving 'interdepartmental agreement' on those official activities that 'for historical reasons' are the responsibility of ministers not in their departmental roles but as Privy Counsellors (paragraph 1.10). The *Manual* goes on to outline the powers of the Privy Council. They include the ability to produce secondary and even primary legislation; to issue orders proroguing Parliament (paragraph 1.16); to oversee regulators and 'Chartered bodies' (paragraph 1.17); and to consent to 'Proclamations for new coinage' and some bank holidays (paragraph 1.18), all on a quorum of three (paragraph 1.15). The monarch is present, and ministers attend, for whom a summons to Privy Council takes priority over any other commitments (paragraph 1.16). So-called 'Privy Council terms' are a means by which government can communicate in confidence with senior members of the Opposition who are themselves Privy Counsellors (paragraph 1.12). The Council also has standing committees, among which the Judicial Committee of the Privy Council is the final court of appeal for some Commonwealth states, and for all Crown Dependencies and Overseas Territories (paragraph 1.14). One-off committees of Privy Counsellors may form to investigate specific issues (paragraph 1.19). Codification, then, has deep roots, in the types of functions it performs, and even the institutions involved.

II. THE CIVIL SERVICE AND CODIFICATION

To understand why codification in its current form came about, it is important to recognise structural tendencies within governmental institutions. Support staff can be important to this process. A political leader wishing to produce a written statement of rules is likely delegate the work. Indeed, without the existence of such assistants to execute it, codification would be less likely to occur. Officials may not

[8] 'Certain Articles devised and delivered by the King's Majesty for the quicker, better, and more orderly dispatch of Causes by his Majesty's Privy Council', reproduced in Tanner, above n 5, 223–24.

always welcome the task. However, from their point of view, it can have benefits. They have some opportunity, within practical limits, to shape the document in ways that may suit them. An important purpose of many texts is the regulation of the same support personnel that help draft them. The end product may perform a clarifying function with respect to roles, relationships and procedures that makes their job more straightforward and protects them from possible criticism. Potentially, a text setting out principles and arrangements can strengthen the place of officials within a governmental system by giving a firmer definition of their positions, perhaps expanding their remits in the process. For these reasons, staff within public institutions may be not only important participants within the codification process, but also a source of encouragement for it. As well as taking part in the drafting and updating of documents, officials are often central to the practical use made of them. Through applying codes, staff can maintain the relevance of these texts. The particular way in which they deploy them is also important, helping to determine the precise impact they have. Public officials, then, are crucial to codification.

A historic development in the UK constitution, the emergence of a politically impartial, career Civil Service, that gained pace from the mid-nineteenth century onwards, was a key development.[9] It meant the emergence of a body of employees who—whatever the possible shortcomings in terms of policy expertise—possessed strong literary skills, enabling them to produce codes, and perhaps even disposing them to do so. They remained in their posts even when ministers moved or governments fell, meaning that they could become the keepers of texts, maintaining and updating them as required. The developing Civil Service became a more clearly defined institution, with increasingly complex bureaucratic structures and procedures. That such trends might lead on to the production of a growing volume of written guidance on good practice should not be difficult to comprehend.

Confirming the importance of war to constitutional change in general and codification in particular, an important event for the developing structure of the Civil Service was the appearance of what became the Cabinet Office. It began as a secretariat to the War Cabinet that David Lloyd George created upon becoming Prime Minister late in 1916, and acquired a central role in the coordination of government activity. At the time the secretariat was formed, the only written record of Cabinet proceedings was the letter the Prime Minister wrote to the monarch after each meeting describing what had taken place. The informality this approach engendered was conducive to chaos and increasingly intolerable during a time of consuming military conflict. Lloyd George created the entity that became the Cabinet Office to minute War Cabinet meetings, ensure that written decisions were circulated as appropriate, and manage communications and the paper-based

[9] For the development of the Civil Service, see Hennessy, above n 5; R Lowe, *The Official History of the Civil Service*, vol 1: *The Fulton Years: 1966–81* (Oxford, Routledge, 2011).

information flow into the War Cabinet. With hindsight it is not surprising that the Cabinet Office would be a primary driver of codification. The production and distribution of documents intended to attain systematisation of government was the central essence of this entity from the outset. Codification arose because the secretariat was concerned not only to record and transmit the output of the processes it supported, but also to formalise those processes themselves, and assert its own role as the focus for this systematised form of administration. Upon its creation, the secretariat immediately set about producing codes (see section III. below).

The personal approach of Lloyd George was in itself important to the early instigation of codification. Another Lloyd George innovation, carried out shortly after the First World War in 1919, was the creation of a single Head of the Civil Service, a post combined at first with that of Permanent Secretary to the Treasury. Lloyd George thereby created two centralised spheres of activity—the operation of government decision-making and the management of the Civil Service—that would over time generate numerous codes. The Cabinet Office and Treasury have been and remain important players in this process, especially the Cabinet Office, which—from 1983—became clearly responsible for most Civil Service management functions, in conjunction with its ongoing Cabinet role.

Just as they did during the First World War when Lloyd George created the War Cabinet secretariat, military conflict and the requirements of the administrative machine drove the codification process. *Estacode*—the name appears to be an abbreviation of 'Establishment Officers Code'—appeared during the Second World War. It was a time of turbulence within the Civil Service, with the import of vast numbers of temporary staff from outside combined with substantial structural change within. A Treasury memorandum from July 1943 described a 'proposed Code', the purpose of which was 'to bring some easy intelligibility into the mass of Instructions that have been issued and provide a code of current Instructions' to assist Treasury Officers and Establishments Officers. This Code, then, was not intended to introduce new rules but to provide coherence to those that existed. The initial intended task was to identify all the relevant instructions, including Treasury Circulars and Establishment Officers Circulars, issued as far back as the earliest phase of the centralised Civil Service in 1920, and remove those that were 'dead and moribund'. It was anticipated that the Code might be 'unpopular at the outset', since it would mean presenting some instructions in a new format, breaking up familiar texts. For this reason some 'duplication of information' might be 'desirable to overcome this possible prejudice against the code'. It was 'desirable to popularise the Code' as a means of preventing officials from 'referring back to original instructions'. The Code would not include Orders in Council, readily available elsewhere. The Treasury anticipated that 'in later years a reformer may wish to amend a particular Rule'—in other words, use the Code as a vehicle for change. There might be problems with such an approach if it entailed altering an agreement reached with employee representatives on the 'Staff side'. It was clear that producing what became *Estacode* would be a substantial task, involving an Editing Group creating drafts, checked by Divisional Officers, who might suggest changes.[10] In July 1944 a Treasury 'Office Notice' announced that 'Estacode, a standard reference book of the more important directions and decisions on Establishment matters promulgated by the Treasury from time to time should be available for distribution to Divisions and Departments at an early date.'[11] It was issued in 'loose leaf', and demand for copies from the departments seems to have been high.[12]

A precursor to texts such as the *Civil Service Management Code*, *Estacode* was still in use in the 1970s. By this point it had progressed beyond being a mere compendium of circulars, and had moved into the territory of prescribing core values. It included within it a section on 'Conduct and Discipline', which sought to set 'out the rules which govern the conduct of civil servants'.[13] The opening passage betrayed the tensions that are inherent in seeking to encapsulate in writing constitutional understandings, particularly within a constitutional tradition that makes a fetish of its supposedly 'unwritten' quality. It conveyed the sense that the task was impossible and unnecessary, and verging on impolite because it implied that there were participants in the process who did not understand, or did not wish to abide by, the rules, therefore necessitating their express iteration. As *Estacode* put it:

> No attempt has ever been made to prepare a complete list of matters which, because of the particular character and duties of the Civil Service, require regulation, nor has it ever been thought necessary to lay down a precise code of conduct because civil servants jealously maintain their professional standards. In practice, the distinctive character of the British Civil Service depends largely on the existence and maintenance of a general code of conduct which, although to some extent intangible and unwritten, is of very real importance. There are however a number of things on which it has been found expedient from time to time to issue general instructions …

The core rules the text was able to elucidate were that civil servants had a 'first duty' of 'undivided allegiance to the State'. They were prohibited from placing private gain over their public duty. While 'the State' was largely uninterested in their 'private activities', officials should avoid behaving in a way that might damage the reputation of the Civil Service, for instance 'heavy gambling and speculation'—especially if they were based in a role that gave them access to commercially sensitive information. Officials should ensure not only that they behaved well, but also that they were perceived as doing so. If they fell within the 'politically restricted' category, that is if they were advising on and implementing the decisions of ministers, they should avoid becoming drawn into 'matters of public and political controversy, so that their impartiality is beyond suspicion'.

[10] The National Archive/Public Record Office (TNA/PRO), T162/953, 'Code of Rulings for the Guide of Establishments Officers and Treasury Officers', 22 July 1943.

[11] TNA/PRO, T162/953, 'Office Notice: Estacode', 31 July 1944.

[12] TNA/PRO, T162/953, 'Establishment Officers Circular No 737 (Amended): Estacode, Revision of Method of issuing Establishment Officers Circulars', 28 July 1944.

[13] TNA/PRO, PREM 16/104, 'Excerpt from Estacode Vol 2/Amendment No 614', January 1972.

III. *QUESTIONS OF PROCEDURE FOR MINISTERS*

Another text that became established from the 1940s onwards was *Questions of Procedure for Ministers* (QPM). It proved to be one of the defining texts of the codification period. Fortunately, in 2000 Amy Baker published a full history of this document. In the following passages I draw on her account and supplement it with additional analysis and research.[14] The origins of QPM lie in a text entitled *Rules of Procedure* that the Secretary to the War Cabinet, Maurice Hankey, produced in January 1917, distributing it to all government ministers. The Rules were, therefore, an outcome of the Lloyd George reforms discussed in section II. above. Just 10 paragraphs long, they marked the beginning of codification as defined in this book. The text began abruptly, with paragraph 1 informing the reader that '[q]uestions may be referred for decision by the War Cabinet by the Prime Minister, or by Members of the War Cabinet, or by any Member of the Government, or by any Government Department'. The document stated that the 'normal procedure' for such a referral was through the 'Secretary, accompanied, when practicable, by a short Memorandum containing a summary of the points on which a decision is required'.

With its invocation of 'normal procedure' this passage conveyed a sense of firmly established practice. Yet the existence of the Secretary, along with the War Cabinet and its procedures, was new. An important function of codification has always been to manage or even bring about change, though perhaps not to do so openly. It has never—despite implications or claims the documents sometimes make—involved simply describing the already prevailing position. Some of the key principles set out in the Rules are recognisable in the Cabinet system of today. Codification therefore proved an effective tool in helping form lasting rules—or even conventions. The institutional agenda associated with the new arrangements set out in 1917 was also significant, and another foretaste of future codification. Not only did the Rules seek to impose the practices that fitted with the preferences of staff within the official machine (and in particular the most senior secretary, Hankey), they also directly asserted the role of the Secretary as filter and central figure within the nascent system, with the insistence that matters should be raised through him.

Paragraph 2 referred to a practice 'as a general rule' of the War Cabinet's consulting ministers who led departments, and making available to them the relevant information, before reaching a decision. This stipulation must have arisen from a desire to reconcile the decision of Lloyd George to use a small inner War Cabinet of mainly non-departmental ministers with the need to maintain wider government cohesion. Paragraph 3 dealt with another key procedure. The Secretary was required to send copies of the draft minutes of each War Cabinet meeting to its members, to enable them to comment. Additional ministers attending particular

[14] A Baker, *Prime Ministers & The Rule Book* (London, Politico's, 2000). For 'Rules of Procedure' see TNA/PRO CAB 21/102, 'The War Cabinet: Rules of Procedure', 24 January 1917.

meetings would also have this opportunity. After the recipients of these papers responded, the Secretary would send a 'final draft of the Minutes' to the Prime Minister. The crucial point then follows: 'After the Prime Minister has initialed the Minutes of the War Cabinet, the conclusions formulated therein will become operative decisions to be carried out by the responsible Departments.' The premier could, if necessary, 'delegate' his power of authorisation.

Paragraph 4 continued to provide an important role for the Secretary as facilitator of collective government. Having received prime ministerial approval, 'the decisions of the War Cabinet will be communicated by the Secretary to the Political and Civil Heads of Departments concerned, who will be responsible for giving effect to them'. Furthermore, paragraph 5 explained, the Secretary would circulate the minutes to all War Cabinet members and other senior ministers and officials. Availability could be limited over 'decisions of extreme secrecy', including 'dates of forthcoming operations, new engines of war, &c'. As well as depicting the Secretary as a communicator of instructions, the Rules, in paragraph 6, gave him a role in the monitoring of their implementation:

> In order to keep the Committee fully informed, the Head of the Department responsible for action on any of the War Cabinet's decisions is to notify the Secretary as to the action taken, or, if for any reason action is found impossible or unnecessary, is to notify him accordingly.

The text stipulated a preference for copies of orders 'actually sent'.

Moving on to the actual business of War Cabinets, paragraph 7 provided a list of individual post-holders directly involved in war policy, who would 'ordinarily' attend the beginning of War Cabinet meetings to provide an update on developments. Furthermore, 'Other experts may be summoned as required.' Paragraph 8 stated that heads of departments must provide the War Cabinet regularly with relevant information, again via the Secretary, and that the War Cabinet would also 'have the right to call for any information from Government Departments'. Paragraph 9 provided more detail on the sorts of material the War Cabinet had to receive, and from whom. Lastly, paragraph 10 noted that 'Meetings of the War Cabinet will be held at 10 Downing Street. All communications in regard to the circulation and distribution of Papers should be addressed to the Secretary at 8 Whitehall Gardens, S.W.' In producing this text, Hankey left no doubt about his centrality to proceedings. The tendency for Cabinet Office documents to emphasise the importance of the secretariat and the Cabinet Secretary to the proper functioning of government persists today.

The National Archive file containing the Rules includes another document, also dating from January 1917, under the heading 'Notes on the machinery of the British War Cabinet: The War Cabinet'. In its 23 paragraphs it provided information about the membership of the War Cabinet, its meetings, its procedures, its place within government and the organisation of the secretariat. The propensity of the body soon known as the Cabinet Office to produce multiple codes, sometimes with overlapping content, was always present. So too was the practice of regularly updating texts. From 1919 *Rules of Procedure* became known as *Instructions to the Secretary*. Hankey initially pursued a practice of presenting it to ministers for their agreement when a new Cabinet was formed, but this custom then tapered off. The transition of *Notes on War Cabinet Procedure*, as it was labelled during the Second World War, into QPM provides further evidence of how military conflict, personality and underlying institutional imperatives could combine to drive forward codification. There was a general disposition towards codification, but the precise way in which it manifested itself depended upon how it intersected with major external circumstances, and the approaches of particular individuals such as prime ministers. Baker explains that in August 1945 the new Labour Prime Minister, Clement Attlee, issued the first edition of QPM. It combined *Notes on War Cabinet Procedure* with an added annex compiling a series of prime ministerial procedural instructions issued during the War. The Cabinet Secretary, Edward Bridges, secured the agreement of Attlee to the new document, and it was then disseminated to all ministers in the incoming Labour Government. Bridges had begun this initiative in advance of the General Election, which produced a Labour victory that was surprising to many. The use of such a text suited the temperament of Attlee better than it did the ousted Winston Churchill, who is known for his less formal approach. Attlee placed a premium on efficient, orderly government, a goal QPM could help him pursue. In 1946 an updated version incorporated his numerous additional directives, and they were now added to the main body of the text, rather than being confined to an annex. Baker recounts how it continued to grow and took on the character of an assorted collection of operational stipulations and guidance on ministerial behaviour, such as prohibitions on the leaking of confidential information, a concern that remains with us today, as does QPM itself, under the title attached to it since 1997, the *Ministerial Code*.

A comparison of the 1949 edition of QPM with the most recent edition of its successor text, the *Ministerial Code*, is instructive. The 2015 document[15] opens with a 'Foreword', attributed to the Prime Minister, David Cameron. It reads:

> This Government was elected with a clear set of instructions from the British people. To back working people. To deliver security at every stage of their lives. To build not just a stronger economy, but a stronger society, too. And to govern for one nation: England, Scotland, Wales and Northern Ireland.
>
> People didn't just tell us what to do, but how to go about it. They want their politicians to uphold the highest standards of propriety. That means being transparent in all we do. It means rooting out any form of misconduct. It means spending every pound carefully—because it's not our money; it's taxpayers' money.
>
> This is good government. And it is precious. Around the world, Parliaments have copied the Westminster system. But they also want to copy the way we conduct our politics, because they see that transparency and openness go hand in hand with progress and prosperity.

[15] Cabinet Office, *Ministerial Code* (London, Cabinet Office, 2015).

> So in every decision we take, every speech we make, every policy we formulate, we must keep in mind who put us here and why. If we remember that, if we carry out our duty with the utmost integrity, then together we can make our vision a reality: and make Great Britain greater still.

The 'Note by the Prime Minister' that opened the 1949 edition of QPM set a different tone. There was no attempt to link the text to a vision for society, the economy, the country or the democratic well-being of the entire world. Instead, the then premier, Clement Attlee, wrote:

> My colleagues may find it convenient to have this consolidated and revised statement of the directives which I have issued from time to time on points of procedure and other similar matters. Special attention is drawn to the instructions in paragraph 40 regarding references in Ministerial speeches to Commonwealth affairs, which have not been included in any of my previous directives … I should be glad if Ministers in charge of Departments would bring to the notice of Junior Ministers and officials such sections as concern them. For this purpose additional copies may be obtained from the Cabinet Office.[16]

Cameron, of course, was writing in a text that had, since 1992, been publicly available, encouraging—but not justifying—his hyperbole. Attlee had a narrower internal audience. But whether it would have made any difference to his style were Attlee knowingly addressing a potential audience of millions is doubtful. Yet though this contrast is unavoidable, the main bodies of the two documents, one from 1949, the other from 2015, share important core features, in particular their concern with internal procedure and etiquette, and communications between government and the outside world.

Baker reminds us that it would not have been obvious in the early phase that QPM would become a permanent fixture, and it could well have appeared a document specific to the Attlee Government. This realisation is important. Retrospectively the rise of codification may seem inevitable, but it did not appear so when it was underway. We can now identify some of the trends that drove it, but they were not necessarily plainly apparent all along. Moreover, individual codes have in some cases failed or disappeared, as we shall see. When Churchill returned in 1951, QPM was heavily pruned at the outset, and then left unchanged. But it survived. Anthony Eden (1955–57) did not produce a version of QPM. However, Harold Macmillan (1957–63) introduced a new text in 1958. The fresh provisions incorporated into it that Baker highlights provide an example of the relationship between codes and constitutional change. They included guidance on television appearances, a medium of growing significance. Here was an instance of the creation of completely new rules in response to an external trend. A second type of change involved the clarification of regulations that had previously been more vague in nature. In a climate of rising scrutiny of the personal conduct of ministers, the 1958 QPM incorporated provisions intended to make clear how they

[16] Reproduced in Baker, above n 14, 135.

could avoid financial conflicts of interest. Third was the incorporation of rules that were already firmly accepted, such as the prohibition on ministers bringing civil servants with them to party conferences. Baker's work shows that, generally, alterations to the code in the years that followed were pre-emptive—that is seeking to avoid particular problems in advance—or reactive—that is, responding to a difficulty that had manifested itself.

The text was becoming a fixture, retained through the 1960s and 1970s by successive Conservative and Labour Governments. In 1979, a Conservative Prime Minister, Margaret Thatcher, came to power. Despite her reputed disregard for traditional principles of collective decision taking, she retained in QPM a text that regulated the system within which this form of government operated. From less than secure beginnings, though with consistent support from officials at high level in the Cabinet Office, QPM had managed to survive changes in the party of government and transitions to prime ministers of varied dispositions. By this point—though it lacked legal underpinning—QPM was in practice a firm part of the system. Moreover, while it was confidential, knowledge of its existence began to seep out. An important moment came in 1975. In this year, though it did not formally publish the text until 1992, the Government submitted QPM as evidence as part of its legal attempt to prevent the publication of the diaries of the former Cabinet minister, Richard Crossman. The Government held that Crossman had breached the confidence of Cabinet proceedings. The press, referring to 'a secret document called Questions of Procedure for Ministers', quoted the Attorney-General, Sam Silkin, as explaining that 'The Queen … had given permission for this [the production of QPM as evidence] to be done.'[17] Later governments were insistent that codes should not be used against them in court proceedings, but this case suggests that deploying a text in support of the administration was considered acceptable.

IV. THE *PRECEDENT BOOK*

Another important code from the post-Second World War period was the *Precedent Book*, the earliest existing version of which dates from 1954. This text comprises one of the most important codifications of all, dating from an era when the practice, driven by bureaucratic imperatives, was taking hold, though still a secretive activity internal to the executive. The book consists of a collation of different sets of already existing guidance to the conduct of Cabinet government, for use within the Cabinet Office, primarily, it seems, by the Cabinet Secretary. The name creates the implication that past practice and circumstances are an important guide for future action, and perhaps the main or only basis for legitimate conduct. Analysis of what appears to be the 1954 edition is revealing regarding the nature of codification and the system of government as it operated around this time.

[17] G Parry, 'Silkin hits at diaries', *The Guardian*, 23 July 1975.

Part I, 58 pages long, dealt with 'The Cabinet'.[18] At the outset, in paragraph 1, it reminded the reader of the relatively informal nature of Cabinet, and that there was no statutory reference to it until the Ministers of the Crown Act 1937 (which provided extra income to some ministers inside the Cabinet). Evidently written from the vantage point of the immediate post-Second World War period, it noted that 'in the last thirty or forty years a more formal system has developed', yet that the precise way in which Cabinet operated could alter 'to suit particular circumstances and particular Prime Ministers'. Paragraph 1 then made further important constitutional observations. While Cabinet lacked 'statutory powers or functions', because it comprised senior figures from the group that is pre-eminent within the House of Commons it was able to act as 'the directing body of national policy'. Cabinet, the *Precedent Book* stated, offered a means of reconciling two potentially conflicting constitutional requirements: that a minister at the head of a particular department was individually responsible to Parliament, but at the same time that members of the government were responsible for policy collectively. Alongside these statements of central principle, it contained a large body of description of practice and procedure, including accounts of who made up the Cabinet, who could go to Cabinet meetings, the business of Cabinet, when it convened, and how the conclusions it reached were recorded and put into action. This part referred to authorities such as Ivor Jennings and parliamentary sources, as did other portions of the book. They also made references to a 'Downing Street Handbook', that the present author has not yet located, though it may well be the so-called 'Bible' that the No 10 private secretaries maintained.[19]

Part II of the book covered 'Ministers'.[20] Totalling 59 pages, it considered their appointment, their removal, and various rules and procedures surrounding their activities. In assessing the role of the monarch in the appointment of prime ministers, Part II contained a relatively direct statement of the rights of and limitations upon the ruler, that would be less likely to appear in a document were it intended for public dissemination, then or now. Paragraph 2 tells us that the selection of a Prime Minister by the monarch 'is not made on formal advice or submission'. While frequently the person who would be made Prime Minister was obvious, 'the King has an absolute right in all cases to consult anyone he pleases' over this matter. This discretion in seeking counsel, the book noted, could be of particular use when there was room for uncertainty about who should become premier, for instance if an incumbent had died or decided to stand down unexpectedly, or perhaps because there was 'a complicated political situation'. While this paragraph did not deal expressly with a House of Commons lacking a single-party majority, the term 'complicated political situation' could encompass this eventuality.

[18] TNA/PRO, CAB 181/2, 'Precedent Book, Part I, The Cabinet', undated.

[19] For the history of rule-keeping within No 10, see A Blick and G Jones, *At Power's Elbow: aides to the Prime Minister from Robert Walpole to David Cameron* (London, Biteback, 2013).

[20] TNA/PRO, CAB 181/4, 'Precedent Book, Part II, Ministers', undated.

Notwithstanding the possession of the right to obtain advice, since a monarch 'should not exercise, or appear to exercise, any political bias, he would normally choose as Prime Minister the leader of the Party having the largest number of seats in the House of Commons'. In these straightforward circumstances the ruler would not make 'any overt or personal consultations', because to do so might create an undesirable impression of 'personal partisanship'. In other words, the monarch might appear to be considering the possibility of circumventing an election result. The book went on to state that '[n]o Peer has been chosen as Prime Minister since the end of Lord Salisbury's administration in 1902'. However, it did not offer any explicit conclusions about whether it would still be possible for a premier to be appointed from, or continue to sit in, the Lords rather than the Commons.

'Cabinet Committees' were the subject of Part III (31 pages).[21] It contained in its opening paragraph a justification of their role. They were needed, it explained, as a means of dealing with the 'mass of business engaging the collective responsibility of Government' that would swamp 'a single body', that is, the full Cabinet. Cabinet committees lessened the pressure on Cabinet as a whole and on individual ministers. Furthermore, they made it possible for 'Ministers of Cabinet rank who are not members of the Cabinet to take their share in the formulation of Government policy'.

Part IV dealt in depth over 53 pages with the handling of Cabinet documents, demonstrating the importance to codification of administrative imperatives that might not seem of the highest constitutional significance.[22]

Part V (21 pages) returned to the sensitive, complex and difficult-to-define constitutional role of the monarchy.[23] The Annex to this part, entitled 'The King and the Prime Minister', contained passages that merit reproduction as exemplifying an orthodox view of the UK constitution. It suggested that the authors were encountering similar strains to those suffered by the drafters of the 'Conduct and Discipline' section of *Estacode* (discussed in section III. above):

> The British constitution is unwritten and is built upon on practice and precedent over very many years. Its procedure is well defined in some respects; in others less so; new situations arise and to meet them there are modifications, often imperceptible, which in themselves become precedents and part of established practice. For these reasons it is impossible in many cases to be dogmatic on broad constitutional issues, and it may well be misleading to say, for example, that 'the King must do this' or that 'the Prime Minister must do that.' It will often be found that there is an exception or that an exception can be made which in itself will prove a precedent.
>
> Therefore, to define in precise terms the general relationship between the King and the Prime Minister is difficult even if the matter were to be set out at length … What follows is only a brief and simplified outline of the main principles of this relationship.

[21] TNA/PRO, CAB 181/5, 'Precedent Book, Part III, Cabinet Committees', undated.

[22] TNA/PRO, CAB 181/6, 'Precedent Book, Part IV, Documents', undated.

[23] TNA/PRO, CAB 181/7, 'Precedent Book, Part V, Relations with Buckingham Palace', undated.

The Annex then sought to define what was meant by a constitutional monarchy. The first key feature it identified was that ministers had to be ready to take 'responsibility for every act or omission of the King which has any political significance'. As a consequence of this 'fundamental constitutional doctrine', ministers were able to offer advice on these matters; and there was a 'well-established tradition that in the last resort the King accepts the advice of his Ministers'. Yet he also had a 'right and indeed duty to make known to Ministers his views about or objections to' their proposals. A second crucial principle was that monarchs 'should not take sides in party politics'. The Annex replicated the material in Part II about choosing prime ministers. One important area in which it expanded upon this account involved the issue of prime ministers and the House of Lords. It stipulated that there was 'no constitutional bar' to a Peer's becoming premier. But such an outcome, it noted, had not taken place since the time of Salisbury. An important addition to Part II then followed, when the Annex remarked that 'the passing over in 1923 of Lord Curzon in favour of Lord (then Mr) Baldwin may possibly mark a constitutional convention excluding a Peer from being Prime Minister'. The Annex dealt with prime-ministerial recommendations for ministers. The monarch 'may exercise a considerable influence' in this area, but ultimately had to accept the wishes of the premier 'or find another Prime Minister who can command the support of the House of Commons or the country'. No such breakdown had occurred in 'recent years', the book noted.

Regulating the flow of information to the outside—and keeping it to a minimum—was an important concern for the Civil Service in the post-Second World War era. A later part of the book, Section 5 of Part VII, demonstrated this point.[24] It consisted of 142 pages of guidance on 'Handling Requests for Information' pertaining to 'The Cabinet, Cabinet Committees and the Cabinet Office'. It displayed what might today seem to be a preposterous level of reticence regarding key operational features of a democratic government, and revealed that there was a privileged group of individuals regarded as more worthy and trustworthy than others with respect to some knowledge. Paragraph 3 described the procedure to follow when 'ordinary members of the public' asked about the functioning of the Cabinet system. They were allowed to know the answer to some questions, such as whether minutes were kept at Cabinet or the point at which the post of Cabinet Secretary was created. But if the inquiry extended further than already publicly available knowledge, the usual response was to be 'that information about the procedure of the Cabinet, the organisation of Cabinet Committees, etc is confidential and cannot be made available'. When approaches came from 'specialists' it was possible to be more helpful, but not in an entirely straightforward way (paragraph 4). The precise method of dealing with requests for details about the operation of Cabinet for the purposes of research publications 'depends largely on the standing and

[24] TNA/PRO, CAB 181/10, 'Precedent Book, Part VII, Miscelleaneous (Contd)', Section 5, 'The Cabinet, Cabinet Committees and the Cabinet Office', undated. For 59 further pages on 'Use of Official Information in Private Publications', see CAB 181/11 'Precedent Book, Part VIII', undated.

purpose of the enquirer'. So even within this small group there were subdivisions of importance. The book did not elaborate on how these distinctions were made. A person—or rather a 'he'—who passed whatever obscure, informal screening process was applied then received a flattering reception. But it was not entirely freely given. The book explained:

> Unless this is for some reason undesirable, the enquirer would normally be seen by the Secretary of the Cabinet or his deputy and given, in general terms, information on the developments or aspects in which he is interested. (This interview serves also to elicit the intentions of the enquirer.) If appropriate, he would be offered a short memorandum or a note of references to published material which he may not have seen.

At the meeting with the Cabinet Secretary or deputy, 'the suggestion would be made that he should submit a manuscript, or at least a printed proof, of any material which he intends to publish'. For the author, the guidance suggested, it would be a means of avoiding 'misstatements', while for the Cabinet Office it would provide the possibility of 'seeking the modification of any passages which may be objectionable'. Yet while the Cabinet Office might be willing to provide and verify accounts of how it operated, it would not wish publicly to appear to do so. The standard practice was, according to the book, 'to make it clear to the author that he must himself take full responsibility and must not refer to the Cabinet Office, directly or indirectly, as the source of his information'. The Cabinet Office found this overall approach satisfactory in that 'there has always been the fullest co-operation'. The main problem, it noted, was in deciding how far it should draw back the curtain and make 'information not previously published ... available'. But there were benefits in a degree of openness. The book referred to the 'considerable advantage to the Cabinet Office itself' of there being 'an authoritative textbook to which enquirers can be referred'. Given the general outlook regarding outside access to internal information about the way the system operated, the idea of the *Precedent Book* itself's being available potentially to be viewed anywhere in the world, instantly, free, on demand on a screen—which it now is—would be difficult to comprehend.

As the Annex to Part V on the monarch and the Prime Minister revealed, even the apparently more obscure parts of the *Precedent Book* contained within them valuable seams of systemic guidance. Part I of the book also has a series of annexes.[25] The first was a list of Cabinet posts held since 1916, presumably to inform senior staff involved in making appointments of the range of titles held by Cabinet members and the implications for precedence. These issues are important in the frenetic circumstances of Cabinet formation or reshuffles, when various competing political, personal and administrative needs must be fulfilled in a way that appears proper. The past could constrain, through suggesting norms, but also provide opportunities to justify courses of action. In this sense the *Precedent Book*

[25] TNA/PRO, CAB 181/3, 'Precedent Book, Part I, Annexes', undated. Information contained within it runs up to 1950.

was potentially a powerful tool for those who had easy access to it, presumably a small group centring on the Cabinet Secretary, a post held at this point by Norman Brook, the master-manipulator of the bureaucratic machine. It is easy to see how this text could both guide him and strengthen his case when proposing particular courses of action to others.

Annex II was entitled 'Submission of Business to the Cabinet: Action in the Cabinet Office'. Apparently dating from 1949, it shows how far Cabinet business had become codified by this point, even if such guidance was not widely available beyond (and perhaps even within) Whitehall. Despite the typically mundane title, this document dealt with high-order constitutional matters. Moreover, it tended to present its account as a description of practices as they were, rather than as they had been, the implication being that the version it offered was one that should be followed. The Annex began with an account of the purpose of Cabinet: to consider 'major issues of policy', or significant issues over which there is disagreement within the government that can only be settled through 'reference to the highest authority'. There was also 'a considerable variety of miscellaneous business' (paragraph 1). This 'wide range of miscellaneous problems, often unforeseen, thrown up in the day to day activities of Departments' should not be neglected, even if Cabinet faced a consuming emergency demanding its attention. The implication was that senior Cabinet Office officials needed to ensure that distracted ministers avoided overlooking the less attention-grabbing but nonetheless important issues. 'Thus the Cabinet may often have to turn from discussion of some vital economic or international problem to consider some item of domestic legislation or some relatively long-term administrative issue', or papers produced by Cabinet Committees. Given the hard-to-predict nature of Cabinet work, papers should only be sent to Cabinet if 'essential and then in clear and concise terms' (paragraph 2). The text proceeded to provide detailed guidance about the handling of business, including means of ensuring that an issue reached Cabinet only if it had to, and that appropriate advance consultation with relevant Whitehall departments took place. It firmly fixed the role of the Cabinet Office at the centre of the process.

Memorandums, the Annex tells us, should normally be circulated at least two full days in advance of the Cabinet's taking them (paragraph 13). While Parliament was meeting, the document went on, Cabinet normally convened on Mondays and Thursdays, though if parliamentary business permitted, Tuesdays were preferred to Mondays (paragraph 16). The normal venue was the Cabinet Room on the ground floor at the back of No 10 Downing Street, the official residence of the Prime Minister (in the role of First Lord of the Treasury). If circumstances required, Cabinet could take place in the House of Commons, in the Prime Minister's room there. Paragraph 20 was a fascinating account of how the Cabinet Office, no doubt with the Cabinet Secretary in the lead, and Prime Minister's Private Secretary met on Thursdays to agree between them a proposal regarding 'when … Cabinet should meet and what business should be taken'. It included a 'draft of the Agenda' for the initial Cabinet of the following week, as well as a '"provisional programme" indicating in general terms the business for both meetings'. It was then sent to the Prime Minister for agreement. Paragraph 21 described another proposal drafted following the Monday Cabinet, with a 'draft Agenda' for Thursday. This description demonstrated the importance of officials in No 10 and the Cabinet Office in supporting prime ministers in their role as chair of the Cabinet. Civil servants had (and still have) a crucial part in framing the way in which political discussions at the highest level were framed. They could also use texts such as the *Precedent Book* to assert their position in writing. However, while officials were influential figures, it should not be assumed that they could exploit or would even attempt to utilise their position nakedly to pursue their own particular goals. Prime ministers, who are by definition skilled politicians, would not be likely to submit to such abuse, and civil servants would know that to engage in it would be to risk the closeness of their relationship with the premier on which their status was dependent.

The *Precedent Book* was in use for four decades. But in 2015, the House of Commons Political and Constitutional Reform Committee (PCRC) revealed that it had learned from the Cabinet Secretary, Sir Jeremy Heywood, that since 1992 the Cabinet Office had ceased formally to maintain the book. It had come instead, the Committee found, to rely 'on a more nebulous concept of unwritten corporate memory'.[26] Heywood explained in oral evidence to the PCRC:

> How we deal with these issues now is on the basis of experience of how the ministerial code, for example, has been interpreted in the past, what the recent precedents have been, but we don't collect these together into something called the precedent book. In a sense, the corporate memory is there in the Cabinet Office and in my office but we have not gone to the trouble of bringing all of those individual cases together into a new version of the precedent book.[27]

The Committee noted that it was uncertain whether any clear method had appeared in place of the *Precedent Book* to store and place in context events of constitutional significance. The post-1992 disappearance of the book shows that, even as the practice of producing published codes was in the ascendant, an older method of internal storage declined. The Committee expressed unease regarding the fate of the book, regretting that it was no longer apparent how the Cabinet Office and the Government would store its 'corporate memory'.[28]

V. CODIFICATION AND PUBLIC MONEY

Often codes are issued by individual institutions, frequently but not exclusively the UK executive. However, they can entail agreements between different

[26] House of Commons Political and Constitutional Reform Committee, *Revisiting the Cabinet Manual* (HC 2014–15, 233) para 27.

[27] ibid, 13.

[28] ibid.

constitutional players. The 1932 *PAC Concordat*[29] is a code of the latter type. As a document it remains to the present day central to the financial relationship between Parliament and the executive, and is part of the contemporary canon of codes. The circumstances in which the Concordat came about suggest another important observation: that codification does not take place in a vacuum, and that it tends to arise in the intersection between long-run tendencies and more immediate pressures. The background to the Concordat was sustained apprehension on the part of Parliament, stretching back at least as far as the middle of the nineteenth century, regarding the executive practice of spending money from the Contingencies Fund without deriving express authorisation through specially designed legislation. Parliament objected to this approach because it created difficulties for the task of holding government to account for the use of public funds, since the purpose for which this money was provided was not as clearly defined as it otherwise would be. The House of Commons Public Accounts Committee (PAC), established in 1862, became a persistent critic of this habit. Against this general concern, the immediate driver of the Concordat was an upturn during the 1920s in the government practice of spending money in ways for which it had not obtained specific prior statutory authority. The global economic downturn following the Wall Street Crash of 1929 played its part. After PAC had already objected to government practices in 1930 and 1931, the final trigger for the understanding of 1932 came about as a consequence of Ministry of Labour spending on assistance projects for unemployed people, for which it had no precise legislative power.

The text known as the 1932 Concordat consists of an exchange of letters between PAC and the Treasury. The Parliamentary Committee insisted that if it were intended

> that continuing functions should be exercised by a government department, particularly where such functions may involve financial liabilities extending beyond a given financial year, it is proper, subject to certain recognised exceptions, that the powers and duties to be exercised should be defined by specific statute. (A2.3.6)

The Treasury responded with a minute stating that, though Parliament could provide authorisation through an annual Appropriation Act, 'constitutional propriety requires that such extensions should be regularised at the earliest possible date by amending legislation, unless they are of a purely emergency or non-continuing character'. In other words, following the prompting of PAC, the Treasury was acknowledging in written form the existence of an established understanding, or perhaps even a constitutional convention, that—though not possessing a firm legal basis—was accepted as having force nonetheless. As would often prove to be the case, the authors of the text sought to ensure that,

[29] See HM Treasury, *Managing Public Money* (London, HM Treasury, 2013, revised 2015), Annex 2.3, 'PAC Concordat of 1932'.

while committing to a restriction, they preserved a degree of latitude for themselves. The minute went on to assert that the government needed to retain 'a certain measure of discretion' in being able to seek power through an Appropriation Act, something—the Treasury noted—that Parliament was certainly able to grant. However, through the minute the Government acknowledged its agreement that 'continuing functions'—especially those involving 'financial liabilities extending beyond a given financial year'—ought to 'be defined by specific statute'. The Treasury agreed that it would, for its 'part, continue to aim at the observance of this principle'.

Though there will always be potential for disagreement around some of the concepts the Concordat defines, it has broadly proved successful and lasting. As a Treasury text most recently updated in 2015, *Managing Public Money*, puts it, 'With this Concordat, the matter still lies.'[30] In 2013, the House of Lords Select Committee on the Constitution described the Concordat as 'a self-denying ordinance by the Treasury, which has in general worked well'.[31]

Another text dealing with related issues has proved more problematic. The so-called 'Ram Memorandum' was a letter from Granville Ram, First Parliamentary Counsel, dating from 2 November 1945.[32] A crucial difference between this text and the 1932 Concordat was that the former was a unilateral act of drafting within the executive, while the latter involved an exchange of views between two institutions. Though it became crucial to executive understandings of the extent of its financial power, the Memorandum did not become public until 2003.[33] It was an opinion given by a lawyer (Ram) to a client (the Government), and as such had no legal authority of its own. Yet the Memorandum acquired in practice an exalted status inside the executive. Indeed, regardless of its actual legal grounding, it became a constitutional text—as far as those within Whitehall were concerned at least. It was the basis for the so-called 'Ram Doctrine', though the doctrine as often understood was possibly a misrepresentation of the views of Ram as he expressed them in the Memorandum.

Ram commenced by explaining that he was responding to a request to explain 'how far legislation is necessary to authorise any extension of the existing powers of a Government Department'. He immediately identified a need 'to draw a sharp distinction between what is legally possible and what is permissible having regard to established practice'. This issue is perennial within any political system—perhaps particularly so for the UK with its 'unwritten' constitution—and a reason for codification as defined in this book. Beginning with the 'Legal Position', Ram explained that a Minister of the Crown differed from a corporation founded in statute. While the latter was 'entirely a creature of statute' and possessed only

30 See ibid, A2.3.8.

31 House of Lords Select Committee on the Constitution, *The pre-emption of Parliament* (HL 2012–13, 165) para 13.

32 'Text of memorandum from Granville Ram, First Parliamentary Counsel, 2 November 1945'.

33 House of Lords Select Committee on the Constitution, above n 31, para 50.

authorities derived from statute, the former 'as an agent of the Crown', could 'exercise any powers which the Crown has power to exercise, except so far as he is precluded from doing so by statute'. There was, Ram recognised, potential for discussion about whether statutory authorisation could bring with it implied restrictions. However, 'the governing principle', Ram held, 'is that express statutory provision is not necessary to enable a Minister to exercise functions'.

The manifestation of this doctrine in financial terms was that 'a Minister may do anything which he is not precluded from doing', but 'he will only be able to pay for what he does if Parliament votes him the money'. Ram noted that, in its interactions with PAC—including those embodied in the Concordat of 1932—the Treasury had been careful to assert the basic principle that, whatever the ideal practice might be, Parliament nonetheless possessed the power to support government activities solely through Appropriation Acts. Ram found fault with some of the arguments PAC had advanced in the past, including its view that if a grant was derived exclusively from an Appropriation Act, it 'had no statutory basis whatever'. He expressed the view that 'the use of the Appropriation Act without previous general legislation however objectionable it may be is not illegal and therefore not unconstitutional'. Whatever the merits of Ram's legal point, the claim we can infer from the point he made here, that a practice that is legal is by definition constitutional, is difficult to reconcile with widely shared understandings of the UK system. While universal consensus over what precisely is the constitution is absent, many would agree that the constitution has both legal and non-legal manifestations. It would seemingly be legal, for instance, for the monarch to dismiss a sitting Prime Minister who still possessed the confidence of the House of Commons, and to appoint a successor of her choosing.[34] But it would surely not, in the perceptions of many, be constitutional to do so. Ram concluded that 'Legislation is not legally necessary to authorise an extension of the existing powers of a Government Department except where such an extension is precluded by a previous statute either expressly or by necessary implication.' However, 'If the extended powers involve an annual charge extended over a period of years' then 'legislation though not required by law, is required by established practice formally recorded in the transactions between the Public Accounts Committee and the Treasury.' What for Ram was an 'established practice' was probably for others 'constitutional'.

The Ram Memorandum provides us with evidence of how a text can become influential over a sustained period—surely to a greater extent than its author could have imagined. At the same time, problems connected to a document can fester, only fully becoming apparent a substantial period of time after it is issued. In 2013, the same House of Lords Select Committee on the Constitution report that broadly praised the 1932 Concordat expressed more concerns about the Ram Memorandum and its usage. The Constitution Committee stressed that, regardless

[34] See para 2.9 of *The Cabinet Manual*, above n 6.

of its revered standing within the executive, Ram was 'not a source of law' (paragraph 52). Furthermore, events had rendered it out of date. Ministerial activity was now subject to additional constraints, including 'public law limitations … as enforced through judicial review; human rights law; the pre-existing rights and significant interests of private persons'; and the rules included in the Concordat of 1932 and the Treasury text *Managing Public Money*. The Committee objected more forcefully to the idea of a 'Ram doctrine' founded in the Memorandum. It understood the doctrine, as described to it by the Treasury, as meaning that 'ministers can do anything a natural person can do, unless limited by legislation' (paragraph 55). One problem noted in evidence to the Committee, aside from this view being legally incorrect, was that it misrepresented Ram, who had not held that governments could do anything that private people could (paragraph 56). In response to the Committee, the Government recognised that the relevance of the Ram Memorandum was limited by changes in public law and by the introduction of the Human Rights Act 1998. But it maintained that the basic principle expressed by Ram still stood, namely, that the Government was in possession of common law powers, though limited by the law.

VI. CONCLUSION

From the First World War onwards, Whitehall began to acquire the habit of producing texts setting out key constitutional understandings and governmental practices. Some of the main documents that appeared—*Estacode*, the *Precedent Book* and QPM—were important forerunners to the texts of the contemporary codification era and clearly within the overall phenomenon discussed in this book. But there were important differences from the present. Most of these texts were not intended for public consumption, and their availability might be restricted even within Whitehall. With the exception of the *PAC Concordat*, they were issued by the executive alone, and tended to focus on its internal concerns. Nonetheless, they had implications for constitutional power relationships. *Estacode* was intended to ensure adherence throughout Whitehall to edicts issued by the Treasury in its bureaucratic management role. The purpose of the *Precedent Book* was partly to ensure consistency and continuity in the practice of government. It could also be seen as assisting senior permanent officials, in particular the Cabinet Secretary, as guardians of proper practice in their dealings with the temporary component of government, the ministers; and in promoting good practices connected to collective government, part of the institutional interest of the Cabinet Office. Furthermore, the book managed the relationship with outsiders seeking information about the way in which the system worked. QPM and its predecessors similarly served the interests of the Cabinet Office and of officialdom, as well as being tools with which prime ministers might impose behavioural standards on ministers.

The *PAC Concordat*, however, was not purely executive property. It dealt with the relationship between the executive and Parliament in the crucial area of financial control; and it emerged out of a negotiation between different constitutional branches. It can be contrasted with the Ram Memorandum. That dealt with similar subject matter, but Parliament played no a part in its production and was not even made aware of its existence. Such secretive practice was well within accepted standards of the time. But the constitutional system is never entirely static. It was, by the end of the 1970s, already subject to pressures and transformations that would bring with them an acceleration and broadening of, and a change in the nature of, the codification process. Not only would texts proliferate, but they would become public documents, with players beyond the executive increasingly engaging in their manufacture, and in commentary upon them. The outside world became a key player in a process that was previously largely the internal business of Whitehall.

2

Codification Since 1979

I. CODIFICATION IN THE PUBLIC DOMAIN

SOME OF THE main components of the contemporary codification trend had established themselves by the opening decades of the post-1945 period. They included the practice of creating documents depicting various understandings and principles for use within the UK executive. A series of constitutional forces then built, which served to stimulate the codification process further, as well as altering its nature and expanding its scope. From the late 1950s onwards, the UK system of government became the subject of pronounced controversy and political pressure, and underwent change on an unsurpassed scale. These processes had multiple dimensions to them, including UK participation in European integration, the status of the nations and regions that make up the UK, relations between the different branches of the constitution and public scrutiny of governmental institutions. Codification became a characteristic component of this new environment, both a consequence and a manifestation of the transformations that were underway.[1] It arose from and demonstrated the complex network of overlapping power bases comprising the UK constitution, and the way in which they and the relations between them morphed. It could be a source of strength and a sign of weakness on the part of all involved. Yet though these texts became a prominent part of UK governance, they were not an irresistible force. They could at times fail or be diluted. While starting points can have an arbitrary quality (for instance the 'Croham Directive',[2] discussed in section II. below, dates from 1977), some important developments began to occur in the period from 1979.

A. The Barnett Formula

A growing source of constitutional tension, helping drive codification, has been the multinational character of the UK, with demands from within some territories for more attention to their specific needs, for political autonomy of some kind or

[1] See A Blick, *Beyond Magna Carta: a constitution for the United Kingdom* (Oxford, Hart Publishing, 2015), especially pt 2.

[2] See P Hennessy, 'Whitehall brief: How public right of access to official information is curtailed', *The Times*, 27 November 1979.

even for secession from the union.[3] The so-called 'Barnett Formula' differs from the other codes considered here in that it is, as the name suggests, a mathematical formula. However, it merits consideration because it shares qualities with these codes. It is non-statutory and came about in a casual fashion. But nonetheless it has acquired a prominent public status, and has become a significant part of UK constitutional arrangements. The formula has precursors. In 1888, George Goschen, as Chancellor of the Exchequer, applied a formula to the distribution of public funds between Scotland and Ireland on the one hand and England and Wales on the other hand, derived from relative population sizes. It became known as the 'Goshen Formula'. Barnett itself was devised in 1978, replacing the complicated process of negotiating individual parts of the budget for the Scottish Office that had established itself by this time. Part of its purpose was to help restrain public expenditure, particularly in the wake of the International Monetary Fund crisis of 1976.[4] It began to function for Northern Ireland and Scotland in 1979, and expanded to cover Wales in 1980.[5] Initially the new formula was confidential, and it did not become public until 1980, when the Select Committee on Scottish Affairs managed to secure its clear avowal by the Government. It was subsequently labelled the 'Barnett Formula', after the Chief Secretary of the Treasury at the time of its invention, Joel Barnett. By the 1990s this name found its way into public consciousness.[6] Initially the intention was that the formula would be a temporary arrangement.[7] As Barnett (by this time Lord Barnett) told the House of Lords Select Committee on the Barnett Formula in 2009, 'I thought it might last a year or two before a government would decide to change it. It never occurred to me for one moment that it would last this long.'[8]

By the time the House of Lords Select Committee on the Barnett Formula came to examine the subject in 2009, the formula was used to determine funding for the three devolved systems in Northern Ireland, Scotland and Wales that had been introduced in the late 1990s. Using population sizes in its calculation, it allocated changes in funding to the devolved territories on a basis of alterations to spending programmes in specified policy areas for England. In certain instances England and Wales, or Great Britain, were treated as a single unit, rather than just England. Some areas of spending, such as on defence, were treated as not possible to attribute to UK sub-territories; while others—especially social security—could be attached to different parts of the UK, but were excluded from the Barnett calculation. The basic effect was that if spending increased—or decreased—in one of the specified policy areas in England, it would increase—or decrease—proportionately in the devolved territories. The precise allocation of funds between projects,

[3] See V Bogdanor, *Devolution in the United Kingdom* (Oxford, Oxford University Press, 2001).

[4] House of Lords Select Committee on the Barnett Formula, *The Barnett Formula* (HL 2008–09, 139) 19.

[5] ibid.

[6] See, eg, P Hetherington, 'Funding doubt as Scots' 20pc is threatened', *The Guardian*, 7 April 1992.

[7] T Edmonds, *The Barnett Formula* (London, House of Commons Library, 2001) 7–8.

[8] House of Lords Select Committee on the Barnett Formula, above n 4, Q2.

once the total was worked out, was a matter for the devolved area concerned.[9] Barnett himself had pressed for the formation of the Lords Committee on the formula because he was concerned about the differentials in per head public expenditure it produced. He noted to the committee in 2009 that for 2007–08 it was £1,600 lower for England than it was for Scotland. Barnett was concerned that 'the figures would so upset people in England' that they could threaten the future existence of the UK.[10] Ultimately the Committee recommended the replacement of the Barnett Formula with a new system of allocation based on needs. However, such a task would be complex, inevitably controversial and carry political risks for whoever undertook it. By the time of the Scottish Independence Referendum of September 2014 there had been no change. At this point the Barnett Formula appeared to attain an even firmer status. Shortly before the vote, the leaders of the three main parties in the UK Parliament, David Cameron (Conservative), Nick Clegg (Liberal Democrat) and Ed Miliband (Labour), as part of a late pro-union drive, committed to retaining the formula permanently. Yet whether it will survive the substantial expansions in devolution that followed the referendum, particularly in Scotland, is uncertain.[11]

At the time of the introduction of Barnett, devolution was on the agenda of the Labour Government, but ultimately the programme fell when it failed to meet the referendum requirements set for it in Scotland and Wales. The formula was not designed directly for devolution, but it came to be the means of determining financing for this system of government. The advent of devolution from the late 1990s, however, necessitated detailed codification of the relationship between the respective administrations at the UK and devolved levels, and the mechanisms they established for its maintenance. In particular it led to the production of the *Memorandum of Understanding*, considered in detail in Part Two (Chapter 10, section II.) of this book. Centrifugal pressures within the union, whether leading ultimately to a decentralised UK or an actual break-up, were a definite source of momentum for the codification process. Furthermore, the devolved systems developed their own codes. Today, for instance, there are *Ministerial Codes* in force in Wales, Scotland and Northern Ireland, applying to the respective executives in these territories.[12]

B. The *Civil Service Code*

Consideration of the *Civil Service Code* helps illustrate some of the paths of development that codification can follow. The values of the Civil Service have developed

9 ibid, 13–18.

10 ibid, Q1.

11 For a discussion of these issues, see V Bogdanor, *The Crisis of the Constitution*, 2nd edn (London, The Constitution Society, 2016).

12 For a comparative assessment, see O Roberts, *The Welsh Ministerial Code* (Cardiff, National Assembly for Wales, 2012). See also *Scottish Ministerial Code* (Edinburgh, Scottish Government, 2008); *Ministerial Code* (Belfast, Northern Ireland Executive, 2007).

over a long period, with an important stage in this process being the so-called Northcote-Trevelyan Report of 1854, a publication that in time came to wield significant influence. The decades that followed Northcote-Trevelyan saw the slow emergence of a permanent bureaucracy, the officials working within which were distanced from attachment to political parties and individual politicians. To retain these qualities, an understanding developed that civil servants should loyally serve the given ministers to whom they were attached, while preserving the ability to provide the same support to whoever succeeded those ministers. These principles could always potentially be subject to strain. Officials might, on the one hand, pursue their own agendas or those associated with their departments, or, on the other hand, might come to be too closely associated with an individual politician or seemingly supportive of a particular party. The advent of a Conservative administration under Margaret Thatcher in 1979 saw a sharp change in the style and policy of the UK Government. For some officials it became difficult to reconcile private conscience with public duty. Robert Armstrong, Cabinet Secretary from 1979–87, and from 1983–87 the sole Head of the Home Civil Service (he shared this role with Douglas Wass, Permanent Secretary to the Treasury, from 1981–83), began preparing a statement of the constitutional position of the Civil Service, to assist those employed within it to feel that they could work to support the government of the day without compromising their personal integrity. In doing so he was not breaking into completely fresh territory, as demonstrated by texts such as *Estacode*, cited in Chapter 1, section II.

Publication of this statement was held back until after the trial of Clive Ponting under the Official Secrets Act 1911. Ponting had leaked information about the sinking of the Argentine warship, the *General Belgrano*, during the Falklands conflict of 1982. The Ponting affair raised the question of whether civil servants might be subject to a higher public duty that overrode responsibility to the government of the day.[13] The publication of what became known as the 'Armstrong Memorandum', following the acquittal of Ponting in March 1985, led to an interpretation that the text was a response to this particular case. In fact it was the product of a desire to restate existing values of the Civil Service in the general atmosphere of the Thatcher premiership, something the Ponting case only served to delay. Some, however, construed the memorandum, with its insistence on the need for officials to serve the government of the day, as a attack on conventional understandings of their proper role, and as a tilt towards politicisation.[14] It was published as a written answer by the Prime Minister on 26 February 1985, expressly described as a 'Note by the Head of the Home Civil Service' and attributed personally to Armstrong.[15] This public association with a specific official was ironic given the emphasis that the memorandum placed on the lack of distinct personality on the part of civil servants.

[13] For Ponting's version of events, see C Ponting, *The Right to Know: the inside story of the Belgrano affair* (London, Sphere, 1985).

[14] A Sofer, 'In neutral—with drive', *The Times*, 18 November 1985.

[15] HC Deb, 26 February 1985, vol 460, cols 128–30W.

The text opened with an explanation from Armstrong that in recent months civil servants had put it to him that

> it would be timely to restate the general duties and responsibilities of civil servants in relation to Ministers. Recent events, and the public discussion to which they have given rise, have led me to conclude that the time has come when it would be right for me, as Head of the Home Civil Service, to respond to these suggestions.

Armstrong noted that he had received the approval of departmental permanent secretaries to the text (paragraph 1). The first principle it expressed was that civil servants were 'servants of the Crown. For all practical purposes the Crown in this context means and is represented by the Government of the day'. There was in this formulation no higher force. The general rule, with limited exceptions, was that the wielding of 'the executive powers of the Crown' took place in accordance with 'the advice' of ministers, who answered for their conduct to Parliament. The Civil Service 'as such' lacked 'constitutional personality or responsibility separate from the duly elected Government of the day'. The task of the Civil Service was to supply that government 'with advice on the formulation of … policies', to help execute them, 'and to manage and deliver the services for which the Government is responsible'. Another task in which it might engage was 'presentation' (paragraph 2).

Officials served the entire government, and the Prime Minister held the post of Minister for the Civil Service, but the primary 'duty' was to the minister at the head of the department in which they worked (paragraph 3). The Civil Service was 'non-political'. Staff had to support whatever government held office at the time, and behave in a fashion that made it possible for them to assist a different future government in the same way. Confidence on the part of ministers was critical (paragraph 4). Decisions about policy were a matter for the minister, operating within the wider framework of collective Cabinet responsibility. Officials had 'no constitutional responsibility or role' of their own separate from the minister. They had to support ministers fully in their decisions, providing all the relevant materials. But their duty also extended to speaking the truth as they saw it. In a passage Armstrong seems consciously to have modelled on the Privy Councillors Oath (the spelling used in the reproduced historic source) from the sixteenth century (see Chapter 1, section I.), Armstrong referred to the need 'to give the Minister honest and impartial advice, without fear or favour, and whether the advice accords with the Minister's view or not'. But once a decision was reached, whatever officials thought of it, they had to act upon it (paragraph 5). Further similarities to the Privy Council oath came with a reference to the need to maintain appropriate secrecy (paragraph 6). Ultimately a civil servant who could not comply with an instruction—assuming it did not entail breaking the law—had no option other than to resign from post (paragraph 11).

With the official Civil Service version of its values placed in the public domain, it was now possible for other players to scrutinise and contest it. The debate that followed, described by Oonagh Gay,[16] demonstrates the blurring of objectives that

[16] O Gay, *The Civil Service Code* (London, House of Commons Library, 2006).

can occur in connection with attempts to define constitutional understandings such as conventions. It can be difficult to determine whether those who seek to change codes are attempting to state the existing position more accurately, or alter it in accordance with their own favoured programme for change. In 1986 the First Division Association (FDA), the trades union that represents senior Whitehall officials, called for the introduction of an ethical code for civil servants, proposing its own draft. Writing in the *Guardian*, John Ward, General Secretary of the FDA, complained that the 'central message' contained in the Armstrong Memorandum 'was that civil servants' loyalty is to ministers … Morality and ethics are conspicuous by their absence.'[17] The House of Commons Treasury and Civil Service Committee considered issues connected to the Armstrong Memorandum.[18] In 1987, in accordance with a recommendation from the Committee, the text was altered to allow for appeals to be made by officials to the Head of the Home Civil Service about violations of principles.

Select committees emerge as another important driver of codification. They have pressed for the introduction of texts, scrutinised their operation, made recommendations for changes in their content and the way they function, and have sometimes created a need for codes relating to their own activities. In 1994 the Treasury and Civil Service Committee made further proposals regarding the Civil Service, including an enhanced process for appeals, a full ethical code for Whitehall—for which it produced a draft—and an Act of Parliament to provide a basis for the Civil Service. The final recommendation was not realised until 2010. But the *Civil Service Code*—also advocated by the recently-formed Committee on Standards in Public Life—appeared more swiftly. Coming into force at the outset of 1996, it was an important moment in the history of codification. In 2006 the Government consulted on and issued a new version of the Code that updated the language.[19] Ultimately, in accordance with repeated recommendations, including from the Treasury and Civil Service Committee and the Committee on Standards in Public Life, Part 1 of the Constitutional Reform and Governance Act 2010 provided the Civil Service, and its regulatory codes including the *Civil Service Code*, with a statutory grounding. The text of the current code is considered in Part Two (Chapter 7, section II.) of this book.

C. The Osmotherly Rules

The need to manage the relationship between different parts of the constitution was an important driver of the codification process. During this period, there

[17] J Ward, 'Whitehall's "no" to the inquisitors from the House of Commons', *Guardian*, 7 November 1986.

[18] House of Commons Treasury and Civil Service Select Committee, *Ministers and Civil Servants* (HC 1985–86, 92) especially xv–xvi.

[19] This account draws upon Gay, above n 16.

is evidence of the different branches, such as the UK executive, Parliament and the judiciary, becoming more assertive in their dealings with each other, and of increased tension developing.[20] Codes could take on pronounced salience if they dealt with interactions involving groups between which trust and mutual deference had declined. These texts, however, did not necessarily end the conflicts that had encouraged their development, and could become a focus for and source of further dispute.

The Osmotherly Rules[21] illustrate how these forces could play out. They involve a scenario that is inherently complex and tests one of the key tension points in the most important of constitutional doctrines, ministerial responsibility, and in particular its sub-component, individual ministerial responsibility (the other half of the doctrine being collective responsibility).[22] The broad constitutional position—as set out in the Armstrong Memorandum discussed in section I.B. above—is that ministers at Secretary of State level answer to Parliament for the policies and the activities of departments and agencies within their portfolios, and that the staff within these bodies—the civil servants—are in turn responsible to ministers. But once we scrutinise a general constitutional principle—particularly in its relationship with other systemic tenets—complications tend to arise. It is a task of many of the codes considered in this book, in the UK and elsewhere in the world, to describe and explain the nuances, and to reconcile them with the overall principles involved and the constitutional system as a whole. The particular complication that the Osmotherly Rules address involves the position of officials within the operation of individual ministerial responsibility.

In many ways, individual ministerial responsibility is supportive of an associated key feature of the UK system, executive accountability to Parliament, a principle that in turn is crucial to the facilitation of democracy itself, in as far as one of the chambers of Parliament, the House of Commons, is directly elected (while the executive is not). Individual ministerial responsibility, when it functions properly, means that Parliament has the benefit of being able to identify a specific person it can seek to hold to account for government activity in a given area of operation. We should not underestimate the value of the existence of a clear focal point for Parliament. It is a key strength of the UK constitution. It necessitates (with limited exceptions) the suppression to some extent of the individuality of civil servants to ensure that it is ministers alone who define the outward posture of the government. But another feature of the system of parliamentary government that individual ministerial responsibility furnishes is that the executive must be cooperative with Parliament in performing its accountability function. One manifestation of this helpfulness involves officials providing oral evidence to parliamentary committees. Yet while they might appear in front of committees, it is important,

[20] For instance, increased rebelliousness among MPs from the governing party. The classic study of this phenomenon is P Cowley, *The Rebels: How Blair Mislaid His Majority* (London, Politico's, 2005).

[21] The source of the name is explained below.

[22] See G Marshall (ed), *Ministerial Responsibility* (Oxford, Oxford University Press, 1989).

from the point of view of individual ministerial responsibility, that in such circumstances civil servants should normally provide evidence only on behalf of ministers, and not on their own account.

Osmotherly seeks to ensure that these various—and potentially competing—principles are adhered to. The text appeared in the wake of the introduction from 1979 of a new system of departmental select committees, each monitoring specific departmental policy areas.[23] Rules already existed internally, but the process leading to the setting up of the committees triggered scrutiny of what they were and whether they were appropriate, and brought to public attention that such regulations existed. They were written and owned by the executive. Parliament has never given formal approval to the Osmotherly Rules. As the House of Commons Liaison Committee stated in 2012, 'The Osmotherly rules are merely internal for Government. They have never been accepted by Parliament.'[24] But the text concerned the relationship between the executive and Parliament in a fundamental constitutional sense, and it was understandable that Parliament should show an interest in them, as it did. The appearance and development of the Osmotherly Rules was, as already noted, connected to a rising tension between branches of the constitution, in this instance the executive and legislature. It was also associated with the possibility of divisions within one of these branches itself. Osmotherly sought to avoid the exposure of disagreements between departments inside Whitehall, or between ministers and their officials.

As parliamentary assertiveness grew over the decades that followed, the Rules became increasingly relevant, and subject to inquiry and challenge in Westminster (particularly by the new select committees themselves), with the executive either hardening its stance in response, or making certain concessions. Problems that might arise involved whether a committee should be able to take evidence from a particular individual official, possibly on her own account, or even inquire into her particular actions in a given circumstance, and whether they were appropriate. An associated issue was whether ministers should be able to enlist civil servants in their efforts to deprive select committees of what might be regarded as a sufficient level of cooperation, perhaps even to the extent of misleading a committee. A similar dilemma had appeared in relation to the Ponting case (section I.B. above), and engaged matters that the Armstrong Memorandum, and later the *Civil Service Code*, also addressed. It involved a clash between constitutional principles: the accountability of civil servants to ministers, individual ministerial responsibility and parliamentary government. Though they were potentially mutually supportive they were distinct, and questions could arise in some circumstances about how they should be interpreted and which should override the others in a given circumstance. Lastly, a related problem from the point of view of Parliament was

[23] See, eg, G Drewry (ed), *The New Select Committees: a study of the 1979 reforms* (Oxford, Clarendon Press, 1989); MA Jogerst, *Reform in the House of Commons: the select committee system* (Lexington, KY, University Press of Kentucky, 2006).

[24] House of Commons Liaison Committee, *Select Committee Effectiveness, Resources and Powers* (HC 2012–13, 697) 40.

the idea that it was the ultimate authority within the UK constitution, and should be able to obtain whatever information it sought, from whomever it wished to obtain it. Moreover, it was a crucial part of its historic 'privilege' that Parliament have 'exclusive cognisance' of its own business, and that it should not be hampered by external limitations, such as the Osmotherly Rules. Hence the dilemma Parliament faced when scrutinising the Rules. Parliamentarians did not wish to imply endorsement of this text and by extension the acceptance of an outside restraint upon themselves (nor did they want to be seen to become involved in the internal management of the executive). But they knew that in practice the Rules had important practical implications for their ability to perform their constitutional role, and therefore could not ignore them.

Gay provides an account of the conception and development of the Osmotherly Rules.[25] In 1978 the House of Commons Select Committee on Procedure, as part of its inquiry that ultimately recommended the formation of a group of select committees focused on particular Whitehall departments, managed to obtain a copy of the rules that were a precursor to Osmotherly.[26] The official files now available reveal that the then Prime Minister, James Callaghan, was reluctant to release them, but decided that a refusal to disclose would contradict public undertakings he had made to more open government.[27] In its report the Liaison Committee found the rules, that dated from 1976, 'broadly unobjectionable' (paragraph 7.12), though it recorded certain reservations about them, including the breadth of the definition of matters over which civil servants should not reveal information. In 1980, with departmental select committees having begun their work, EBC (Edward) Osmotherly, an Assistant Secretary responsible for the the Machinery of Government Division of the Cabinet Office, produced a new document. Issued on 16 May 1980, it was intended to be confidential, but it soon leaked into the public arena. The full title was *Memorandum of Guidance for Civil Servants Appearing before Select Committees*. But—like the Barnett Formula—it became known by the name of the person to whom it was attributed, although Osmotherly was seemingly unhappy about the notoriety he thereby attained.[28] The following pattern manifested itself. First there were objections that certain rules were secret. Then, once they became public, critical scrutiny shifted to the actual contents of the document, with demands for their alteration. Opposition parties and observers argued that the Rules denied meaningful insight into policy formation discussions and internal processes of decision-making. Hennessy writes that he regarded the Rules 'as an attempt to stymie the reforms of the 1980s with the rules of the 1940s or even the 1250s'.[29] But in 1987, following the Westland scandal, an affair that was

[25] O Gay, *The Osmotherly Rules* (London, House of Commons Library, 2005).

[26] House of Commons Select Committee on Procedure, *First Report* (HC 1977–78, 588-I) xci. The Committee reproduced the rules in Appendix D.

[27] See The National Archive/Public Record Office PREM 16/1788.

[28] P Hennessy, *Whitehall* (London, Pimlico, 2001) 361–62.

[29] ibid, 363.

the subject of close select committee interest,[30] the executive hardened its stance. The Government tightened the Osmotherly Rules to stress that parliamentary committees should not investigate the activities of individual civil servants, which were a matter for ministers to deal with.

Eventually, a further scandal forced the Government to concede ground. Gay describes how the 'arms to Iraq' affair[31] prompted changes to the Osmotherly Rules, accepting limitations on the authority of ministers. It also spurred a parliamentary intervention in the sphere of activity with which the Rules dealt. In 1996 the Scott Report into the matter, the product of a judge-led inquiry, criticised the prevention of former officials from giving evidence to the Commons Trade and Industry Committee. The Commons Public Service Committee then recommended later in the same year that the Osmotherly Rules stipulate that, if select committees ask them to do so, Chief Executives should provide them with evidence. The Government accepted this proposal. Further changes arose partly as a consequence of circumstances surrounding the invasion of Iraq of 2003. This operation was controversial, both as an action in its own right and because of constitutional issues it raised regarding the authority under which military action takes place, and the accountability to which it is subject. Following pressure from within Parliament, including from the Commons Foreign Affairs and Liaison Committees, in 2005 the Government revised the Osmotherly Rules to include express reference to a presumption that if committees asked to take evidence from a named civil servant, they would receive cooperation. This rule covered special advisers—a subject of concern at the time because of an increase in their numbers and perceived importance—as well as permanent officials. Another presumption incorporated into the new version of the Rules was that of supplying information requested by committees.[32]

The most recent set of updates to the Rules came in 2014. They dealt with the exceptions to the principle that civil servants do not answer directly to Parliament. It was long established that departmental Accounting Officers appeared before committees—especially the Public Accounts Committee—on a personal basis. The 2014 update, following pressure from within Parliament and from outside groups, made it possible for Accounting Officers who had moved on to a different role to provide parliamentary evidence about their earlier activities. It also allowed for Senior Responsible Owners involved in running major projects on behalf of the Government to answer directly to Parliament for their performance.[33]

[30] See D Oliver and R Austin, 'Political and Constitutional Aspects of the Westland Affair' (1987) 40(1) *Parliamentary Affairs* 20; House of Commons Defence Select Committee, *Report from the Defence Committee of the House of Commons* (HC 1985–86, 519) especially lxv–lxvi.

[31] See, eg, R Norton-Taylor, *Truth is a difficult concept: inside the Scott Inquiry* (London, Fourth Estate, 1995).

[32] This account draws upon Gay, above n 22.

[33] A Horne, *The Osmotherly Rules* (London, House of Commons Library, 2015); A Paun and P Barlow, *Civil Service Accountability to Parliament* (London, Institute for Government, 2014).

II. CODIFICATION FROM THE 1990s

The 1980s had seen the appearance of important 'name' codes—Barnett, Osmotherly and Armstrong—that, unlike key earlier texts, *Questions of Procedure for Ministers* (QPM) and the *Precedent Book* (see Chapter 1, sections III. and IV. respectively), entered the public domain soon or immediately after being devised. During the following decade codification became an increasingly prominent part of political life. One motive for this tendency was the personal outlook of John Major, who succeeded Margaret Thatcher as Conservative Prime Minister in 1990. A central part of his agenda was the idea that government should become more transparent in its interactions with the public, especially in the provision of public services.[34] One manifestation of this approach was the publication, following the 1992 General Election, of QPM. Peter Hennessy, an influential figure as both a commenter on and influencer of codification, played a part in bringing about this decision.[35] As we have seen, a public outing of the *existence* of the document, but not its contents, had taken place as early as 1975 at the time of the Crossman case; and the retention of its confidential status had been a subject of criticism for some time. During the 1980s, the public atmosphere was different from that of the 1940s. Demands for greater openness had gained force, with the Campaign for Freedom of Information and various journalists in the vanguard. In this environment it seemed reasonable to question why a text relating to the operation of a democratic constitution should be kept secret from the public. Providing an example of this attitude, noting that he had obtained a copy, the political journalist Hugo Young wrote in 1985, 'Although lacking even the vestige of a security aspect, this intriguing state paper has, curiously, never been published. It is time to bring it out of the closet.'[36] Now, following the Major initiative, QPM was fully in the open. The subsequent development of the text is considered below.

At the same time that it published QPM, the Government began issuing lists of Cabinet committees and their members that had previously been confidential, another shift towards openness. Any Cabinet decision, whether taken at committee level or by full Cabinet, is supposed to have equal force. Yet publicising the existence of differentiated Cabinet bodies and their membership potentially demystified Cabinet and the idea that it was an homogeneous, monolithic entity. A further initiative in this area was the introduction of the *Code of Practice on Access to Official Information*, which came into force in April 1994.[37] This text entailed

[34] See, eg, A Bevins and N Timmins, 'Waldegrave opens chink in Whitehall', *Independent*, 20 May 1992. For Major's outlook, see House of Commons Public Administration Select Committee, *The Ministerial Code: Improving the Rule Book* (HC 2000–01, 235) vi.

[35] For Hennessy on this period of codification and his role in it, see P Hennessy, *The Prime Minister: the office and its holders since 1945* (London, Allen Lane, 1999) 451–52.

[36] H Young, 'The secret code that locks the Cabinet door against 50 million enemies', *Guardian*, 5 September 1985.

[37] See O Gay, *The Code of Practice on Access to Official Information* (London, House of Commons Library, 1997).

the codification of openness itself. It had a precursor in the 'Croham Directive' of 1977, requiring officials, when writing submissions, to separate their recommendations from the evidential material on which they rested, so that the latter could be released in public. The Directive took its name from the former head of the Home Civil Service who devised it, Lord Croham (Douglas Allen), and was in this sense another 'name code'.[38] The 1994 document provided for members of the public to apply for particular information to be released. Once again, Parliament took a close interest in this Code, and was a source of recommendations for its better operation. The Code was subsequently superseded by the Freedom of Information Act 2000, evidence of a possible dynamic leading from non-statutory code to framework contained in an Act of Parliament, as would take place later in a slightly different fashion with the *Civil Service Code*.

Codification during the 1990s also had a reactive dimension to it. During the middle years of the decade in particular there developed a mood of public concern regarding probity in political and official life. Drivers of this trend included the aforementioned 'Arms to Iraq' scandal, and revelations about MPs receiving payment in return for tabling questions in the House of Commons ('Cash for Questions'). Against this background, Major established in 1994 the Committee on Standards in Public Life, an extra-parliamentary body reporting directly to the Prime Minister. Part of its impact has been upon codification, making various recommendations about the content and operation of these documents. The Committee also produced a text of its own in 1995, that remains to this day widely referred to within official codes, *The seven principles of public life*, applying to those who occupy public offices.[39] It became another 'name code', known colloquially as the 'Nolan Principles' after the first chair of the Committee, Lord Nolan. As the title suggests, the seven principles provide an example of a text focused on overarching values rather than practicalities. In a sense they sought to fill the ethical void some identified in texts such as the Armstrong Memorandum. The first principle is 'Selflessness', requiring conduct always to be in accordance with 'the public interest.' Second is 'Integrity', meaning not becoming subject to improper external influences. Third is 'Objectivity', entailing taking 'decisions impartially, fairly and on merit, using the best evidence and without discrimination or bias'. The fourth principle is 'Accountability', stipulating that those who hold public office 'are accountable to the public for their decisions' and that they 'must submit themselves to the scrutiny necessary' to achieve this outcome. Fifth is 'Openness', referring to 'open and transparent' decision-making, with a predisposition towards making information publicly available. 'Honesty' requires that those subject to the principles 'be truthful'. Lastly, 'Leadership' stresses the importance of adhering to the principles and promoting them among others.

[38] See, eg, 'Let the people know', *The Observer*, 6 January 1985.

[39] M White and P Wintour, 'Nolan acts to stamp out sleaze: Seven principles of public life', *Guardian*, 12 May 1995.

A. The *Ministerial Code*

The publication of QPM—in accordance with a Conservative Party manifesto pledge of 1992—was the beginning of a new phase for the text.[40] In an act one newspaper described at the time as 'a laudable exercise in open government',[41] QPM became a public document. The prolonged suppression of QPM up to 1992 may have given it a mystique that the actual text, once published, could not sustain. As we shall see, it contained many important statements of principle and practice. However, rather than being used as a means of better understanding the UK constitution, the most notable purposes towards which the newly available QPM was deployed were less lofty, unsurprisingly. The purpose of publication may have been to encourage improved perception of the probity of government. Whether it achieved this goal, or indeed improved the actual conduct of ministers, is difficult to establish with certainty. Indeed the document became a focus for debate about the conduct of particular politicians, and a weapon to use against the government of the day.[42]

Over the years, discussion in the media and Parliament of possible violation of QPM and then the *Ministerial Code* has figured in the build-up of pressure on numerous ministers, sometimes ending in their loss of office, as the account provided by Lucinda Maer and Ed Faulkner demonstrates.[43] Those who fell from office after becoming embroiled in criticism in which QPM was at some point invoked have included David Mellor, Secretary of State for National Heritage under John Major.[44] A casualty of the Labour period of government from 1997 was David Blunkett. He resigned from Cabinet twice, in 2004 and again in 2005.[45] Blair himself was accused of violating the code in his conduct regarding the decision to participate in the invasion of Iraq in 2003.[46] In the coalition era of 2010–15 the *Ministerial Code* continued to play a part in public judgements of ministerial fitness for post. But alleged violations of the rules described in the text did not necessarily lead to the loss of office. Much depended on the political circumstances of the time, and the extent to which the Prime Minister was inclined to withstand pressure on behalf of a particular colleague in a given difficulty. Nonetheless, it is reasonable to conclude that many ministers and their officials were aware of the way in which the Code could figure in political difficulties. A desire to avoid such

[40] This account draws on L Maer and E Faulkner, *The Ministerial Code and the Independent Adviser on Ministers' Interests* (London, House of Commons Library, 2015).

[41] 'From the Independent Archive', *Independent*, 4 December 2004.

[42] A Blick and P Hennessy, *The Hidden Wiring Emerges: the Cabinet Manual and the working of the British constitution* (London, IPPR, 2011) 30.

[43] Maer and Faulkner, above n 40.

[44] *Anthony Bevins*, 'Major "must check if Mellor broke rules"', *The Independent*, 16 September 1992.

[45] 'What is the Home Secretary accused of?', *Independent on Sunday*, 5 December 2004; F Elliott, 'Revealed: Blunkett broke rules with job at DNA firm', *Independent on Sunday*, 30 October 2005.

[46] See, eg, M Woolf, 'Blair broke code to keep war advice from Cabinet', *Independent*, 9 March 2005.

problems for themselves might influence their behaviour, and in this sense promote adherence to the Code and its contents.

Another focus of controversy was the way in which the Code was enforced. The post of Independent Adviser on Ministers' Interests came into being during 2006–07. Before the creation of the Adviser, the practice had developed for the Prime Minister to entrust investigations into specific incidents to particular individuals. The Adviser represented the permanent presence of a new player in the process of enforcing the Code, strengthening its autonomy, and therefore potentially a lessening of the role of the premier. Yet equally a referral to the Adviser could be the means of passing on some of the responsibility for awkward decisions, potentially providing a useful shield for the Prime Minister. Furthermore, though supposedly 'Independent', the Adviser—who was selected purely at the discretion of the premier, with no statutory framework for the appointment—lacked autonomy, being unable to initiate inquiries, carrying them out only when the Prime Minister decided they were necessary. This arrangement was subject to criticism. For instance, in 2012 the House of Commons Public Administration Select Committee pressed for the Adviser to be able to trigger inquiries; and for the holder to be recruited through an open competition, with a parliamentary select committee holding a pre-appointment hearing. The Committee also favoured the creation of a statutory framework for the Adviser.[47] The Government rejected these proposals, stressing the centrality of the Prime Minister to the application of the relevant rules.[48]

But that an official post-holder with a specific and publicly avowed role in enforcing the Code even existed was evidence of a transformation in the status of this text since the publication of QPM in 1992. It lacked firm constitutional autonomy, and had no direct legal force. But, though senior officials protested otherwise, the Code became in practice something more than merely an internal management document for the executive. Less than a decade after Major's decision, the House of Commons Select Committee on Public Administration had noted that while the document 'may have developed in a private and ad hoc way', it had become 'an integral part of the new constitutional architecture'.[49] The document seemed only to receive attention in circumstances of controversy regarding ministerial conduct, or over supposed inadequacies in its own provisions or the means for their enforcement. But below the surface, as the Committee recognised, the changing nature of the *Ministerial Code* and its associated paraphernalia amounted to a far more substantial constitutional development, which continues today.

[47] House of Commons Public Administration Select Committee, *The Prime Minister's adviser on Ministers' interests: independent or not?* (HC 2010–12, 1761) 20–21.

[48] House of Commons Public Administration Select Committee, *The Prime Minister's adviser on Ministers' interests: independent or not? Government response to the Committee's of Twenty Second Report of 2012–12* (HC 2012–13, 976) 20–21.

[49] House of Commons Public Administration Select Committee, above n 34.

B. Codification after Major

The impetus and new patterns that codification acquired during the 1990s continued after the fall of John Major. Under the leadership of Tony Blair, who became Prime Minister in May 1997, Labour presented itself as the scourge of the 'sleaze' that supposedly characterised the outgoing Conservative Government.[50] Codes played a part in the new approach. Therefore, in seeking to attain and convey the impression of a break with the Major years, the Labour Government used some of the same techniques the Major administration had developed. Early examples of Blair-era codification, both dating from 1997, are the *Model Contract for Special Advisers* and the rebranding of QPM as the *Ministerial Code*. Yet these documents and others discussed so far from the 1990s onwards were only the more prominent manifestation of a far larger and intensifying process.

A two-volume text that appeared in 2000, the *Directory of Civil Service Guidance*, gives an idea of the scale on which codification was taking place, generally without attracting parliamentary or media attention.[51] Like *Estacode*, QPM and the *Precedent Book* at their inception (see Chapter 1), the *Directory* represented an effort to collate existing guidance into a single document. It described itself as superseding an earlier text, the intriguingly titled *Guidance on Guidance*, the final edition of which appeared in February 1996; and it also included a significant amount of the contents of another previous volume entitled the *Head of Department's Personal Handbook*. In the Foreword, the then Head of the Home Civil Service and Cabinet Secretary, Richard Wilson, depicted the *Directory* as intended to make it easier for civil servants to obtain an account of the 'principles and practice' informing how their institution operated. In this sense the *Directory* was not conceived of with an external audience in mind but as intended to disseminate knowledge within Whitehall. Though it was seemingly not classified—as QPM had been up to 1992—the *Directory* was not actively promoted to the public in the name of greater transparency, a contrast with a later publication, *The Cabinet Manual* (see section VI. below), for which outward exposition was an avowed purpose.

A problem that many codes face is that they describe rules that are supposed to be flexible, but writing them down can make them less so. Wilson was careful to emphasise that the text was only '**guidance** [emphasis in original]. It reflects important and useful accumulated wisdom which has been built up over the years, but it should not be regarded as a rigid set of rules.' It could set out 'key principles' but not 'provide a blueprint for every situation'. Lastly, Wilson promised ongoing updates of the text 'in the light of experience'. It is not clear how far this plan manifested itself, and the document available online today appears to be the 2000 issue, though the *Directory* is referenced in the 2011 *Cabinet Manual*.

[50] See, eg, the Labour General Election manifesto of 1997, *New Labour: because Britain deserves better* (London, Labour Party, 1997), especially the section headed 'We will clean up politics'.

[51] Cabinet Office, *Directory of Civil Service Guidance*, vol 1: *Guidance Summaries* and ibid, vol 2: *Collected Guidance* (London, Cabinet Office, 2000).

The first volume, 71 pages in total, consists of 'Guidance Summaries', that is shortened versions of longer texts; while the second volume, at 57 pages, is a compendium of those documents referred to in the first volume that are not widely available, reproduced in full. Both cover a wide span of issues, some seemingly less consequential, others more obviously important, but all with constitutional connotations of some kind. They take in matters of propriety, such as, in volume 1, how civil servants should approach 'events run by organisations with party political links' (p 9); the taking up of private sector posts after having left public service (p 10); payment for public appearances (p 12); engagement in political activities by officials (p 47), and travel arrangements for ministers, their advisers (p 62) and the partners of civil servants (p 63). More definitely overarching constitutional issues (again in volume 1) include the business of Cabinet committees (p 11); the *Civil Service Code* (p 12) and *Civil Service Management Code* (p 13); the handling of contacts with opposition parties (p 18); devolution (p 23); the European Union (p 28); freedom of information (p 29); the Human Rights Act 1998 (p 32); the advice of the Law Officers (pp 35–36); ministerial accountability and the *Ministerial Code* (p 39); referendums (p 54); parliamentary select committees (p 57); obligations under international agreements (p 63); and whistle-blowing (p 64). There are some now dated references to specific initiatives from the time of publication (such as 'Information Age Government', p 33) and practical matters that may seem parochial to the outsider but were of great importance to the readership, in particular pay (pp 44–45). Some of these subject areas, such as the Human Rights Act, freedom of information and devolution, were connected to legislative changes that were recent in 2000, demonstrating how constitutional change drove codification. Suggesting the overall scope and complexity of codification at this point, there are well over 100 individual subject entries in volume 1. Though earlier texts such as the *Precedent Book* and *Estacode* reveal the Civil Service as an institution that had already provided for a range of circumstances and activities in written form, the overall detail (in areas such as financial propriety) and breadth had expanded. Again like the *Precedent Book* and *Estacode*, the *Directory* represented an attempt to systematise and impose some kind of order on the mass of documentation.

The full reproductions of actual texts contained in volume 2 deal with such complex areas as how accountability is possible for events that took place under an earlier government of a different complexion, given that present ministers are not directly responsible for them and are not generally even able to view the papers involved (pp 11–14). How should ministers who feel they are the victims of defamation respond? The guidance included in the *Directory* on this matter reminds the reader that '[s]uccessive Law Officers have generally discouraged Ministers from bringing defamation proceedings' (p 20). The *Directory* contains an account of the cycle and content of honours lists, and includes a stipulation that 'The Honours List should be as representative as possible of outstanding service and achievement across the whole of the country's life, whether in the public, private or voluntary fields.' It cautions departments against 'any undue bunching … in a particular field of activity, geographical area or age group' when making recommendations for recognition (p 27).

One interesting discussion in volume 2 of the *Directory* involves the legal implications of a vacancy in a senior ministerial post after a General Election, a resignation or a death; or during the period before formal appointment procedures, such as swearing in and receiving the seals of office, are complete. Both officials and junior ministers, the document explains, need to exercise caution in carrying out actions in the name of a minister who heads their department. It is possible that 'an instrument made or action taken' will be the subject of a successful legal challenge. Possible means of bypassing difficulties include finding another Secretary of State to authorise a course of action, since formally any Secretary of State can carry out the functions of another. If the minister is legally defined as a 'corporation sole', it may be possible to act, for instance through utilising the 'corporate seal' (pp 44–45). This guidance, then, deals with precisely the kind of contingency that may occur only rarely but that officials must know how to handle in order to preserve the outward veneer of continuity and stability in governmental institutions. Codification could help ensure that the necessary steps were taken at critical moments, thereby shoring up the system further. Yet at the same time, in as far as it revealed—to use the Hennessy phrase—the 'hidden wiring'[52] of the constitution, it could deplete the mystique these procedures were deployed to preserve. The authors of the *Directory* neither sought nor achieved wide public exposure for their work, but for other codes the story was different.

III. CODIFICATION BEYOND THE EXECUTIVE

By the early twenty-first century, codification had begun to spread beyond the UK central executive to different branches of the constitution. The House of Commons Liaison Committee, a committee including the chairs of all the Commons select committees, first promulgated the *Core Tasks for Select Committees* in June 2002.[53] As Richard Kelly and Agnieszka Suchenia show, it was the product of a combination of influences.[54] The first was pressure for change from outside Parliament and government, including the Conservative Party Commission to Strengthen Parliament, the chair of which was the constitutional expert Lord Norton.[55] The Hansard Society Commission on Parliamentary Scrutiny issued a

[52] The title of a collection of essays on the constitution: P Hennessy, *The Hidden Wiring: unearthing the British constitution* (London, Phoenix, 1996). The phrase was reused for a pamphlet written by Hennessy and the present author dealing directly with the codification phenomenon: Blick and Hennessy, above n 43.

[53] House of Commons Liaison Committee, *Annual Report 2002* (HC 2002–03, 558).

[54] R Kelly and A Suchenia, *Select Committees—Core Tasks* (London, House of Commons Library, 2013) 8–11.

[55] Commission to Strengthen Parliament, *Strengthening Parliament* (London, Conservative Party, 2000).

report in 2001 making proposals for more methodical committee working that included the phrase 'core tasks' within them.[56] Second was a political dispute between Parliament and the Government over the status of select committees and their vulnerability to executive interference. Third was the determination of the Leader of the House of Commons, Robin Cook, to bring about change. The Modernisation Committee, of which Cook as Leader of the House was chair, issued a set of recommendations in May 2002, providing direct impetus for the *Core Tasks*.[57]

The *Core Tasks* as issued in 2002 divided into four lettered 'objectives'. Objective A described the role of examining and commenting on departmental policy. It had four sub-tasks, including addressing specific courses of action stated by the UK Government or European Commission (Task 1), considering policy that was developing, or where it was needed but did not presently exist in satisfactory form (Task 2), examining draft bills falling within the remit of the particular committee (Task 3) and scrutinising departmental publications (Task 4). Objective B was the consideration of departmental expenditure. It consisted of one task: examining planned expenditure and 'out-turn' of the relevant departmental and associated institutions (Task 5). Objective C, comprising four tasks, involved departmental administration. It included reference to scrutinising departmental Public Service Agreements (PSAs), a public management tool then in use under New Labour (Task 6). The reference to PSAs serves to illustrate one of the hazards involved in codification when it focuses on aspects of official activity that—though they may seem important at the time—are not of a lasting quality. By the time the core tasks were renewed a decade later, PSAs had ceased to exist, superseded by other management vogues that themselves would probably prove fleeting. Task 7 required that committees consider the activities of bodies connected to the department, such as Executive Agencies, Non-Departmental Public Bodes and regulators. Task 8 was to scrutinise important departmental appointments, while Task 9 was the assessment of how key policies and legislation were implemented. Lastly, Objective D described the function of supporting the Commons in debating and making decisions. The task it proposed was that of issuing reports appropriate for being discussed in plenary, Westminster Hall 'or debating committees' (Task 10).

A new version of the *Core Tasks* appeared in 2012, the text of which is considered in Part Two (Chapter 8, section III.) of this book. It came about partly at the prompting of the Select Committee on the Reform of the House of Commons, which recommended an overhaul in its 2009 report, *Rebuilding the House*.[58] Once again the Hansard Society contributed to the pressure for change from outside Parliament. A common thrust to these assessments was that the *Core Tasks* needed

[56] Hansard Society Commission on Parliamentary Scrutiny, *The Challenge for Parliament—Making Government Accountable* (London, Hansard Society, 2001).

[57] For an account of the development of the *Core Tasks for Select Committees* drawn upon here, see Kelly and Suchenia, above n 54.

[58] Select Committee on the Reform of the House of Commons, *Rebuilding the House* (HC 2008–09, 1117).

to avoid being overly prescriptive, placing excessive demands on committee members, and should allow each individual committee a significant degree of flexibility as to its precise programme.

Another constitutional branch to develop the codification habit was the judiciary. The first edition of the *Guide to Judicial Conduct* appeared in October 2004, drawing on an earlier report from November 2002, 'Guidelines to Judicial Ethics'.[59] The *Guide to Judicial Conduct* describes its purpose as 'to offer assistance to judges about their conduct and to set out principles on the basis of which judges can make their own decisions'.[60] In his Foreword to the 2013 issue, the then Lord Chief Justice of England and Wales, Lord Judge, emphasises that it is not intended 'to prescribe a detailed code'. One motive for the *Guide* was a need to respond to social trends. As Lord Judge puts it, 'the responsibilities and the public's perception of the standards to which judges should adhere are continuously evolving'. To illustrate the point, he recalls that when he 'first came to the Bar it was considered in order for a son to appear before his father. This would be unacceptable today.'[61]

Appendix 4 to the 2013 judicial guide provides an example of how a code can allow for responses to changing patterns of behaviour, driven by underlying social change. Entitled 'Blogging by judicial office-holders', it comprises guidance from the Senior Presiding Judge and the Senior President of Tribunals. Applying to all occupants of judicial posts, it is 'effective immediately', suggesting a degree of urgency to prevent any problems that might occur. It begins by defining a 'blog' as a 'personal journal published on the internet'. Importantly, blogs 'tend to be interactive, allowing visitors to leave comments', and can include links to other material elsewhere. While noting that blogging is not prohibited, the guidance states that those to whom it applies must 'be acutely aware of the need to conduct themselves, both in and out of court, in such a way as to maintain public confidence in the impartiality of the judiciary'. When blogging, those who hold judicial offices should not describe themselves as such, yet at the same time should keep in mind the need to avoid creating reputational problems, even if blogging anonymously. The guidance also recommends deleting any historic blogs that could be problematic. Failure to abide by the rules, it threatens, could lead to 'disciplinary action'.[62]

The *Guide* also presented itself as part of an international trend, noting the appearance of a series of equivalent texts in the Commonwealth. The most significant was a work by Mr Justice Thomas, *Judicial Ethics in Australia* (1988). There followed texts including, in 1998, the Canadian Judicial Council's *Ethical Principles for Judges* and, again in Australia, a *Guide to Judicial Conduct* (2002) and a *Code of Conduct for Judicial Officers of the Federal Republic of Nigeria* (undated). Further encouragement came from a United Nations-inspired exercise that began in 2001. It involved collaboration between senior judicial figures across different types of

[59] Judiciary of England and Wales, *Guide to Judicial Conduct* (London, Judiciary of England and Wales, 2013) 4.
[60] ibid, 5.
[61] ibid, 3.
[62] ibid, 37.

legal system, eventually leading to the endorsement by the United Nations Human Rights Commission in April 2003 of the so-called 'Bangalore Principles of Judicial Conduct'. The six 'values' it entailed were: independence; impartiality; integrity; propriety; equal treatment; and competence and diligence. They form the core of the *Guide to Judicial Conduct*.[63] As Lord Judge put it, 'the recent adoption of written codes of conduct throughout the world' and the Bangalore Principles 'have indicated that a written Guide for England and Wales would now be desirable and in accord with international practice'.[64]

Publication of the *Guide to Judicial Conduct* was more than simply an occasion: it had a lasting institutional structure created around it. It was the product of a working group under Lord Justice Pill. It is notable that the judicial guide, listing the members of this body, is open about process and about who sat on the various groups that produced it in a way that executive texts such as *The Cabinet Manual* are not. Consultation followed with the Court of Appeal and High Court Benches, and with the Circuit and District Benches. The Lord Chancellor then had an input.[65] After the judicial guide appeared, the Judges' Council then formed a Standing Committee tasked with monitoring the text with a view to identifying necessary alterations and additions, intended to meet at least every six months. Once again, the *Guide* names the members.[66]

Another judiciary-related document had appeared earlier the same year as the *Guide to Judicial Conduct*, in January 2004. Entitled *The Lord Chancellor's judiciary-related functions: Proposals*, it became known as 'the Agreement' or 'the Concordat'. It was issued in the wake of the announcement by the Government in June 2003 that it intended to abolish the office of Lord Chancellor, as part of a wider programme to create a UK Supreme Court and Judicial Appointments Commission. Unlike other texts discussed here, much of the Concordat consisted of government commitments to the judiciary regarding what it would include in forthcoming legislation intended to provide for the reformed framework. Provisions from this text were duly included in the Constitutional Reform Act 2005. In addition to the content that was legislated for, the Concordat included some significant statements, for instance its reference to the need to safeguard the 'separation of powers' between executive, judiciary and legislature. This interpretation of the constitution is questionable. Traditionally in the UK the three powers are fused in one institution: Parliament, though the 2005 Act, in creating an independent Supreme Court, represented some movement towards a 'separation' model.[67]

[63] ibid, 7–8.
[64] ibid, 3.
[65] ibid, 4.
[66] ibid, 5.
[67] For discussion of the 'Concordat', see House of Lords Select Committee on the Constitution, *Relations between the executive, the judiciary and Parliament* (HL 2006–07, 151) 9–11. For guidance to civil servants on issues connected to judicial review, see Treasury Solicitor's Department, *The judge over your shoulder* (London, Stationery Office, 2006).

By the beginning of the twenty-first century, codification had extended altogether beyond the field of official authority as conventionally understood, as demonstrated by a text purporting to be an agreement between government and civil society, *The Compact*.[68] The most recent edition of this 16-page document, dating from 2010, opens with a 'Message' from the Prime Minister, David Cameron, and the then Deputy Prime Minister, Nick Clegg. Cameron depicts the purpose of the Compact with reference to his 'Big Society' initiative, 'getting citizens more engaged, involved and responsible for the communities around them'. Clegg, on the other hand, does not mention the Big Society, describing the 'Power Shift the Coalition Government is committed to, transferring power away from central government to local communities'. Next there follows a 'Foreword' by Nick Hurd MP, described as the 'Minister for Civil Society'. Curiously, given the title of this ministerial brief, the document concedes in footnote 1 on page 6 that 'civil society is a contested term'. It goes on to state that, 'for the purposes of the Compact, civil society organizations include charities, social enterprises and voluntary and community groups'. In another 'Foreword', Simon Blake, 'Chair of Compact Voice', explains that the document 'is now in its twelfth year'. The text is an accord between central government and its various agencies on the one hand, and civil society organisations (as defined in the text) in England (not the UK) on the other hand (p 6).

Part of the text proper is concerned with the terms on which central government and so-called 'civil society' interact. It engages an important area of constitutional concern. If, through the 'Big Society' or similar initiatives, central government takes on the services of outside organisations in return for providing them with money or some other benefit in kind, there is a risk that the independence of these groups will in some way become compromised. Consequently, government undertakes, for instance, to 'Respect and uphold the independence' of these groups, 'including their right to campaigning', notwithstanding 'any relationship, financial or otherwise, which may exist' (paragraph 1.1). The Compact requires civil society organisations, for their part, if 'campaigning or advocating', to 'ensure that robust evidence is provided, including information about the source and range of people and communities represented' (paragraph 1.7). What these stipulations mean in practice is open to question, as is their enforceability. Nonetheless, they represent how far codification has progressed in its scope from its origins as an internal attempt to organise the operation of the War Cabinet.

IV. THE LIMITS TO CODIFICATION

A. The *Central-Local Concordat*

Consideration of the historic development of constitutional codes might create the impression of a Whig or Hegelian process, an irresistible march towards

[68] HM Government, *The Compact* (Cabinet Office, London, 2010).

ever-more-extensive, comprehensive and detailed incorporation of rules into textual form. Even if there is strong evidence of a broad tendency in this direction, there have been important exceptions to it. An important corrective comes with the case of the *Central-Local Concordat* of 2007.[69] The context within which the Concordat came about was the centralised nature of UK constitutional arrangements. While local government has ancient lineage, today it lacks a firm constitutional foundation. Drawing on the doctrine of parliamentary sovereignty, the Westminster legislature can alter, modify or remove the powers of local government and change its structure, even to the point of creating or abolishing whole tiers. Over time the tendency has been for Parliament to use its legal authority (in England at least) to reduce the autonomy of local government, in the realms both of policy and finance. International comparisons reveal that the UK is exceptional for its degree of central control.[70] From the late 1990s, devolution to Scotland, Wales, Northern Ireland and Greater London created new poles of political authority. However, it did not augment the strength of local government in the territories concerned—indeed it may have encouraged its deterioration. Furthermore, much of England lacks any form of devolution on anything like the scale existing elsewhere. In the post-devolution era, central government brought forward schemes presented as intended to enhance local democracy in England. Yet in practice they often involved imposing new burdens and conditions upon it, alongside any new powers they created. The concept of 'double devolution', for instance, entailed local government having to commit to involving local communities—however defined—in its activities, alongside a limited relaxation of control from the centre.

Institutional pressure for the 2007 Concordat came from the Local Government Association (LGA), which formed in 1997 following an amalgamation of different bodies operating in the field. A civil society initiative, the Power Inquiry, advocated in 2006 a 'Concordat between central and local government setting out their respective powers'.[71] It would 'confirm where key powers lie and … enshrine the process of decentralisation'.[72] The Inquiry presented such a text as a means of enforcing the *European Charter of Local Self-Government*, a Council of Europe document to which the UK had assented in 1998, 'but which seems to have been growing mould on a shelf in Whitehall and to have had limited impact on policy'.[73] The Inquiry anticipated the introduction of 'Parliamentary Acts'—presumably meaning primary legislation—to give effect to a concordat, something that did not happen.[74]

69 See N Headlam, *The Central-Local Concordat* (London, House of Commons Library, 2008).

70 See, eg, House of Commons Political and Constitutional Reform Committee, *Prospects for codifying the relationship between central and local government* (HC 2012–13, 656-I).

71 Power Inquiry, *Power to the People, The Report of Power: an independent inquiry into Britain's democracy* (York, Power Inquiry, 2006) 159–60.

72 ibid.

73 ibid.

74 ibid.

The Concordat was between the LGA, the body that represents local authorities throughout the UK, and the UK Government as a whole. It arose from a pledge contained in the *Governance of Britain* paper issued in July 2007 setting out the constitutional reform programme of the incoming Prime Minister, Gordon Brown.[75] This document contained a commitment to 'establish a concordat to govern the relations between central and local government', intended to 'establish for the first time an agreement on the rights and responsibilities of local government, including its responsibilities to provide effective leadership of the local area and to empower local communities where possible'.[76]

As the Power Inquiry reference to the *European Charter of Local Self-Government* indicates, there was international influence at work. The Charter dates from 1985, but the UK ratified it only after 13 years and the changeover from a Conservative to a Labour Government. It notes in its preamble that 'local authorities are one of the main foundations of any democratic regime' and that 'the right of citizens to participate in the conduct of public affairs' is a shared value of all the member states of the Council. The most immediate means of realising this entitlement, the preamble continues, is through activity at 'local level', a tier that operates in a form 'both effective and close to the citizen'. The Charter preamble goes on to depict local government as playing a part in the objective of 'the construction of a Europe based on the principles of democracy and the decentralisation of power'. This goal in turn necessitates democratic institutions' enjoying 'a wide degree of autonomy with regard to their responsibilities, the ways and means by which those responsibilities are exercised and the resources required for their fulfilment'. This description would be hard to apply to local government in the UK at the time of the introduction of the Charter in 1985, at the point when the UK ratified it in 1998 or in the period since.

Article 2 of the Charter—'Constitutional and legal foundation for local self-government'—calls for the recognition of 'local self-government' in legislation and, if possible, the constitution. This stipulation, repeated in Article 4, paragraph 1 of the main body of the Charter, suggests something more than a non-statutory code is required. Though the UK does not have a written constitution of the sort to which the Charter alludes, it does have Acts of Parliament—such as those providing for devolution—which are in practice constitutional in character, and in theory an Act could express some of the content of the Charter. Article 3 then defines the 'Concept of local self-government'. It entails (paragraph 1) an authority's being able to control 'a substantial share of public affairs' in a way that serves people living locally. Article 3, paragraph 2 then deals with democratic legitimacy, requiring that the bodies exercising these powers be 'freely elected by secret ballot on the basis of direct, equal, universal suffrage', potentially with 'executive organs' answering to them. Another requirement, contained in Article 4,[77] paragraph 2, is

[75] Secretary of State for Justice and Lord Chancellor, *The Governance of Britain* (Cm 7170, 2007).
[76] ibid, para 179.
[77] 'Scope of local self-government'.

that local government should be able to act in any way that does not contravene the law or is not specifically ruled out of its remit. This idea of a 'general power of competence' found expression in section 1 of the Localism Act 2011. Yet how effective it can be in the absence of full protection of other core features of the Charter is questionable.

The Charter creates a predisposition for local-level power with the statement in Article 4, paragraph 3 that 'Public responsibilities shall be exercised, in preference, by those authorities which are closest to the citizen.' The allotting of a particular function to a higher level should follow careful consideration. Article 5—'Protection of local authority boundaries'—states that alterations to local borders should be on the basis of consultation in advance with the areas involved, perhaps through referendums if possible. Article 6,[78] paragraph 1 supports the principle that a local authority should have the ability to decide how it is organised internally, so as best to meet its particular requirements. Article 9 deals with the 'Financial resources of local authorities'. It requires that they should have 'adequate financial resources of their own'—though within the limits of 'national economic policy' (paragraph 1). The finances available to them should match the tasks with which they are charged (paragraph 2). A portion 'at least' of their finance should come from taxes set by local authorities (paragraph 3). Their sources of income, the Charter holds, should be sufficiently 'diversified and buoyant' that local authorities are able to sustain spending at a level that their responsibilities demand (paragraph 4). The text identifies a need for redistribution between more wealthy and poorer areas (paragraph 5). It also states that the provision of grants to local authorities should preferably avoid ring-fencing for specific purposes, so that local autonomy is preserved (paragraph 7). Local authorities, according to the Charter, should be able to raise money on the 'national capital market' (paragraph 8). Article 10—'Local authorities' right to associate'—asserts that local authorities, including those from different countries, should be able to work together on chosen projects. Lastly, Article 11—'Legal protection of local self-government'—iterates that there should be a possibility for a local authority to seek to uphold its rights through the courts.

Despite the UK's having been party to the Charter for nearly a decade by the time of the *Central-Local Concordat*, the latter text did not purport to reflect its content in full, nor did it in fact do so. Dated 12 December 2007, it was an agreement between 'Her Majesty's Government and the Local Government Association', creating 'a framework' for interactions between central and local government. Rather than depicting itself as bringing about change, the Concordat simply claimed to depict the manner in which the relationship operated at the time of its being reached.

As opposed to local government as an entity in and for itself, much of the focus of the Concordat was on the idea of providing services, and on the notion that central and local government have a shared responsibility to ensure that they reach a quality that matches the expectations of the public (paragraph 1). After making

[78] 'Appropriate administrative structures and resources for the tasks of local authorities'.

reference to the then recent Local Government and Public Involvement in Health Act 2007 and other policy initiatives (paragraph 2), the Concordat made the constitutionally significant statement that (paragraph 3):

> Central and local government both derive their legitimacy from Parliament and the electoral mandate granted to them by individual citizens who look to central and local government to take the lead in ensuring better places and better services.

This statement had the effect of qualifying the significance of the local electoral mandate by implying that Parliament is at least as significant a source for its authority, and perhaps even more important. In strict constitutional-legal terms this view might have reflected the true position. But it is hard to imagine a similar claim about a devolved assembly appearing in an official document. Nor did this depiction of the basis for local government reflect the *European Charter of Local Self-Government*, with its emphasis on local autonomy and a preference for the position of local government to derive ultimately from a written constitution. Moreover, the reference to 'better places and better services' was both prescriptive and restrictive, predetermining what should be the priorities of local government, and doing so in a narrow fashion.

Paragraph 4 advanced the concept of central and local government as 'partners in delivering improved services and in strengthening our democracy', then listing a series of shared policy objectives to which it would be as hard for anyone to object as it would be to discern precisely what they mean in practice. They included the creation of 'thriving communities, where people want to live, work, bring up their families and retire', better 'outcomes for children, young people and families', 'creating wealth and rising prosperity, shared by all', and promoting 'high standards of conduct in public life'. Once again, the mood was one of denial of an autonomous role for local government, depicting it as a partner of another tier, engaged in the fulfilment of a programme both detailed and empty of meaning.

Paragraph 4 did then make a more significant statement that is more promising from the perspective of the supporter of enhanced local government. It held that in attaining these goals, 'there should be a presumption that powers are best exercised at the lowest effective and practical level'. However, the passages that follow, describing the respective roles of central and local government, placed the former in a position of primacy. They portrayed central government as possessing both 'the responsibility and democratic mandate' to pursue the 'national interest', with 'over-riding interest' in areas including 'national economic interest, public service improvement and standards of delivery, and taxation' (paragraph 5). Paragraph 6, setting out the corresponding position of local government, made no mention of its enjoying a democratic mandate of its own, dwelling merely on its responsibilities. While it referred to a programme of ensuring that local government would 'conduct a growing share of the business of government', it would not in this model be able to fix its own distinctive parameters. Paragraph 8 attributed to central government the right to determine 'minimum standards of services' and, 'as a last resort, to intervene' in the localities 'to avoid significant underperformance'. It could, the

Concordat noted, bring forward legislation determining the framework for the operation of local government. In exercising its rights, central government was, according to paragraph 9 of the Concordat, supposed to consult with local authorities and lessen central bureaucratic demands upon them. Councils for their part had a 'right to address the priorities of their communities as expressed through local elections'—the first clear reference since paragraph 3 to local elections as a source of legitimacy (paragraph 10). They were required to be 'accountable, visible and responsive to their communities' (paragraph 11). There were then further allusions to the 'double devolution' concept (see, for example, paragraph 16).

Paragraph 15 included the sole mention in the Concordat of the *European Charter of Local Self-Government*, a text that—as we have seen—is difficult to reconcile with the Concordat, despite the UK's being a signatory to this international agreement. In this paragraph the two parties to the Concordat agreed to 'work towards' providing local authorities with greater 'flexibility in their funding', making possible the 'wide degree of autonomy referred to in the' Charter. This statement would appear to amount to an admission that at the time of the drafting of the Concordat, the Charter remained unfulfilled. When investigating the relationship between central and local government in a 2009 report, the House of Commons Communities and Local Government Committee confirmed this view of the status of the Charter in the UK.[79] The Committee saw potential, in theory, for the Charter to 'protect the autonomy of local government' (paragraph 131). However, it doubted that 'the prescriptive nature of the English system' was reconcilable with the Charter, which it regarded as a 'constitutional dead letter' (paragraph 132).

The Committee judged the Concordat potentially to be a means of enhancing the status of local government relative to central government (paragraph 127). However, it took the view that in practice, 'nothing much appears to have changed as a result of the Concordat'. Indeed one witness who was a Vice-Chair of the LGA, the co-signatory organisation, Councillor David Shakespeare, told the Committee inquiry that 'the concordat was signed with a flourish, but if I got out my microscope and looked at the outcomes, they would be very tiny indeed'. Whitehall departments other than Communities and Local Government seemed to pay scant regard to the Concordat; indeed the Committee doubted whether the Health Minister, from whom it had taken evidence, knew that the text even existed (paragraph 128). One individual expressed the view to the Committee that the LGA had been pressurised into accepting the Concordat (paragraph 86). The Committee noted that a number of evidence-givers to its inquiry 'have called for the Concordat to be put on a statutory basis, to turn its good intentions into statutory facts' (paragraph 129). It concluded that the Government seemed, through the Concordat and Charter, 'to have created a constitutional settlement, but in practice can ignore its strictures with impunity' (paragraph 132). The Concordat subsequently disappeared from view.

[79] House of Commons Communities and Local Government Committee, *The Balance of Power: Central and local government* (HC 2008–09, 33-I).

B. Codification and Consultation

The *Central-Local Concordat* (section IV.A. above) was a codification exercise that proved to be flawed, had no significant impact and soon became defunct. Another example of how codification does not represent a smooth progression comes from the field of official consultation practice. While governments may enjoy electoral legitimacy providing them with an authority to act, it is often regarded as good democratic practice that, before it makes important decisions, the executive should seek and take into account the views of interested members of the public and certain corporate bodies and groups—a practice known as consultation.[80] Failure to do so may bring policy-making into disrepute, through creating aggrieved parties who feel they were excluded and promoting the idea that government takes place in closed circles, with access available only to officials and ministers and selected privileged outsiders. Consultation, furthermore, can improve the quality of particular proposals, and potentially even avert major dysfunctions.

The UK Government first issued a *Code of Practice on Consultation* in 2000. The third and final edition, itself revised following a consultation process, a 16-page document, appeared in July 2008.[81] At the core of the Code were the 'Seven Consultation Criteria', which the Code required should be included with all official consultations. The Code opened its 'Introduction' by asserting the importance of two-way communication between government and 'stakeholders'. The stakeholder concept is important but sometimes difficult to define. It implies that some groups and individuals have a heightened importance in relation to certain areas of policy, perhaps because government deems them so, or perhaps through self-selection. There are certain tensions between this idea and the principle that, on some level, all are politically equal in a democracy. This friction surfaced in the statement that consultations 'should be open to anyone to respond but should be designed to seek views from those who would be affected by, or those who have a particular interest in' a given decision. The 'Introduction' distinguished between different types of continual discussion between government and 'stakeholders'. Sometimes it needed to be 'more formal and more public in nature'. If government was working on a fresh proposal or altering its present approach, 'it will often be desirable to carry out a formal, time-bound, public written consultation exercise'—the subject of the Code. The value of this method, the text noted, was that it could facilitate scrutiny of government ideas at a formative stage, and the different possible approaches that could be taken.

The next section was headed 'Status of the Code'. The document applied to a variety of departments and agencies that adopted it, and other public sector bodies could use it. The Code stated that it contained 'the approach the Government

[80] R Manwaring, *The search for democratic renewal: the politics of consultation in Britain and Australia* (Manchester, Manchester University Press, 2014).

[81] HM Government, *Code of Practice on Consultation* (London, Department for Business, Enterprise and Regulatory Reform, 2008).

will take' when holding a 'formal, written, public consultation exercise'. On this evidence, it was an important text. It appeared to entail a range of public agencies abiding by specific procedural rules and standards in their dealings with the public over policy. Yet the Code then made the familiar qualification often found in these documents, noting that it 'does not have legal force and cannot prevail over statutory or mandatory requirements'. As discussed elsewhere in this work, whether or not a code has 'legal force' is ultimately a decision for the judiciary, not the executive as issuer of it. A court may take the view that it can use such a text in judicial review. While it is true, as the Code noted, that such a text cannot override an Act of Parliament, the document and others like it could conceivably have played a part in the interpretation of statute during a legal proceeding, or in the scrutiny of executive conduct. The Code also noted that it set out 'the Government's general policy' on consultations. Perhaps the word 'general' was intended to discourage the impression of absolute applicability.

Further executive flexibility was sought through the assertion that ministers remained able to choose not to run a consultation of the type to which the Code would apply at all, and might seek some other form of engagement. Circumstances in which this course of action might be appropriate could include when more informal contributions were sought 'very early in policy development' (though a formal consultation could follow), or when an area being covered was relatively obscure. Qualifying itself still further, the Code insisted that it 'is not intended to create a commitment to consult on anything, to give rise to a duty to consult, or to be relied on as creating expectations that the Government will consult in any particular case'. The 'creating expectations' phrase seems to be another effort to preclude use in judicial review, in this instance over the issue of *whether* a consultation should take place, rather than the manner in which it should be run. In any given instance, the Code went on, it was the particular circumstances that would determine whether a consultation occurred. The Code stipulated that there would be points at which it was not possible to adhere fully to its terms, but that, when departing from it, departments should be clear that they *were* doing so, should account for *why* and what action they were taking to ensure that any problems were avoided.

The Code then set out its seven criteria in turn, with explanatory statements under each. Criterion 1 was entitled 'When to consult'. This specified that the consultation should occur at a point when some kind of meaningful impact on the form of the contemplated action remained possible. Crucial here was that the Government should have developed its thinking far enough to provide useful material to respond to, but that it should not have reached a stage when it had finally fixed its views. Within these limits, consultation should take place as early as possible (paragraph 1.2). The Government should not generally initiate consultations 'during election periods' (paragraph 1.6).

Criterion 2 was entitled 'Duration of consultation exercises'. Such exercises should usually last 12 weeks as a minimum, and longer if possible. Departmental planning should allow for the consultation phase as part of time-planning (paragraph 2.1). Consultation periods that ran over times of year such as the summer or Christmas season, or that involved complicated issues, should preferably allow longer periods for their consideration (paragraph 2.2). At times, because of contingencies or legal requirements, it might be necessary to have a period that was shorter than 12 weeks. The consultation document should make the reasons for this compression clear (paragraph 2.3). Those who developed consultations should give attention to means by which they could bring themselves to the attention of likely respondents, including publicising the launch, either at the time it took place or beforehand (paragraph 2.4).

'Clarity of scope and impact' was Criterion 3. It required the papers issued as part of the consultation to 'be clear' about the process itself, the idea that is being put forward, the potential for those responding to wield influence upon it, and the anticipated 'costs and benefits' involved. The guidance to this criterion placed special emphasis on the need to establish the different groups and parts of society most likely to be affected by a particular intended course of action, and what the effect on them would be (paragraphs 3.1–3.5).

Criterion 4, 'Accessibility of consultation exercises', dealt with the need to ensure that the intended participants in a consultation were deliberately and effectively targetted and engaged. The guidance referred to the importance of identifying the appropriate people and groups, and not simply working within the usual circles (paragraph 4.1). It held that active promotion of the occurrence of a consultation was important (paragraph 4.3).

Criterion 5, 'The burden of consultation', dealt with the need to minimise the work pressures created for those expected to respond to consultations. Criterion 6, 'Responsiveness of consultation exercises', then covered a crucial component of a consultation process if it was to be meaningful: taking the responses seriously, with the arguments and evidence carefully scrutinised (paragraph 6.1). After it had consulted, the document required government to produce an account of the submissions it had received and who wrote them (paragraph 6.4); and possibly to publish the submissions (paragraph 6.5). Lastly, Criterion 7 dealt with the internal 'Capacity to consult' of Whitehall.

In July 2012 the Government launched a new 'Consultation Principles' document on its website,[82] superseding the *Code of Practice on Consultation*. It had a number of similarities to this earlier text. But it was not as long—only three pages in total—nor as detailed. Generally it suggested greater flexibility for government over how it went about consulting—and indeed whether it did so at all formally. The text describes itself as 'not a "how to" guide' but instead as seeking 'to help policy makers make the right judgments about when, with whom and how to

[82] The document cited here dates itself as October 2013. It is no longer available online and is superseded by 'Consultation Principles 2016'.

consult'. It describes its 'governing principle' as 'proportionality of the type and scale of consultation to the potential impacts of the proposal or decision being taken.' It notes the importance of 'real engagement' over 'merely following bureaucratic process'. The implication here could be that rules can be a barrier to rather than a facilitator of involvement. The document closes its first paragraph by referring to the possibility of consultation's not being appropriate, describing a 'wider scheme of engagement' against which 'decisions on whether and how to consult' should be taken. The following paragraph continues to downplay the importance of consultation, stressing the importance of 'open policy making' on an ongoing basis, rather than 'just at set points of consultation'. It describes the importance of 'real discussion with affected parties', and notes the role of 'Modern communications technologies' in facilitating dialogue 'more quickly and in a more targeted way than before', rendering 'the traditional written consultation' less relevant. The overall tone, then, is one of questioning the value of formal written consultations and proposing increased flexibility for the maker of decisions—that is, the Government—about how to engage.

A significant difference from the 2008 Code in terms of content is the view it presents on the appropriate length of consultations. In this regard the main text of the 2012 document, in the section 'Timing of Consultation', refers to *The Compact* between the community and voluntary sector and the Government (section III. above), stating that its 'principles … must … be respected'. It then includes a footnote that cites the following provision from *The Compact*: 'Where it is appropriate, and enables meaningful engagement, conduct 12-week formal written consultations, with clear explanations and rationale for shorter timeframes or a more informal approach.'[83] Yet further on in the 'Timing of Consultation' section, the 'Consultation Principles' document informs the reader that the 'amount of time required' derives from the kind of action under contemplation and the effect it is likely to have, and that it 'might typically vary between two and 12 weeks'. In this formulation, 12 weeks appears to be a standard maximum, at the end of a scale of acceptability that begins at two weeks. The footnote seems to assert that 12 weeks is the norm; while in the 2008 *Code of Conduct*, 12 weeks is the usual minimum. On this issue, then, 'Consultation Principles' is both internally contradictory and brings about change with regard to earlier rules. It elaborates by emphasising context specificity, stating that 'there is no set formula for establishing the right length'. Indeed, in certain instances, no consultation is needed at all. If a proposal is 'new and contentious', however, '12 weeks or more may still be appropriate'. This language is difficult to reconcile with *The Compact*. Like other codes, including the consultation *Code of Conduct*, 'Consultation Principles' is keen to play down the idea that it might be binding—not that it makes many firm commitments—with the insistence that '[t]his guidance does not have legal force'.

[83] ibid, 1, fn 1. For the Compact, see above n 68.

V. THE CONSTITUTIONAL REFORM AND GOVERNANCE ACT 2010

Two codes that appeared during the premiership of Gordon Brown—the *Central-Local Concordat* of 2007 and the 2008 edition of the *Code of Practice on Consultation*—were in different ways doomed. The first was flawed from the outset, while the latter gave way to a weaker successor. However, the legacy of the constitutional reform programme that Brown set out as his central agenda upon becoming Prime Minister in mid-2007 was more extensive, significant and lasting than these two texts alone. It included within it a statute, the Constitutional Reform and Governance Act 2010, that represented an important development in the process of codification, since it provided previously existing documents with a new basis in an Act of Parliament, rather than—as had been standard practice for such texts up to this point—resting in the Royal Prerogative as their legal source. Perhaps the clearest precursors to this development were the introduction of the Freedom of Information Act 2000, supplanting the 1994 *Code of Practice on Access to Official Information*, and the inclusion of some of the core content of the 2004 judicial concordat in the Constitutional Reform Act 2005. At devolved level, the Northern Ireland *Ministerial Code* has a statutory foundation in the paragraph 4 of Schedule 1 to the Northern Ireland (St Andrews Agreement) Act 2006.

Part 1 of the 2010 Act deals with the Civil Service. Its general effect was to place this institution on a statutory basis for the first time. As part of this task it obliges the Minister for the Civil Service (the Prime Minister) to 'publish a code of conduct for the civil service' (section 5(1)), with an option to introduce distinct codes for officials supporting the Scottish and Welsh governments (section 5(2)), subject to consultation with the relevant First Ministers (section 5(3)). The code would be known as the 'civil service code', which—as we have seen—had existed under the prerogative since 1996 (section 5(4)). The Prime Minister, as Minister for the Civil Service, had to lay it before Parliament (section 5(5)). The code is part of the 'terms and conditions of service' of civil servants (section 5(8)). A similar code applies to the Diplomatic Service (section 6). The Act then sets out certain 'Minimum requirements' for these two codes (section 7). They must place an obligation on civil servants to 'carry out their duties for the assistance of the administration as it is duly constituted for the time being, whatever its political complexion' (section 7(2)). Codes must also 'require civil servants to carry out their duties ... with integrity and honesty, and ... with objectivity and impartiality' (section 7(4)). The codes 'need not' apply the objectivity and impartiality stipulations to special advisers, but this wording leaves open the possibility that they could do so.

Section 8 of the Act deals with the 'Special advisers code'. It requires the Prime Minister to publish this code (section 8(1)), with the option of separate versions for Scotland and Wales (section 8(2)), subject to approval from the respective First Ministers (section 8(3)). This code is required to stipulate that special advisers must not

> authorise the expenditure of public funds ... exercise any power in relation to the management of any part of the civil service of the State ... [or] otherwise exercise any power

> conferred by or under this or any other Act or any power under Her Majesty's prerogative. (section 8(5))

It can, however, allow special advisers to carry out management of other special advisers (section 8(6)). The code, which again the Prime Minister must lay before Parliament (section 8(8)) is 'part of the terms and conditions of service' of special advisers.

The Act, in creating a power for the Prime Minister to 'manage the civil service' (section 3(1)) makes possible the publication of further codes, and the already-existing *Civil Service Management Code* subsequently drew on this new authority. The Act also creates a new legal basis for a long-established body with a role in upholding these codes. It gives the Civil Service Commission, first formed under the Royal Prerogative in 1855, a statutory grounding. One of the tasks the Act attaches to the Commission is to deal with complaints from civil servants in relation to Civil Service codes of conduct. Section 9 stipulates that a civil servant to whom a given code applies, who thinks she is being required to violate a code, or that another civil servant subject to the code has transgressed it, can take the matter to the Commission. The provision for complaints contained in the Act is narrow in the sense that it seems to mean that the only people who can object to what they perceive as conflicts with a code are those who come under its remit. Members of the public, for instance, could not complain. Nonetheless, the Act gives the process a firm basis in an Act of Parliament, requiring the Commission to create a handling mechanism and obliging others in the Civil Service to cooperate in providing evidence.

VI. *THE CABINET MANUAL*[84]

Brown instigated a further, major act of codification that reached full fruition only after he had left office.[85] *The Cabinet Manual* represented a culmination of the different strands of development towards codification of the preceding decades. It had both an open, transparent and yet an executive-steered, opaque quality. Of all the codes produced up to that point, it was probably the most outward-facing. In the early phases of the trend, the documents—such as QPM and the *Precedent Book*—were intended for internal executive purposes only, and might be available only to a limited number within Whitehall itself. Some began to find their way into the public domain after being introduced, for instance the Barnett Formula (section I.A. above). Others were issued in public immediately, for instance the Armstrong Memorandum (section I.B. above) and QPM (or, as it became from

[84] Cabinet Office, *The Cabinet Manual: A guide to laws, conventions and rules on the operation of government* (Cabinet Office, London, 2011).

[85] The following draws on Blick and Hennessy, above n 35; and A Blick, 'The Cabinet Manual and the Codification of Conventions' (2014) 67 (1) *Parliamentary Affairs*, 191.

1997, the *Ministerial Code*—see section II.A. above) from 1992 onwards. Those who issued codes began to deploy them partly as a means of attaining a desired impression outside government, for instance of openness, or of being attentive to the maintenance of standards of integrity. With *The Cabinet Manual*, that its contents would be available to the public was integral to its purpose. It was intended not only to ensure that the Government was perceived in a certain way, but also to help secure common understanding, without as well as within Whitehall, around certain key constitutional arrangements. The production process itself had an open dimension. Gordon Brown, then Prime Minister, announced the plan to issue the *Manual* in February 2010. Or at least, it appears to have been what he was alluding to. The Cabinet Office, which had central responsibility for the *Manual* within government, provided the House of Commons Justice Committee with a preliminary version of one of the sections shortly afterwards. A complete draft appeared late in 2010, with a consultation being held on it. Various interested parties responded, and three parliamentary committees, two in the House of Commons and one in the House of Lords, produced reports. The Cabinet Office produced a response to these public and parliamentary submissions when it published the full first edition of the *Manual*. However, it had ultimate control over drafting the final product, and some of its decisions appeared arbitrary.

The *Manual* came into being as a consequence of a specific intersection of long-term tendencies, short-term pressures, and particular personal and institutional influences. For Brown—whose authorisation was needed as Prime Minister—the project he unveiled in February 2010 was part of his wider constitutional reform agenda. Amid a range of other changes he envisaged, some of which have already been discussed, he hoped to be able to generate movement towards the introduction of a written constitution for the UK. The project that eventually led to the appearance of the *Manual* was, as Brown conceived it, intended to provide an account of the existing system as a starting point for a debate about the possibility and content of a written constitution. How far the *Manual* as it emerged would have been a suitable document for a constitutional design process is a different debate. But even before the 2010 General Election took place, the plan Brown had developed for a written constitution had lost impetus, partly because he could not secure the cooperation of opposition parties. The coalition that formed in May of that year did not seek to sustain the Brown written constitution initiative, though one of the participating parties, the Liberal Democrats, was in theory committed to this outcome. But the coalition retained the ongoing *Cabinet Manual* project. We can view this continuation of the process across different administrations—evidence of the importance of the permanent Civil Service to the sustained momentum of code production in the UK—as helping create for it the aura of a lasting, impartial document. But why had it survived?

In parallel to the ideas of Brown, there were other motives for the production of the *Manual*. One was the view that it would be appropriate to import the New Zealand *Cabinet Manual* into the UK. Gus O'Donnell, then the Cabinet Secretary and Head of the Home Civil Service, acknowledged the existence of this text in the Preface to the first edition of the *Manual*.[86] This approach had support from the think tank community, in particular the Institute for Government and Constitution Unit, and from within the Civil Service itself, including at the top, in the person of O'Donnell. It should be noted, however, that some of the functions of the New Zealand *Cabinet Manual*, discussed in Chapter 3, were already fulfilled by UK texts such as the *Ministerial Code*. Indeed, one New Zealand commentator has likened the New Zealand *Cabinet Manual* to the UK *Ministerial Code*.[87] Another more immediate driver of the *Manual* arose from a judgement that no party might win the next General Election, due to take place in 2010, outright, and that it was important to clarify the rules surrounding the government formation process in such circumstances. The Government published a draft of the part of the *Manual* dealing with this subject early, in advance of the poll. This imperative gave relevance, purpose and momentum to the project that it might not otherwise have possessed. Therefore while *The Cabinet Manual* outlasted the tenure of the Prime Minister who instigated it, the character of the project became different from that which he initially envisaged. Later accounts of the *Manual* omitted any specific reference to this initial purpose. In his Preface to the first edition of the *Manual* in October 2011, O'Donnell simply stated that in advance of the most recent election, Brown had 'asked that I lead work to produce a Cabinet Manual', but did not explain why.[88]

Subtitled *A guide to laws, conventions and rules on the operation of government*, the main document is 94 pages long, plus a Foreword by the then Prime Minister, David Cameron, and a Preface by O'Donnell. The *Manual* has references at the end of each chapter, a glossary, and a list of online links to 'Reference Documents'—that is, other official guidance—and an annex setting out the timetable surrounding general elections. Its main focus is on the workings of central government. But it extends far beyond this immediate remit, though all of it is—the *Manual* holds—'from the view of the Executive'.[89] After an introductory chapter, it deals with the monarch—described as 'The Sovereign' (Chapter One); 'Elections and government formation' (Chapter Two); 'The Executive' including 'the Prime Minister, ministers and the structure of government' (Chapter Three); 'Collective Cabinet decision-making' (Chapter Four); 'The Executive and Parliament (Chapter Five); 'The Executive and the law' (Chapter Six); 'Ministers and the Civil Service' (Chapter Seven); 'Relations with the Devolved Administrations' (Chapter Eight); 'Relations with the European Union and other international institutions (Chapter Nine); 'Government finance and expenditure' (Chapter Ten); and 'Official information' (Chapter Eleven). The content of this text is considered in detail in Part Two of the present book.

[86] Cabinet Office, above n 84, v.

[87] G Duncan, 'New Zealand's Cabinet Manual: How Does It Shape Constitutional Conventions?', *Parliamentary Affairs*, Advance Access published 6 November 2014, 2.

[88] Cabinet Office, above n 76.

[89] Cabinet Office, above n 76, iv.

VII. CONCLUSION

In the period from 1979, cumulative pressures on the UK constitution and the changes they triggered brought about a transformation in the subject matter of this book. There was a proliferation of codes, an expansion in the breadth of subject matter they addressed, an intensification of their detail and an increase in the range of institutions issuing them. Texts such as the *Directory of Civil Service Guidance* and *The Cabinet Manual* represented attempts within the executive to codify codification itself, as did *Estacode* and the *Precedent Book* in earlier times. These processes occurred across governments involving three different parties, showing that constitutional transformation can take place under any type of administration. The particular qualities of this trend also brought about changes in the nature of documents themselves. Codes had become by the early twenty-first century a regular feature of the UK polity, issued to facilitate the internal organisation of different branches of the UK constitution, and to handle their relations with outside. The production of codes was now a standard part of the repertoire of politicians and other public office holders. They figured prominently in public political discourse and were a fixed part of the constitution they served to describe. Furthermore, the more that was published, the more was demanded. In 1994, William Waldegrave, Chancellor of the Duchy of Lancaster and a central figure in the Major drive for openness, took a question asking him whether he would 'place a copy of the "Permanent Secretary's Handbook" in the Library [of the House of Commons]'. His answer was blunt, but also enabled him to highlight how much had changed over the past decade or so:

> No. The handbook referred to is a compendium of guidance and other documents which heads of departments and others with similar responsibilities find useful to have collected together. Much of the material in it is already in the public domain—for example, 'Questions of Procedure for Ministers', the 'Armstrong Memorandum' on the duties and responsibilities of civil servants, the memorandum of guidance for officials appearing before Select Committees, guidance on Government publicity and advertising, the 'Radcliffe Rules' on ministerial memoirs, and guidance on access by Ministers to documents of a previous Administration. Other material, for example on security and vetting procedures, is justifiably confidential.[90]

Codification played a subtle role in the complex power relations of the UK constitution. It could serve both to manage interactions and to assert particular interests, sometimes at the same time. Osmotherly, for instance, both presented the executive view of how the provision of evidence to parliamentary select committees should take place, and (over time) sought to establish a basis for the accountability process that was acceptable both to government and legislature. As the history of the Osmotherly Rules demonstrates, the servicing of these dual objectives contained tensions within it, and could lead to controversy. The institutions

[90] HC Deb, 9 March 1994, vol 239, cols 255–56W.

issuing codes were not entirely homogeneous, and the texts they produced could reflect these internal contrasts. Differentiation within the executive was particularly apparent. As a governmental entity it included within it ministers, permanent civil servants and special advisers; and a structure of departments headed by politicians, each with different perspectives, that needed to be reconciled collectively at Cabinet level.

Codes also tell us about the multidimensional power balance of the UK constitution. No group could completely dominate. Given the inbuilt majority in the primary parliamentary chamber, the House of Commons, that governments possess, and the lack of a written constitution, the UK executive may appear from an international perspective to possess unusual strength and discretion. These documents are in some senses indicative of the autonomy it possesses, mainly issued unilaterally under the Royal Prerogative. But they are also suggestive of weakness, of the pressures to which the executive is subject, for instance from Parliament in carrying out its accountability role; or arising from the territorial dynamics of the UK, which have intensified over time and prompted the Barnett Formula. The attempts to assert that documents are not legally binding shows a sense of the importance of the judiciary. There are also forces beyond the immediate realm of governmental institutions to be contended with. Pressure for openness and to demonstrate probity has come from the media, driving codification further; and the relationship with civil society and the wider public is important, encouraging such codes as those dealing with policy consultations. In issuing documents, the executive helped create the impression that such publications were good practice that ought to be adhered to. Codification thereby acquired its own momentum, and was beyond the control of any one institution. Other players at UK level have entered the game—in particular Parliament and the judiciary—demonstrating not only that they feel a need to assert their positions, but also that they have the ability to do so. But was the UK unique in having acquired this codification habit? What did it actually mean? And what sort of constitution, between them, did these texts delineate?

3

Codification in Perspective

THE URGE TO codify in the UK has become powerful. But we should not assume that the practice is unique to this country. It exists in a variety of comparable developed world democracies. This chapter considers a range of codes from foreign states.

Research produced by the Politics and Public Administration Section (PPAS) of the Parliament of Australia demonstrates that the use of codes is a phenomenon common to many democracies in the English-speaking world.[1] For instance Article I, Section 5 of the United States Constitution contains a stipulation that each of the Houses of Congress, the House of Representatives and the Senate, 'may determine the rules of its proceedings, punish its members for disorderly behavior, and, with the concurrence of two thirds, expel a member'. Accordingly, PPAS informs us, the House of Representatives has a Committee on Ethics that produces and enforces internal regulatory documents; while the Senate Select Committee on Ethics performs a similar role in relation to the *Senate Ethics Manual* and the *Senate Code of Official Conduct*. In 2009, President Barack Obama issued Executive Order 13490 that obliged political appointments to commit to an 'Ethics Pledge', focused on the regulation of lobbying.

This chapter has a special focus on the three Commonwealth countries with developed economies and stable democracies: Australia, Canada and New Zealand. The UK has a shared heritage, derived from the imperial past, with each of these states. Yet they have all developed along their own paths, while retaining similarities, direct links and mutual influence upon one another. By examining these documents we can learn much, not only about the arrangements of the specific countries involved, but also about the common features between them all and the nature of codification.

I. AUSTRALIA

The case of Australia demonstrates that, even in a country with a written constitution, conventions can be of pronounced importance to the operation of the system, and disagreements about them can produce demands for codification.

[1] The following draws upon D McKeown, *Codes of conduct in Australian and selected overseas parliaments* (Canberra, Parliament of Australia, 2012).

(Clearly, lack of consensus about the precise meaning of the words of a written constitution is possible too, though at least there can be an umpire in such disputes in the form of the courts.) In 1975 Australia saw 'a series of four interlocking [constitutional] crises'.[2] They involved the ability of the second chamber of the Commonwealth Parliament to deny financial supply to the Government; the filling of vacancies in the Senate; and the powers of the Governor-General, in particular with respect to the appointment and dismissal of prime ministers. Conventions surrounding these different issues were unclear and came to be fiercely disputed in the circumstances of 1975. The outcome was the removal in November of that year of the Labor Prime Minister, Gough Whitlam, by the Governor-General, and his replacement by the Liberal, Malcolm Fraser. An election to both chambers of Parliament followed, won by the Liberal and National Country parties. Those on the Labor side who felt aggrieved by what had happened called for codification of the relevant relationships and practices to prevent abuse. In 1985 a constitutional convention convened to 'recognise and declare' conventions. It identified 18 in total, though more sensitive suggestions pertaining to the authority of the Governor-General in relation to government were not adopted. The proposals were not incorporated into the full written constitution.[3]

Subsequently, a growing tendency towards codification has become detectable in Australia, gaining particular momentum from the 1990s, as the account provided by Deidre McKeown shows.[4] The States in some cases led the way. As early as 1978, Victoria had established a code of conduct applying to members of its parliament as part of a *Members of Parliament (Register of Interests) Act* of that year. New South Wales saw the establishment of a *Code of Conduct for Ministers of the Crown* in 1988. The Australian Capital Territory saw the promulgation of a code of conduct that applied to ministers in 1995. Ultimately, all the States would introduce codes applying variously to ministers and parliamentarians. At the federal level, in 1996, John Howard, who was then Australian Prime Minister, introduced a text called *A Guide on Key Elements of Ministerial Responsibility*. Subsequently, a series of ministers who had failed to comply with the rules it set out were compelled to leave office. Howard then produced a new version of the text that proved less stringent. In 2007, Kevin Rudd, successor to Howard, supplemented this guide with *Standards of Ministerial Ethics*, dealing with matters such as financial interests, lobbying and the taking up of posts after leaving office. While this document promulgated more stringent standards in the areas it dealt with, it

[2] N Barry and N Miragliotta, 'Australia' in B Galligan and S Brenton (eds), *Constitutional Conventions in Westminster Systems: Controversies, Changes and Challenges* (Cambridge, Cambridge University Press, 2015) 207. See also JR Archer and G Maddox, 'The 1975 Constitutional Crisis in Australia', *Journal of Commonwealth Politics* XIV, 1976, 141; P Kelly, *November 1975: The Inside Story of Australia's Great Political Crisis* (Sydney, Allen & Unwin, 1995).

[3] Barry and Miragliotta, above n 2, 207–15. See also C Sampford, 'Recognise and Declare: An Australian Experiment in Codifying Constitutional Conventions' (1987) 7(3) *OJLS* 369; C Sampford and D Wood, 'Codification of Constitutional Conventions in Australia' [1987] *Public Law* 137, 231–44.

[4] McKeown, above n 1.

lacked independent enforcement. Ultimately the premier would judge whether a violation had taken place and, if so, what the consequence should be.

Gaining in pace and extent from the closing decades of the twentieth century, codification in Australia built on already existing tendencies. A federal document, the *Cabinet Handbook*, appeared in its eighth edition in 2015.[5] In its Foreword the Prime Minister, Tony Abbott, traces its origins to 1927 and the issue of the 'first set of rules to guide the Cabinet'. Abbott describes the purpose of the *Handbook* as being to set out 'the principles and conventions by which the Cabinet System operates'. It depicts the Cabinet as 'the council of senior ministers who are empowered by the Government to take binding decisions on its behalf' (paragraph 1). The following paragraph notes that any reference to Cabinet is absent from the Australian Commonwealth Constitution, and that even statutes dealing with Cabinet are lacking. Cabinet, the *Handbook* notes, is 'a product of convention and practice'. Consequently, it goes on, the premier who holds office at a given point is responsible for deciding upon its 'shape, structure and operation'. Paragraph 3 emphasises that, given its informal status, Cabinet relies on office holders and institutions in possession of hard power to implement its will, such as the Governor-General, individuals with statutory or constitutional authorities, and Parliament. A later passage describes the office of Prime Minister. It depicts the remit of its occupant as being to determine the personnel of the Cabinet and its committees; and to set the overall operation of Cabinet and the Government (paragraph 6). The Prime Minister, the *Handbook* goes on, 'advises the Governor-General' on the appointing of ministers, the particular functions attached to them and their job titles. Premiers also decide who of these appointees will sit as members the Cabinet (paragraph 7). They are responsible for setting when and where Cabinet meets, and what the agenda will be. The premier 'leads and guides discussion to achieve a collective response'. Yet in the unusual event of such an outcome proving unattainable, 'the Prime Minister's view is authoritative' (paragraph 8).

The *Handbook* describes Cabinet committees, the Ministry as a whole, the Cabinet Secretary and the Cabinet Secretariat. In a section on 'Cabinet conventions and principles' it states that 'A Westminster-style Cabinet is defined by adherence to the principles of collective responsibility and Cabinet solidarity' (paragraph 19). The text therefore consciously locates itself within a wider international model of governance, deriving from a colonial historic heritage. There then follows a description of collective responsibility. It is, the *Handbook* tells us,

> a long standing and integral part of the Cabinet system. It requires that whatever the range of private views put by ministers in Cabinet, once decisions are arrived at and announced they are supported by all ministers. It ensures that the Government is accountable and responsible, as a collective whole, to the Parliament and, through the Parliament to the people of Australia. (paragraph 20)

[5] Department of the Prime Minister and Cabinet, *Cabinet Handbook* (Canberra, Australian Government, 2015).

The *Handbook* adds an important corollary to the principle of outward loyalty in paragraph 21: that 'Issues may, and should, be debated vigorously within the confidential setting of Cabinet meetings.' The purpose of these discussions 'is to reach some form of consensus', enabling the Prime Minister to make a summary. We have already seen the proviso contained in the *Handbook* that, in the event of failure to agree, the Prime Minister has the power to override, perhaps suggesting that premiers are both part of and, when required, above the collective. The *Handbook* defines three 'operational values' upon which collective responsibility rests: 'consultation, confidentiality and respect for the primacy of Cabinet decisions' (paragraph 24).

After dealing with a variety of procedural matters, the *Handbook* covers 'Caretaker conventions and Cabinet'. It notes that a 'caretaker period' commences when there is a dissolution of the House of Representatives. This phase continues either until there has been a definite election outcome, or until a new administration takes office. The principle that applies is that during this period, the existing Government avoids committing to courses of action 'that would bind an incoming government'. The activities that the Government should seek to avoid include the introduction of large-scale programmes, entering into substantial commercial agreements or making important public appointments. Officials should be protected from taking part in business with implications for the election.

Another code, the *Federal Executive Council Handbook*, deals with a body that exists to manage important manifestations of the status of Australia as a constitutional monarchy, with the head of state represented in country by a Governor-General.[6] The Council in important ways resembles the UK Privy Council (see Chapter 1, section I.). The Governor-General derives from section 61 of the Australian Constitution the right to dispose of the executive authorities. Section 62 then creates the Federal Executive Council, the purpose of which is to 'advise' the Governor General on the deployment of these powers. The Council comprises ministers of state within the Australian Government. The purpose of the *Handbook*, the Foreword explains, is to act as a reference for officials who are drafting documents for submission to the Governor-General in Council. The *Handbook* states an important convention in noting that 'most powers of the Governor-General under the *Constitution*' are in fact 'exercised on ministerial advice' (paragraph 2.1.3). It describes an electoral 'caretaker' phase as applying to the Council, just as it applies to the Cabinet (paragraph 2.31). Over the remainder of its 60 pages, the text then sets out in detail the appropriate operating procedures for the Council.

Public codification, then, has an important role in defining the innermost workings of the Australian Constitution. This pattern is replicated in other parts of the former Empire, as we shall see.

[6] Department of the Prime Minister and Cabinet, *Federal Executive Council Handbook* (Canberra, Australian Government, 2015).

II. CANADA: ACCOUNTABLE GOVERNMENT

Like Australia, Canada has a federal, written constitution, but nonetheless—also like Australia—exhibits a disposition towards codification similar to that found in the UK. A text that covers some of the same ground as the Australian handbooks, but is wider in its scope, exists. Entitled *Accountable Government*, it is intended as guidance for senior ministers and more junior Ministers of State.[7] Issued in the name of the Prime Minister, totalling 82 pages, it seems to have first appeared in 2003. The edition analysed here dates from 2011, since which a 2015 update has appeared, entitled *Open and Accountable Government.*

The 'Introduction' to *Accountable Government* states that the text applies to the Prime Minister as well as to other ministers in the Government. Section I, 'Ministerial Responsibility and Accountability', opens with the statement that Ministers of the Crown—who comprise 'the Ministry'—'are chosen by the Prime Minister' and 'serve at the pleasure of the Prime Minister'. There follows a commitment to the principle that Cabinet determines the policy of the Government, followed by reference to the Ministry executing 'the mandate of the government'—presumably meaning a democratic authorisation derived from voters. The document identifies ministers as being 'responsible and accountable' both to the premier and to Parliament. This responsibility and accountability has two forms. The first is individual, that is, it involves performance within the particular brief the Prime Minister has given each minister. Second is a collective form of accountability and responsibility, 'in support of the Ministry team and decisions of Cabinet'. At no point does *Accountable Government* explain the distinction between 'accountability' and 'responsibility'. Despite the suggestion—through the iteration that both apply to ministers—that they are two different concepts, at other points in the text they appear interchangeable.

Paragraph I.1 covers 'Individual Ministerial Responsibility' in more detail. It explains that the Governor-General appoints ministers 'on the advice of the Prime Minister'—a more nuanced description than that proposed earlier in the text, which does not mention the role of the Governor-General. This discrepancy highlights the perils of summarising in these documents. The more subtle wording continues with the statement that premiers can 'ask for' the 'resignation' of ministers whenever they choose. While asking for a resignation may in practice be the same as removal, it does not fully align with the idea presented earlier of ministers holding office at the 'pleasure' of the premier. Alongside the relationship ministers have with the Prime Minister is their connection to Parliament. The bulk of ministerial authorities, the text notes, derive from parliamentary statute. However, other responsibilities are founded in common law, or are attached to ministers by the premier. Nonetheless, regardless of the particular constitutional source, ministers answer to Parliament for the exercise of all of their responsibilities.

[7] *Accountable Government: A Guide for Ministers and Ministers of State* (Ottowa, Privy Council Office, 2011).

Paragraph I.2 elucidates 'Collective Ministerial Responsibility'. It opens by stating that ministers are jointly responsible for implementing the policies formed in Cabinet. Consequently they are required to operate closely with one another. This tenet, the document states, forms the basis for a central convention of the Constitution: 'Cabinet solidarity'. It flows from this principle that policies as expounded both to Parliament and the wider world have to reflect the decisions taken in Cabinet. Moreover, *Accountable Government* tells us, members of the Ministry may not 'dissociate themselves from or repudiate the decisions of Cabinet … unless they resign from the Ministry'. A further source of Cabinet solidarity, the text explains, is the Oath of the Privy Councillor [*sic*], a device we have already encountered in a UK context (see Chapter 1, section I.). The Oath obliges ministers to state their views on a particular issue as it comes before Cabinet, and to maintain secrecy around discussions. The paragraph closes with an exposition of the value of Cabinet government to 'overall coherence and coordination'. Remits of different ministers can 'overlap' or impact upon each other; and the 'increasing complexity of issues' necessitates their being considered as a whole. There is a territorial dimension. Ministers have different geographical bases, colouring their approaches, which 'inevitably cut across departments'. Collective working is essential to ensure that these divergent interests are reconciled with a cohesive government.

'Ministerial Accountability' to Parliament is the subject of paragraph I.3. It opens by reiterating that ministers answer to Parliament for the way in which they dispose of all their authorities, whatever their precise constitutional origin. For this accountability process to take place, they 'must be present in Parliament' to answer queries about their activities, including expenditure. It falls to the 'political judgment' of Parliament to determine whether or not a particular ministerial activity under consideration is appropriate; and it is for the premier to decide how to respond if there is criticism: in other words, to support or secure the removal of the minister concerned. The text then states the principle of indirect accountability: that every part of the executive machine should be answerable to a minister, who then accounts to Parliament for the department and other agencies that fall within her particular remit. Ministers are required accordingly to exercise 'appropriate diligence and competence'. The precise form the fulfilment of this duty takes varies according to the particular organisation concerned. There is a distinction between core departments and 'arm's-length bodies'. In the case of the latter, direct involvement is more restricted, with 'duties and functions … vested in a deputy head or governing body'. It is not necessary for a minister to be aware of all details of activities within her sphere of responsibility, or 'to accept blame' for all problems that may arise. But she must address such issues in Parliament as necessary, and seek to provide redress if needed.

Section II of *Accountable Government* deals with the responsibilities of ministers and the staff assistance they receive. 'Ministerial Relations with Parliament' are the subject of section III. Section IV deals with 'Standards of Conduct'. There then follow eight annexes, lettered A to H. Annex A, Part I comprises 'Ethical Guidelines', applying to all individuals who hold public office. They are required to uphold 'ethical standards', to behave in a way that withstands 'the closest public scrutiny', to 'make decisions in the public interest and with regard to the merits of each case', and to use public property appropriately. Part II sets out 'Guidelines for the Political Activities of Public Office Holders'. These stipulations do not, however, apply to those whose roles are 'necessarily of a political or partisan character'. It explains that those who are subject to the guidelines 'must … discharge their public duties in a non-partisan manner' to guarantee the public perception of 'integrity and impartiality' on the part of the Government. The basic rule is that individuals who hold public office should not take part in any 'activity that is [compromising], or that may reasonably be seen to' compromise the requirement binding upon them that they should perform the role 'in a politically impartial fashion'. The guidelines then provide an illustrative but not comprehensive list of 'political activities'. They include donating money for party political purposes, joining a party, trying to be nominated as a party electoral candidate, taking part in campaigning and making a public expression of party political views. Those who hold public office retain the right to vote. This guidance intersects with the *Public Service Employment Act* of 2003.

Annex B sets out the preferred approach to be taken by ministers to fundraising and interaction with lobbyists; while Annex C deals with the handling of official information. Annex D contains an important account of 'Cabinet Decision Making'. It describes Cabinet as 'the political forum where Ministers reach a consensus and decide on issues'. In this environment they apply 'political and strategic' perspectives to policy programmes that are under consideration. The Annex refers to an obligation in carrying out this process to 'reflect the views and concerns expressed by Canadians, caucus colleagues and other parliamentarians'. Having arrived at an agreement, it is possible for Cabinet members to 'fulfill their collective responsibility to Parliament'. The Annex (paragraph D.1) then stipulates some underlying operational principles for Cabinet, intended to strengthen both its cohesion and how well it functions. There follows a description of the role of the Prime Minister in Cabinet. 'Decision making', the document recounts, 'is *led* by the Prime Minister' (emphasis in original). A function of the premier is to create, in the form of Cabinet and sub-committees of Cabinet, the 'principal forum' for ministers to reconcile varied outlooks. The Prime Minister performs this role through a number of tasks, that is, '*organizes* Cabinet and Cabinet committee decision making, determines the agenda for Cabinet business and chooses committee chairpersons to act on his or her behalf' (emphasis in original). Staff support for these processes comes from the Privy Council Office.

Cabinet reaches its conclusions through 'compromise and consensus building'. Neither it nor its committees vote on decisions. Instead, the premier, or whoever is in the chair of a particular committee, '"calls" for the consensus after Ministers have expressed their views'. The Privy Council Office staff, acting as secretaries to the meeting, take a note of the outcome. Ministers and departments are required to discuss between them any particular plan before it is brought to Cabinet; and ministers also have to engage 'with their Caucus Advisory Committees at an early opportunity'. The purpose of the meeting of Cabinet or of its committees is to concentrate on particular choices that need to be made, enabling those attending to take part in them. Ministers are entitled to bring a particular plan for consideration, provided it falls within their portfolio and 'subject to the agenda set by the Prime Minister for government priorities'. Confidentiality is vital to the process of collective Cabinet government, facilitating Cabinet cohesion and collective responsibility. It enables ministers to put forward their opinions freely during the process of reaching a conclusion. The guidance goes on to stress that the premier 'expects Ministers to announce policies only after Cabinet decisions are taken'. It then explains a variety of procedures. The account of Cabinet committees notes that most of the work takes place in these bodies rather than full Cabinet. The principle is that the 'system settles as many questions as possible at the committee stage in order to lessen the workload of the Cabinet and allow it to concentrate on priority issues and broad political concerns' (paragraph D.4).

Annex E deals with the staff who support ministers. It draws a key distinction between 'public servants' on one hand and 'exempt staff' on the other hand. The 'public service'—which is a 'professional, non-partisan' entity—is responsible for providing ministers with 'frank and candid policy advice and loyal operational support'. This wording echoes that of texts, including the Privy Council Oath and the Armstrong Memorandum (see Chapter 2, section I.B.). Other than a small group of so-called 'deputy ministers' selected by the Prime Minister, public servants are recruited on a basis of merit. Ministers are required to ensure that their 'political neutrality' is sustained. Serving in the private office of ministers is a category of official known as 'political' or 'exempt' staff. The document explains that the purpose of employing these aides is 'to provide Ministers … with advisors and assistants who are not departmental public servants, who share their political commitment … [T]hey contribute a particular expertise or point of view that the public service cannot provide.' Individual ministers will determine the precise role of exempt staff, but the document proposes some possible activities. These aides might assist their minister in formulating proposals, enabling her to express her particular ideological outlook; work on speeches and other statements of a political nature; scrutinise papers produced by the department; be a source of expert advice; and communicate with other ministerial offices and the caucus.

The description of possible tasks for exempt staff is indicative; the limitations are more precise. The Annex explains that they are allowed to interact with departmental officials—that is, non-exempt staff. They can request information, pass on 'instructions' from the minister, and they can 'be informed of decisions in order to address communications and strategic issues'. But, the text stresses, exempt staff have no 'role in departmental operations and have no legal basis for exercising the delegated authority of Ministers'. Furthermore they cannot 'give direction to departmental officials on the discharge of their responsibilities'. Because of the importance of smooth 'working relations', it is crucial that exempt staff 'respect the non-partisanship of public servants' and do not draw them into activities 'outside their appropriate role'. As we shall see, these kinds of limitations are similar to those applied to special advisers in the UK, in accordance with the terms of codes to which they are subject (see Chapter 7, section II.A.). Indeed, more generally, the parallels between 'exempt staff' in Canada and special advisers in the UK are plain. Furthermore, the move to 'Extended Ministerial Offices' in the UK in recent years appears to be a shift in the direction of the Canadian-style private office.[8]

The office of the minister may also comprise, alongside the exempt staff, a 'limited number of public service' staff, who are subject to the non-partisanship rules that the exempt staff are not. They are known as 'departmental assistants', providing logistical support, 'general assistance' and acting as interlocutors 'with the department'. A crucial figure in the management of relations between the minister's office and the department is the deputy minister. As we have seen above, the holders of this post are chosen by the Prime Minister, rather than being recruited on merit. The department as a whole communicates with the minister through the deputy minister, and when exempt staff seek to engage with the department they are required to do so, as far as realistically possible, 'through the deputy minister's office'. If exempt staff communicate directly with other parts of the department, they are expected to ensure that the deputy minister's office is aware they are doing so.

Paragraph E.4 is entitled 'Supporting Ministerial Accountability to Parliament'. It seeks to resolve a particular constitutional tension, addressed by the Osmotherly Rules in the UK (see Chapter 2, section I.C.). While officials have a central role in facilitating meaningful government accountability to Parliament, they must do so in a way that both maintains the non-partisanship of public servants and upholds the principle that it is ministers, not officials, who are accountable—both individually and collectively—to Parliament. Consequently, at oral evidence sessions with parliamentary committees, public servants can deal with inquiries about matters of fact—but their purpose in doing so is to 'explain rather than defend or debate policies'. They are required in such circumstances to 'maintain the traditional non-partisanship' of their institution. To provide a necessary safeguard, the 'authoritative political presence of either the Minister or his or her political representative ... is required if politically controversial matters are likely to arise'. The representative in such circumstances can be either a junior minister, or potentially a member of the ministerial staff. The underlying principle is that a public servant accounts to ministers, via the deputy minister in the department, 'and not to Parliament'. Even accounting officers—by tradition a role taken on in Canada by the departmental deputy minister—are, under statute, 'accountable *before* committees' yet are not 'accountable *to* committees' (paragraph E.1). Furthermore, paragraph E.4 goes on, public servants are subject to a duty to withhold from parliamentary committees certain categories of information, such as those that engage 'national security or privacy' or that comprise 'advice to Ministers'. As the document concedes, '[t]here

[8] Cabinet Office, *Extended ministerial offices: guidance for departments* (London, Cabinet Office, 2013).

is a tension between that obligation and the request of parliamentarians for disclosure of that same information'.

Though placed towards the end of the *Accountable Government* text, Annex F, 'Federal Government Institutions: The Executive' contains a crucial statement of the nature of the Canadian Constitution. It describes Canada as a 'constitutional monarchy' that is also a 'democracy' and in possession of 'a system of responsible parliamentary government'. The code notes that, in structural terms, the systemic arrangements of the country have two sources. First is the 'written constitution', comprising the two *Constitution Acts* of 1867 and 1982 (as amended). Second is the '"unwritten" constitution', composed of 'conventions and customs first established in the British Westminster model of government'. This second portion of Canadian arrangements has, in the period since 1867, 'evolved … to fit the Canadian context'. It determines the central features of democracy in Canada specifically in relation to 'executive authority in government' as wielded by the Prime Minister and Cabinet, 'who are accountable to the House of Commons', a body comprising 'elected representatives of the people of Canada'. The purpose Annex F sets for itself is to describe 'the basic roles and responsibilities' of the different players within the federal executive.

Annex F begins by drawing a crucial distinction between the formal Constitution and the firmly established practical reality (paragraph F.1: 'The Crown, the Governor-General and the Queen's Privy Council for Canada'). Section 9 of the 1867 *Constitution Act* states that 'The Executive Government and Authority of and over Canada is hereby declared to continue and be vested in the Queen.' But the Governor-General, who is the agent of the Queen on the ground in Canada, under 'Canada's democratic system of government … is almost always bound to act only on the advice of the elected representatives who belong to the party that has the confidence of the House of Commons'. Though central to the nature of Canada as a democratic, post-colonial, constitutional monarchy, this statement does not appear until as far as three-quarters of the way through a document the title of which is *Accountable Government*. 'Advice', then, is, in this context, normally more than a simple suggestion and carries in practice a degree of authority, backed by popular legitimacy. It may come to the Governor-General from the Prime Minister 'on some matters', or is 'provided formally by the Cabinet' as a whole. The text tells us that ultimately it 'is the personal prerogative of the Prime Minister to convey the view of the government to the Governor-General'. Though the Governor-General may not in practice be in a position to reject such advice, forms must be preserved and an action requiring her consent cannot be made public or come into force until her agreement is secured. The Annex then makes another distinction between constitutional theory and practice. While the strict position is that the 'chief advisory body' to the 'Sovereign' is the Queen's Privy Council for Canada, comprising every individual sworn in as a Privy Councillor, this entity meets infrequently and for 'ceremonial purposes' solely. In practice, the text explains, it is the Cabinet that 'acts as the chief advisory body to the Governor-General'.

Paragraph F.2 deals with a further crucial feature of the unwritten portion of the Canadian Constitution. Entitled 'The Prime Minister's Functions and Powers', it opens by describing another convention upon which Westminster-type systems depend: 'The Prime Minister, as the leader of the political party that has the confidence of the House of Commons (usually by holding a majority of the seats), is commissioned by the Governor-General to form a government.' This statement is not so much about the role of the premier as it is about the basis for democratic government. The qualifying word 'usually' is of interest, and is redolent of efforts common in equivalent documents in the UK. These UK texts tend to put forward a broad statement of principle, but qualify it in such a way as to reserve a degree of discretion for those involved in its application. The effect can be to overlay arrangements that may seem pre-democratic in nature with more acceptable contemporary values, but to maintain, through deliberately vague wording, precise in its imprecision, some of the traditional principles that the account appears broadly to displace. Displaying another similarity to stipulations made in UK texts, the Canadian document, in introducing the word 'usually', opens up areas of doubt without seeking to resolve them. While it seems to allude to circumstances in which no one party has a majority in the House of Commons, it does not discuss the principles that apply in such circumstances (in this particular area, the UK *Cabinet Manual* does actually seek to dispel uncertainties, though the account it offers has some difficulties) (see Chapter 9, section IV.).

The central task of the Prime Minister, as depicted in *Accountable Government*, is 'organizing the Cabinet and ... providing the direction necessary to maintain the unity of the Ministry'. Such cohesion is essential, the text notes, to the sustenance of Commons confidence. The 'principal functions and exclusive powers' it sets out for the premier in ensuring the viability of Cabinet government are, first, taking the pre-eminent part in determining the overall course of the policy of the Government. To this end, a premier shapes and oversees the mechanisms whereby choices are made, securing agreement between ministers. Also included in this first category are the functions attached to the Prime Minister of advising the Governor-General on the 'summoning and dissolution of Parliament', and devising the 'Speech from the Throne' that sets out the government programme at the beginning of every session in Parliament. Once Cabinet has agreed in principle to a particular law, the text states, it is for the premier to decide if it will be introduced to Parliament. Lastly, the premier 'approves the Budget' prepared by the Finance Minister. These last two powers are examples of how this document attributes to the premier authorities that place her in some senses above Cabinet, rather than being simply the predominant member of it, the traditional formulation under the UK system.

The second central task of prime ministers is in selecting important public appointments, that is choosing and removing government ministers, and in advising the Governor-General on 'senior public sector appointments'. The premier is also responsible for the way Cabinet operates and who its members are to be. Prime ministers set up Cabinet committees and decide who sits on them, and they convene the full Cabinet. The document offers a 'practical' account of this role: '[T]he Prime Minister forms a team, decides on the process of collective decision making, and builds and adapts the machinery of government in which the team will operate.' Reflecting this last point, the fourth role of the premier is in deciding 'the broad organization and structure of the government' to help achieve the goals set for it. Fifth is 'overall responsibility for the government's relations with Parliament and the Sovereign'; sixth is setting out 'standards of conduct' for government and the wider public sector, including through issuing documents such as *Accountable Government* itself. Seventh and lastly, in their capacity as the pre-eminent member of the Government, premiers have what the document describes as 'special responsibilities'. They cover international relations, national security, and dealings between the federal and provincial levels of government. The document then attributes to the premier a more fluid and potentially expansive ability to intervene across government, asserting that a Prime Minister 'may … take a special interest in any other area of a portfolio responsibility as circumstances require'. The text requires ministers to be closely aware of the parts of their own remit that overlap with the interests of the premier.

Paragraph F.3, 'The Ministry, the Cabinet and the Governor in Council' includes an account of the Cabinet as 'the fundamental and final forum for reaching a politically authoritative consensus', despite—in contrast to the Privy Council in Canada—lacking any statutory basis. Having noted this case of a disjuncture between the legal position and the reality, it then identifies a further such gap, when describing how Parliament attaches authorities neither to ministers as a group nor to the Cabinet, but to an entity known as the 'Governor in Council'. An emphasis on the need for ministers to operate within the law comes in paragraph F.4.

Annex G, 'Central Agencies, Communications and Appointments', describes the different bodies that provide assistance to the premier. They are in particular the Privy Council Office (paragraph G.1) and the Prime Minister's Office (paragraph G.2). The annex also discusses other government bodies, and the handling of appointments and the relationship between different tiers of government within the overall federal system. Paragraph G.5 attaches to the premier a central role in coordinating 'Communications and Public Announcements'.

Lastly, Annex H, 'Portfolio Organizations', describes arrangements for the distribution and deployment of different functions within government.

Accountable Government is clearly a wide-ranging document dealing with many aspects of the Canadian Constitution. It encompasses subjects covered in the UK by many discrete texts. But some in Canada believe more codification is needed. They support their view by reference to a constitutional controversy that developed after the Canadian election of 2008. In November, the Conservative Government issued an economic statement that included a plan to remove public financial subventions for political parties. This proposal led the opposition parties to demand that a confidence vote be held; and three of them agreed a deal that would enable them to construct a government for a two-year period. But the Prime Minister, Stephen Harper, stalled the votes and then stated that he would seek a longer delay by requesting that the Governor-General grant a prorogation of Parliament. The Governor-General subsequently agreed, authorising a suspension of Parliament until the beginning of the following year. Opponents of the Conservative Government portrayed this turn of events as an abuse, but the financial crash of the following year distracted attention from it. One outcome of the controversy was a demand for codification of the conventions in this delicate area.[9]

III. THE NEW ZEALAND *CABINET MANUAL*

Another text providing useful points of comparison with the UK codification process is the New Zealand *Cabinet Manual*.[10] One commentator on the *Manual*, Grant Duncan, describes it as intended to create 'a consolidation of the rules, procedures and conventions of Cabinet'.[11] Known until 2001 as the *Cabinet Office Manual*, this text 'emerged quietly in 1979' as an internal document, only placed in the public domain in 1996.[12] At first it was 'restricted' and 'issued in numbered copies'. Then in 1991 it was made 'available to all public servants'. It was 'published as a bound volume for public sale' in 1996; and the 1996 text appeared online in 1998.[13] Though not possessing full legal force, Duncan argues that the New Zealand *Manual* is 'authoritative' and politically entrenched through its acceptance over time by successive Cabinets.[14] The pattern of development of the *Cabinet Manual*, then, is reminiscent of that for the historical rise of the code within the UK, and especially *Questions of Procedure for Ministers*/the *Ministerial Code*, though in the New Zealand case it was accelerated. Both began as internal texts for the benefit of officials but became public works of reference, even acquiring, in the view of some, a constitutional status of some kind, and—as we shall see—figuring in public controversy. As we shall also see, the New Zealand *Manual* has figured in legal proceedings, a use to which its equivalent in the UK has not been put—yet.

Like the Canadian *Accountable Government*, the New Zealand *Manual* is issued by the executive—or rather a branch within it, the Cabinet Office inside the Department of the Prime Minister and Cabinet. The Cabinet as a whole approves the text. In its 180 pages it covers an even wider constitutional spectrum than *Accountable Government* does for Canada. The *Manual* is a central part of a wider codification trend; the text refers to numerous further documents dealing with specific areas in more detail, often in the introduction to chapters. The introduction to Chapter 8, 'The Executive, Legislation, and the House', for instance, lists

[9] AC Banfield, 'Canada' in Galligan and Brenton (eds), above n 2, 199; PH Russell, 'Codifying conventions' in Galligan and Brenton (eds), above n 2, 233.

[10] Current edition: Cabinet Office, *Cabinet Manual* (Wellington, New Zealand Government, 2008).

[11] G Duncan, 'New Zealand's Cabinet Manual: How Does it Shape Constitutional Conventions?', *Parliamentary Affairs*, Advance Access published 6 November 2014, 5.

[12] Russell, above n 9, 234.

[13] Duncan, above n 11.

[14] ibid, 2, 4.

under 'Related information' such texts as *The Legislation Advisory Committee Guidelines: Guidelines on Process and Content of Legislation*; the *Guide to Working with the Parliamentary Counsel Office*; the 'detailed procedural guidance for submitting bids for the legislation programme' contained in the on-line *CabGuide*; and the *Legislation and House Procedure Handbook*. It seems that the UK has in New Zealand a rival as a bulk producer of constitutional codes.

The 'Foreword' to the current, 2008, edition, by the then Prime Minister, Helen Clark, stresses the value of the Cabinet system to the New Zealand Constitution. It 'provides the forum in which Ministers collectively consider, debate and decide on the key issues facing the nation'—an account that would be familiar in Australia, Canada and the UK. Equally reminiscent of these systems is the observation in the Foreword that 'Cabinet is not a creature of legislation', with no statute regulating the manner in which it operates. The *Cabinet Manual*, then, provides what parliamentary enactments do not: it 'guides Cabinet's procedure'. It describes itself as 'an authoritative guide to central government decision making' for officials and ministers. The remit of the *Manual* also extends further, acting as 'a primary source of information on New Zealand's constitutional arrangements' from the point of view of the executive.

The text claims for itself a self-sustaining legitimacy that arises simply by virtue of its being well-established: 'Successive governments have endorsed the *Cabinet Manual* as a sound, transparent, and proven basis on which to operate.' The use of the word 'proven' is suggestive of circular logic: that it is embedded because a number of administrations have acknowledged certain qualities within it, one of which is that it is embedded. It is also notable that being 'sound'—presumably meaning reliable in its effectiveness—is presented as an important virtue: the *Manual* exists partly to serve a practical purpose within government, that is the smooth running of the system. The extension of this logic is that if it succeeds in this objective, it provides an important argument in its own favour. Lastly, the word 'transparent' is significant. The value of openness is nowadays regarded as axiomatic across the Commonwealth systems considered here, and has provided a key motive for codification. Yet in its early days, the *Manual* was a restricted text. An important change in climate has clearly taken place since 1979, in New Zealand as elsewhere, and codification has both modified to accommodate this shift, as well as helping to propel it. The Foreword then makes an important claim: that it 'does not effect change' but instead reflects gradual alterations that have taken place in government practices. It notes that the present edition records ongoing 'development of the conventions' arising from the MMP (Mixed-Member Proportional) method of electing the New Zealand Parliament, and alterations in the way that public institutions deal with one another following the *Crown Entities Act 2004*. The Prime Minister closes by imploring all participants within government to refer to and comply with the *Manual*.

After the 'Foreword' by a senior politician comes the 'Preface' from a high-ranking official: the Secretary of the Cabinet, Diane Morcom. She begins with another assertion that the *Manual* is a necessary and entrenched component of the New Zealand Constitution. 'Successive governments have' known that they require 'guidance' on how to operate; and the *Cabinet Manual* has provided it for them. Going to even greater lengths to present the document as an established fixture, Morcom states that 'endorsement of the *Cabinet Manual* is an item of the agenda of the first Cabinet meeting of a new government', to ensure smooth continuation of the work of government. Here there appears to be an immediate refutation of the earlier claim that the *Manual* does not 'effect change' and only 'records' it. The regular re-endorsement of the text appears to have created an expectation—perhaps even a rule or convention—that this confirmation should take place. It amounts to a new practice that could only possibly have come into being as a consequence of the *Manual*. We shall explore this point, made well by Grant Duncan, in Chapter 4.

As this observation regarding change demonstrates, efforts to derive constitutional legitimacy from practice and precedent, and to allow at the same time for change and flexibility, can be complex. At what point does it become acceptable to break with the past, if adherence to that which has gone before is the guide to proper behaviour? In the case of the *Manual*, the official position is that the text changes if the position it purports to describe has itself clearly altered. Referring back to wording contained in the previous, 2001, edition of the *Manual*, Morcom notes that it 'has a venerable lineage, but is not set in stone'. Occasional updates take place to bring it into line with 'established changes in Cabinet procedures and constitutional developments'. The following vivid description reflects this view of how the *Manual* operates, 'It is like a dictionary: it is authoritative, but essentially recording the current state of the constitutional and administrative language.' But for arrangements to change in such a fashion that the *Manual* itself must alter to retain accuracy would appear to require constitutional players to behave in ways that violate the stipulations contained in the *Manual*.

There follows an essay entitled 'On the Constitution of New Zealand: An Introduction to the Foundations of the Current Form of Government', first written by Sir Kenneth Keith in 1990, updated for the 2008 edition of the *Manual*. It opens by defining a constitution as something that depicts and forms the most significant governmental institutions, iterating their main authorities and determining the way in which they may be deployed. Keith offers an account of the New Zealand constitution in particular. It is, he explains, 'found in formal legal documents, in decisions of the courts and in practices (some of which are described as conventions)'. This sort of account is familiar to the observer of the UK constitution, sometimes described as 'unwritten'. Though, as in New Zealand, a number of key components are written down in some form, it lacks a fully-blown constitutional text. Some of the main features of the New Zealand system, shared with the UK, are that it is a monarchy, a democracy and that it has a parliamentary model of government. New Zealand does, however, have a formative text, in the shape of the Treaty of Waitangi, as the *Manual* recognises (see below). The text also refers to the importance of international agreements and norms.

The New Zealand constitution has progressed slightly further towards being 'written' than that of the UK, since the *Constitution Act 1986* sets out many of the main systemic features, though most of this statute enjoys a legal status no different from that of any other Act. Having accounted for the 1986 Act, the essay then lists other constitutional sources, including legislation originating from New Zealand, from England and from the UK. The Royal Prerogative is another basis for governmental authority. Deriving from the Queen, in practice it is her Governor-General who deploys the prerogative. Ultimately the prerogative is subordinate to statute, as in the UK. The essay then discusses the special position of the Treaty of Waitangi within the New Zealand constitution. It acknowledges that this agreement 'may indicate limits in our polity on majority decision making', with the special position it provides to Maori. Lastly there are conventions that regulate or even 'transform' how the prerogative or statutory authority are exercised. In a reference to influence from elsewhere in the Commonwealth, the *Manual* cites a famous 1982 statement of the Canadian Supreme Court that 'constitutional conventions plus constitutional law equal the total constitution of the country'.

The document then seeks to convey the nature of the democratic system of New Zealand. It explains, first, that 'The Queen reigns', with responsibility (largely through her Governor-General) for: ministerial and other major public appointments; removals from office; the convening and dissolution of Parliament; and for the granting or withholding of formal approval for legislative measures. Yet while these powers reside with the monarch and Governor-General, they exercise them 'only on the advice of the Prime Minister or Ministers who have the support of the House of Representatives—that is, on the advice of those who are elected by the New Zealand voters' and have secured the acceptance of the House that they should hold office. Consequently there is a permanent need for a 'ministry' to provide the necessary advice to the monarch and her delegate. But, since this special position of influence over the Queen and the Governor-General derives from the House of Representatives, a need to replace a government or an individual Prime Minister can arise if they lose the 'support' of the House. In such circumstances, a new premier or majority group may clearly appear. But potentially a less certain position could present itself, making the position more complicated for the Governor-General. As the essay notes, the advent of a more proportionate electoral system in New Zealand has made outcomes in which no one party holds a majority in the House normal, thereby increasing the chances that the Governor-General will face a less than straightforward position.[15] In such circumstances the Governor-General draws upon the advice of members of the House—in particular leaders of the parties—to discern whether it is possible to assemble sufficient support within the House for a government, or if a new election is necessary to try to resolve the issue. While these discussions are ongoing, the existing ministry continues to serve, subject to a 'convention on caretaker government'.

[15] For the impact of Mixed-Member Proportionality (MMP) on the *Manual*, see G Duncan, 'New Zealand' in Galligan and Brenton (eds), above n 2, 225.

The essay is careful to assert that, despite the need to adhere to democratic principle, the Governor-General retains an 'important role' that encompasses 'being informed and consulted, and advising and warning Ministers'—a formulation similar to those applied to the monarch in the UK, including by the UK *Cabinet Manual*. Moreover, the Governor-General has 'central symbolic, unifying, and representative' functions (the type that are, in the UK, generally attributed to the monarch herself rather than her proxy). But the actual ongoing government of New Zealand is generally the task of the ministry. The members of this body 'must take collective and individual responsibility for their decisions, the decisions that are taken in their name, and the measures they propose'. The essay then draws attention to the distinction between '[r]eal power and legal form'. Government actions 'often take a legal form that departs from … practical and conventional reality'. Cabinet, being 'essentially a body established by convention, has no legal power', and even the House 'acting alone has very limited powers to take decisions with full legal effect'. The legal position is often that the Governor-General, acting alone or in Council, or ministers acting individually, formally select or authorise particular courses of action. Were this position the full reality it would not be democratically satisfactory. Conventions, then, are crucial to reconciling the formal arrangement with widely accepted principles of accountability. The appearance of texts such as the New Zealand *Manual* across the Commonwealth countries considered here suggests a perceived need to provide more clarity around these mediating values. However, a perverse outcome, through giving conventions a more precise and official status, is partially to formalise the informal. One question that arises immediately is whether during this process, certain qualities, such as flexibility, might be lost.

The essay recognises the importance of parties within the political system, for supplying a connection between the public, the Parliament and government. It notes the existence of the Prime Minister, with important functions resting on 'constitutional convention'. In an account of the 'public service', it lists key requirements applying to those employed within it, including that they 'be imbued with the spirit of service to the community' and that they can provide 'free and frank advice to Ministers', yet loyally implement the wishes of ministers once they have reached a conclusion: a familiar formulation across the different countries considered in this book. A passage on 'Individuals, autonomy and majority rule' deals with a key dilemma of democracy: how to reconcile the concept of the rule of the majority with the rights of individuals. The *Manual* states that there is a need for the maintenance of a 'balance … between the sovereignty of the people exercised through Parliament and the rule of law'. Interestingly—and reasonably—the text records that 'The answer cannot always lie with simply majority decision making.' In fact, it goes on, many in positions of power are aware that their capacity to act is circumscribed in various senses: by perceptions of fundamental social values, 'by convention, by the Treaty of Waitangi', by requirements under international law, and by conceptions of what is just and fair. Through these words, the New Zealand *Manual* is more direct in its qualifying of parliamentary authority than its

UK equivalent. It is also notable that it suggests that popular sovereignty underlies parliamentary authority, with its reference to 'the sovereignty of the people exercised through Parliament'.

The essay observes a tendency whereby an increasing volume of law has its origins in international agreements, consequently in effect lessening the scope of official organs operating at national level. In the passage that follows, there is an account of further limitations upon the exercise of parliamentary authority, pertaining in this instance to constitutional modification. As we have seen, like the UK, New Zealand lacks a 'written constitution'. Consequently, core features of its system lack a special legal status distinguishing them clearly from more regular laws. Therefore, as the essay points out, it is strictly possible to change most parts of the New Zealand constitution using standard parliamentary law-making procedure, with a majority of just one sufficient. Yet—once again drawing attention to the distinction between legal form and political reality—the capacity for free alteration of the system is limited in a number of ways, 'by law, convention, practice and public acceptance'.

Some constraints come from international agreements, while others (involving the electoral system) need, under law, to meet referendum or parliamentary super-majority requirements. Potentially, the legal protections referred to here could be removed using simple majorities. It would then be possible to alter the previously protected electoral arrangements in the same way, surely contrary to the intention lying behind the initial law. With the threat of such a manoeuvre in mind, the essay cautiously advances that there is a convention that any attempt to remove safeguards in this way would be subject to the same approval procedure of referendum or super-majority that it was seeking to abolish. Another protective rule to which the essay refers is that the introduction of new parliamentary Standing Orders is subject to 'consensus in the Standing Order Committee'. Other alterations to the constitution may take place subject to less stringent requirements. They can involve normal legislative processes, judicial decisions, the use of prerogative powers and 'changing practices' that can encourage 'new conventions'. Yet in all cases, any change should be 'based on relevant principle'. Further on, in paragraph 5.72 of the *Manual*, the text stresses the importance of giving proper attention to constitutional matters, stating that '[a]ny proposal that will affect New Zealand's constitutional arrangements must be submitted to Cabinet'. Furthermore, paragraph 5.72 insists on handling such business in a fashion appropriate to its importance, including ensuring that proper engagement takes place. It states that if 'significant constitutional change is contemplated, issues of process and appropriate public participation must be clearly and fully addressed in the Cabinet paper'. These stipulations for the handling of such business are far more stringent that those present in the UK *Cabinet Manual*.

Chapter 1 of the *Manual* proper deals with the 'Governor-General and Executive Council'. The rules lacking in direct legal force it sets out include that the monarch appoints the Governor-General 'on the advice of the' premier (paragraph 1.2). A further crucial principle is the 'apolitical' nature of the post of

Governor-General. The *Manual* identifies a 'convention' that, despite being central in a 'formal' sense to the operation of the government, 'the Governor-General avoids becoming involved in the party politics of government' (paragraph 1.11). The Governor-General 'acts on the advice of Ministers' (paragraph 1.12) and of premiers (paragraph 1.13) while they possess the necessary support of the House of Representatives. There are a certain number of instances in which the Governor-General may possess some 'personal discretion', acting using the so-called 'reserve powers', though generally 'convention' will determine the course of action chosen (paragraph 1.15).

Chapter 2 of the *Manual* covers 'Ministers of the Crown: Appointment and Role'. An important passage involves the office of Prime Minister. It explains that the Governor-General appoints the premier, taking into account the outcome of elections and any negotiations 'between political parties' that follow (paragraph 2.2). Though the Prime Minister is 'head of the government', the *Manual* explains, the precise role has developed through history and has no basis in statute (paragraph 2.3). Nonetheless, premiers perform functions crucial to the political system. They are the 'principal adviser' both to the monarch and to the Governor-General (paragraph 2.4). According to 'constitutional convention', the premier handles official 'communication with the' monarch (paragraph 2.5). The premier monopolises the provision of advice to the Governor-General on choosing and removing ministers, and on dissolutions of Parliament leading to general elections (paragraph 2.6). Grant Duncan draws attention to this stipulation as an example of the *Manual*'s stating important conventions that would otherwise 'remain (outside textbooks) largely "unwritten"'.[16] Prime ministers, the *Manual* goes on, act as 'the head of executive government'. In this function they establish and operate administrations, a task that under the electoral system now used in New Zealand generally entails liaising with political parties other than their own. As well as advising the Governor-General on the appointment of ministers, the premier determines what their remits will be and the order of precedence. The *Manual* hints at the limitations that apply to premiers in the exercise of this theoretical power when noting it is deployed 'taking into account practical and political considerations' (paragraph 2.7). It records that the Governor-General 'acts on the advice of the Prime Minister' regarding the appointment (paragraph 2.16) and removal (paragraph 2.18) of ministers. When dispensing with a minister, the premier need not explain the reasons for doing so to the Governor-General (paragraph 2.19). These conventions suggest a position of strength for the premier. But once again the *Manual* indicates limitations. It records again that the decisions the Prime Minister makes are likely to be subject to '[p]ractical and political considerations', including 'internal party rules or the terms of a coalition agreement' (paragraph 2.16).

Acting as chair of the Cabinet, the premier 'approves the agenda, leads the meetings, and is the final arbiter of Cabinet procedure'. Premiers also decide the remits of Cabinet committees and who sits on them (paragraph 2.9). Another function of

[16] Duncan, above n 11, 2.

prime ministers is in 'coordinating the government', taking overall responsibility for the course of government 'policy' (paragraph 2.10). The established practice is that the premier has responsibility for the security and intelligence agencies, and can potentially fill other additional functions (paragraph 2.11). The *Manual* notes that there is a clear distinction between the office of Prime Minister and the position of its holder as the leader of a party (paragraph 2.12). Ministers answer in the final instance to the Prime Minister for their compliance or otherwise with ethical standards (paragraph 2.53). The *Manual* identifies three ways in which ministers operate: as ministers, in a political sense, and as individual people (paragraph 2.52). An area to which it devotes significant attention is the avoidance of 'conflicts of interest' (paragraphs 2.60–2.77).

The subject of Chapter 3 of the *Manual* is 'Ministers of the Crown and the State Sector'. It addresses the relationship between 'Ministers and the public service'. The *Manual* explains that while ministers have overall responsibility for the departments they head, they are not directly involved in 'day-to-day operations'. They set and advocate policy, and answer to the House of Representatives for 'policy and operational matters'. Officials working in the public service, for their part, provide assistance to ministers in performing their roles, helping to devise programmes and put them into practice (paragraph 3.5). A key relationship within a department, the paragraphs that follow reveal, is between the minister and the chief executive, with the latter the 'main point of contact' for the former (paragraph 3.6). This distance between minister and core government department in New Zealand is greater than that prevailing in the UK, and has some resemblance to the relationship between UK Secretaries of State and arm's-length executive agencies.

Convention, alongside statute, plays an important part in the relationship between ministers and the public service (paragraph 3.6). The *Manual* sets out some of the key principles involved. The particular way in which ministers and their departments operate, and how often they interact with each other, is shaped by the particular approach of a given minister. Officials should operate on a basis of what the *Manual* calls the '"no surprises" principle'. It entails ensuring that they swiftly make the minister aware of any important issue that has arisen, especially if it is likely to generate controversy. Chief executives have to use their own discretion over whether to raise with the minister any particular piece of business that comes within the statutory remit of the chief executive. Normally this 'briefing … is … for the Minister's information only', and both the chief executive and the minister are required to support 'the independence of the chief executive's decision-making process'. An important stipulation in the *Manual* is that ministers should be aware that they have a significant impact on the public service. It is important that 'their intentions are not misunderstood, and that they do not inappropriately influence officials' or become engaged in business beyond their proper remit (paragraph 3.16).

Ministers need not obtain support from the established staff in the public service and wider state sector alone. They can also turn to 'other sources, including political advisers in their offices'. These aides are a variant on the type of assistants known as special advisers in the UK and as 'exempt staff' in Canada (see section II. above). The *Manual* lists key functions for these 'political advisers': handling interactions with 'other political parties, to manage risk, and to negotiate support for policy and legislative initiatives' (paragraph 3.19). Ministers can task their political advisers with functions that would normally take place inside the department. It is consequently important to ensure clarity with the chief executive and other officials regarding what precisely the political advisers are authorised to do. There is also a need for clear accountability (paragraph 3.20). The *Manual* records that ministers 'are accountable to the House' for the performance of their departments (paragraph 3.21). This broad position—a minister with political responsibility to Parliament with a non-partisan official machine answering to him, with some support from advisers who are allowed overt party connections—is a familiar one to observers of UK codes (and the Canadian *Accountable Government*). The precise details may differ—for instance the operational independence of the departmental chief executive is a divergence from arrangements in Whitehall—but there is clearly some common heritage and ongoing mutual influence in the approach taken. There are, for instance, safeguards against New Zealand public servants' engaging problematically in public debate. While they retain 'rights of free speech', they should ensure that in so doing they exercise 'discretion' apt to their office (paragraph 3.62). When providing evidence to House select committees, public servants are 'subject to ministerial discretion on answers to be given and information to be supplied' (paragraph 3.63). When they speak to 'caucus' committees of their minister's party, public servants purely supply facts and do not discuss the 'merits' of particular policy ideas (paragraph 3.68). In the New Zealand political environment, because of the electoral system employed, negotiations between parties is the norm. Ministers may require assistance from public servants in this activity, but it may only involve 'factual briefing'. All dealings between public servants and parties are subject to ministerial approval, in advance (paragraph 3.69).

Chapter 4 of the *Manual* is entitled 'Ministers and the Law'. It begins by discussing the role of the Attorney-General, the pre-eminent source of legal advice within the Government. The occupant of this post is a minister who 'almost always' has a place in Cabinet. The Attorney-General provides legal advice at meetings of Cabinet and Cabinet committees, and 'encourages ministerial colleagues' to obtain 'appropriate legal advice' when making decisions. The *Manual* insists that it is necessary to seek the view of the Attorney-General on proposals that engage important legal matters (paragraph 4.2). It describes a special task that falls to the Attorney-General, 'maintaining the rule of law'. The *Manual* does not define 'rule of law', but in the following sentence it describes how the Attorney-General is required to inform the Cabinet if any government plans or intended actions 'do not comply with existing law', and to suggest how to deal with the issue.

This account, therefore, involves focusing on adherence to the law as it is in force at a given time, and does not deal with the idea that rule of law entails conforming to a broader set of underlying principles. However, the *Manual* then refers to a particular statute, the *New Zealand Bill of Rights Act 1990*. Under this Act, the

Attorney-General informs Parliament if a bill contradicts the 1990 Act itself (paragraph 4.3). This provision suggests that there are some underlying norms—in this instance individual rights—that require special protection of some kind. This view accords with many versions of the rule of law, which extend beyond simple compliance with the law whatever it may be at the time. The *Manual*, however, does not make this point expressly. It then seems to suggest, albeit implicitly once more, a further feature that is crucial to the rule of law as many interpret it: that the law should not become subordinate to sectional interests, and should be seen as an impartial force. While the Attorney-General can 'take into account public policy considerations', the individual who holds the post is, according to 'convention … not influenced by party political considerations', and should seek not to create the perception of being so. As a law officer, the Attorney-General is exempt from collective responsibility (paragraph 4.4), though as a minister is subject to this rule in areas of government business that do not engage being a law officer (paragraph 4.5). The complexity of the joint ministerial and advisory role of the Attorney-General—a feature of the equivalent post in the UK—is underlined by the holder's being 'answerable to the House of Representatives in relation to the agencies under the Attorney-General's control', such as the Parliamentary Counsel Office and the Crown Law Office (paragraph 4.9).

A further crucial responsibility for the Attorney-General iterated in the *Manual* is to act as the connection between the executive and the judicial branches. She makes recommendations for judicial appointments and 'has an important role in defending the judiciary'. To this end, the Attorney-General rebuts 'improper and unfair public criticism', and seeks to dissuade other ministers from engaging in censure of members of the judiciary and their conclusions and judgments (paragraph 4.8). A subsequent section headed 'Comment by Ministers on judicial decisions' emphasises that ministers should 'exercise judgment before commenting on judicial decisions', because of the 'separation' of the judiciary and the executive. This principle applies both to broad criticism of the approach of the judiciary, and to negative commentary on features of a particular case (paragraph 4.12). The *Manual* insists that ministers ought not to vent any opinions that might become public if it would be possible to interpret them 'as reflecting adversely on the impartiality, personal views, or ability of any judge' (paragraph 4.13). The text refers to a 'long-established principle' of ministers not engaging in decisions about 'whether a person should be prosecuted, or on what charge'. It then reiterates the point about not issuing statements about the outcomes of individual proceedings. Ministers should not make remarks about sentences and 'should avoid at all times any comment that could be construed as being intended to influence the courts in subsequent cases' (paragraph 4.14). Lastly, while they may speak generally about 'the effectiveness of the law' and other areas in which it is appropriate for the executive to involve itself, they should not do so in a way that casts doubt on the effectiveness of the courts (paragraph 4.15). These stipulations are firm—using words such as 'must'—and clear that not only should ministers refrain from interfering in decisions about prosecutions, they should also not comment on cases after the fact. The overall content comprises a greater set of asserted constraints on how ministers should conduct themselves with respect to judicial activity than those contained in the UK *Cabinet Manual*.

'Cabinet Decision Making' is the subject of Chapter 5 of the New Zealand *Manual*. As already noted in Chapter 2 of that volume, the Prime Minister decides who will be a member of Cabinet, and how many members the Cabinet will have. Generally not every government minister is part of the Cabinet (paragraph 2.26). With prime-ministerial approval, ministers outside Cabinet can go to Cabinet meetings to discuss specific issues relevant to their remit, and they are normally members of at least one Cabinet committee. Collective responsibility applies to all ministers, whether inside or outside Cabinet (paragraph 2.27). But what is the significance of Cabinet? The *Manual* describes it as core to the New Zealand constitution, though 'established by convention, not law'. While individual office holders and institutions have specific authorities vested in them by statute, the reality is that 'all significant decisions or actions taken by the Executive are first discussed and collectively agreed by Cabinet' (paragraph 5.3). It is for Cabinet itself to decide upon the manner in which it functions, with the Prime Minister, who is chair of the Cabinet, having the final word on such matters (paragraph 5.4).

The full Cabinet normally convenes on a Monday (paragraph 5.52). It has, according to the *Manual*, a quorum of 'half the full membership ... plus one'. Furthermore, '[t]he chair of a Cabinet meeting may vary the quorum requirements, if necessary' (paragraph 5.60). In August 1998, the New Zealand *Cabinet Manual* was at the centre of a constitutional controversy involving the breakdown of the National Party–New Zealand First Party Coalition Government, turning on this account of Cabinet quorum. On 12 August, New Zealand First Party ministers left a Cabinet meeting that was discussing the sale of a publicly-owned entity. Within the terms of the coalition agreement, there was now an insufficient number in attendance for the Cabinet to be quorate. However, according to the text of the *Cabinet Manual* of the time, only one more than half the total membership was required, and according to this rule the Cabinet was quorate. The Liberal Prime Minister, Jenny Shipley, had obtained the counsel of the Cabinet Secretary and the Solicitor-General on whether the coalition agreement took precedence over the position stated in the *Manual* and felt confident to proceed. Yet the break with the coalition agreement entailed the end of the coalition. The Government went ahead with the sell-off. Winston Peters, the New Zealand First leader and Deputy Prime Minister, was removed from his post for his public disagreement with the policy, which constituted a violation of the requirement for a unanimous Cabinet.[17]

This incident could amount to a case of the *Manual* doing more than simply reflecting the existing position. There was potential for confusion about what the appropriate practice and rules were around this issue. The *Manual* presented a particular interpretation, and could provide support for those who wished to

[17] Duncan, above n 15, 221.

promote it. Without the *Manual*'s stating the rule expressly in the way it did, perhaps the ground Shipley was on might not have seemed as firm. Codes can make a difference.

The *Manual* goes on to describe how Cabinet committees are a means of addressing matters in detail before taking them to the full Cabinet (paragraph 5.6). They usually focus on a specific 'subject area, such as social policy', or a general issue 'such as expenditure and administration' (paragraph 5.7). Unlike in the UK, Cabinet committees in New Zealand cannot normally make decisions that are regarded in their own right as final Cabinet decisions. They must refer their conclusions on to full Cabinet, to agree to them, alter them or send them back to the committee for more work (paragraph 5.8). Cabinet does sometimes grant the 'power to act' in a specific area to a committee or particular ministers, allowing them to settle a matter at once (paragraph 5.9).

The *Manual* applies what might be termed the 'golden rule' to bringing matters to Cabinet: 'Ministers should put before their colleagues the sorts of issues on which they themselves would wish to be consulted.' Ministers ought to ensure that Cabinet members are aware of issues 'of public interest, importance, or controversy' (paragraph 5.11). Paragraph 5.12 lists the business that 'must', via the relevant Cabinet committee, be referred to Cabinet; paragraph 5.13 those issues that 'should not, as a general rule' be referred. Before a minister takes a proposal to Cabinet, there is a need for consultation with fellow ministers (paragraph 5.14) and other parties involved in government (paragraph 5.16). The same 'no surprises' principle that applies to relations between officials and ministers is deemed relevant here, along with 'careful planning' and 'good faith' (paragraph 5.17). There is an 'informal and confidential' quality to debate in Cabinet and Cabinet committees. Details of matters that are due to come before Cabinet should generally remain confidential, as should 'the nature' and 'content of the discussions', the particular positions taken by ministers and the contributions of officials. These points are not 'formally recorded' or included in the final minutes (paragraph 5.21).

The *Manual* depicts 'collective responsibility' as critical in two senses. It rests, first, on the idea that the House of Representatives has given its confidence to a particular government as a 'whole'. Secondly, collective responsibility ensures that advice passed to the Governor-General is clearly the view of ministers as a group and not simply that of the particular minister supplying the advice (paragraph 5.22). Within Cabinet, there is thorough discussion of issues, after which 'consensus is usually reached and votes are rarely taken'. Ministers are then required to unite behind the conclusion, whether or not they were present at the particular Cabinet meeting and whatever their personal position might be (paragraph 5.23). In circumstances of coalition, there may be differences between the stance of a party and the approach of the Government. The *Manual* reminds ministers of the need 'to show careful judgement' in acknowledging differences in this area. They 'must always be clear' that they adhere to the agreed position of the Government (paragraph 5.25). The *Manual* then refers to what it terms '"agree to disagree" processes'. Under this arrangement, it explains, ministers in coalitions are permitted openly to hold views at variance with one another according to their particular party stance. However, once the matter has been resolved through collective means, 'Ministers must implement the resulting decision or legislation' (paragraph 5.25). The 'agree to disagree' procedure applies only to 'different party positions'. It does not allow 'individual Ministers' to distance themselves from the conclusions of Cabinet that they may dislike (paragraph 5.26). It is also possible in a coalition, the *Manual* informs us, for ministers who are not members of Cabinet to be subject to collective responsibility only as it applies to their specific policy remit. Outside of this regulated area, they can make interventions from a party perspective, and not as part of the Government. Within their brief, they must adhere to collective responsibility (paragraph 5.27).

'Elections, Transitions, and Government Formation' are covered in Chapter 6 of the New Zealand *Manual*. Section 18 of the *Constitution Act 1986* vests in the Governor-General the right to summon, prorogue and dissolve Parliament. But, the *Manual* reminds us, she does so—according to 'convention'—'on the advice of the Prime Minister, the Governor-General's principal adviser' (paragraph 6.3). A central concern of this chapter arises from the system of proportional representation used in New Zealand, which 'lessens the likelihood that one party will win enough seats to be sworn in as a single-party majority government'. The *Manual* refers to three possible outcomes: 'a minority single-party government, or a majority coalition government, or a minority coalition government' (paragraph 6.4). A series of constraints apply to governments around election time. Roughly three months in advance of a poll, they 'have chosen to restrict their actions', not making major public appointments and exercising caution around the use of official advertising (paragraph 6.9). In the period immediately after a general election, a 'caretaker convention' can apply. It is relevant either when one government is clearly being replaced by another, but the changeover has not yet taken place, or when there is a lack of certainty about who will be able to form a ministry. The caretaker convention also comes into force if a government has lost the confidence of the House of Representatives (paragraphs 6.17 and 6.19). When there is a period of uncertainty, the general principle is to avoid, if possible, major, lasting commitments (paragraphs 6.20–6.23). During a straightforward transition (likely to be only of minimal duration), the outgoing government should not embark on fresh programmes, and should act only in accordance with the views of the government in the process of taking up office on unavoidable decisions (paragraphs 6.24–6.25).

How should governments be formed in the non-majoritarian environment of the New Zealand Parliament? The basic principle is set out in a one-sentence paragraph (6.37): 'The process of forming a government is political, and the decision to form a government must be arrived at by politicians.' Without offering more detail, the *Manual* then moves on to consider in paragraph 6.38 what happens once 'the political parties have reached an adequate accommodation'. There is an expectation that the parties concerned will announce their plan, and seek approval for it in accordance with their 'own internal procedures'. But it is the Governor-General who is formally empowered to install governments. The holder of this post, paragraph 6.39 states, is 'to ascertain where the confidence of the House lies ... so that a government can be appointed'. However, it is not a function of the Governor-General 'to form the government or to participate in any negotiations'. Nonetheless, the Governor-General 'might wish' to become involved in resolving a deadlock of some kind, the *Manual* explains, by talking to leaders of different parties if negotiations encounter difficulties. According to the following paragraph, 'convention' determines that the Governor-General will respect the conclusion of the negotiations between parties regarding what should be the complexion of the Government and who should be the premier (paragraph 6.40). The Clerk of the Executive Council is a crucial figure in this process, assisting the Governor-General and facilitating transition if it occurs (paragraph 6.41). Similar principles apply if there is a change of Prime Minister or of government between general elections. The *Manual*, however, identifies one possible area of complication. Normally, if a Prime Minister seeks an early dissolution of Parliament, the Governor-General 'will act on the advice'. However, if the Government has lost the confidence of the House, it becomes subject to the caretaker convention. The *Manual* notes that if a Prime Minister were to seek an early dissolution from the Governor-General then the latter 'would expect a caretaker Prime Minister to consult other parties'. The *Manual* insists that '[i]t is the responsibility of the members of Parliament to resolve matters so that the Governor-General is not required to consider dissolving Parliament and calling an election without ministerial advice' (paragraph 6.58). However, it does not entirely preclude that a Governor-General might act in this way.

Chapter 7 of the New Zealand *Cabinet Manual* is entitled 'The Executive, Legislation, and the House'. Among its various provisions, it includes guidance on 'Effective and appropriate consultation', stressing the importance of consultation to 'good decision making, good policy, and good legislation' (paragraph 7.24). However, most of the guidance in this area involves interaction within the elite—inside the executive, for instance, or with parliamentarians. The *Manual* only introduces the concept of public consultation late on in this section (paragraph 7.40). Chapter 8 is on the subject of 'Official Information', and is focused mainly on the statutory framework operating in this area. It does, however, contain a section dealing with the 'Convention on access to Cabinet records of a previous administration'. It asserts a principle that there is a need for 'continuity of government', despite the occurrence of changeovers in the party political complexion of governments (paragraph 8.75). The New Zealand *Cabinet Manual* then concludes with three appendices on the office of Governor-General, government advertising and Crown legal business, followed by an index.

IV. CONCLUSION

Codification is a widespread phenomenon. As the sample used here demonstrates, it can occur in countries with a range of population sizes, from New Zealand (*c.* 4.5 million) to the UK (*c.* 64 million), with Australia (*c.* 23 million) and Canada (*c.* 35 million) falling in between. Countries with written constitutions (Australia and Canada) and unwritten constitutions (New Zealand and the UK) alike utilise them. Codes have a place in federal systems (Australia, Canada) and in a unitary state (New Zealand), and—in the UK—a constitution to which either description is difficult fully to apply. The documents produced in each of these countries reflect some of the key features of the 'Westminster model' within which they are grouped. They set down in writing principles, rules—some that might be conventions—and practices that do not have immediate legal force, and might once have existed more in tacit form than in texts. A recurring theme is the need to distinguish the legal form from the practical reality. The similarity between the lists of issues they address is striking. Indeed, it is plain that the drafters of these texts in the different countries are drawing on one another's work. Codes deal with the constitutional role of the monarch, or of the proxy for the monarch, the Governor-General. They address the need for government to rest on parliamentary support, and how to handle circumstances when the arithmetic in the legislature makes the position complicated. Another common area of interest is the position of the Prime Minister and the role of the Cabinet. The subject of executive accountability to Parliament arises frequently. This issue leads to the constitutional status of civil servants or their equivalent, and within this body of official staff, the existence of a partisan component such as exempt staff, political staff or special advisers. How, precisely, codes in the UK handle these matters is considered in detail in Part Two of this book.

4

The Impact of Codification

WE HAVE CONSIDERED codification as an historical process in the UK and as a phenomenon across different Commonwealth countries. But to appreciate the significance of this tendency in full, it is important to consider its impact. It has implications for core features of the constitution. Codification has consequences in particular for the way in which we perceive our systemic rules; for the rules themselves; for the way in which they change; and even for their legitimacy. In this chapter, I present ideas that I first proposed in an article written in the wake of the publication of the first full edition of *The Cabinet Manual* (see Chapter 2, section VII.), elaborating upon some of the content using new evidence gathered for the purposes of this book.[1] I then discuss the use another author has since made of my theories, who applied them to the New Zealand constitution.[2]

The most important impact of codification has been upon constitutional conventions. The term 'constitutional convention' applies to systemic rules lacking direct legal enactment but nonetheless vital to the operation of any constitution. For those who accept that they are valid as a tool of analysis (which this author does), there is nonetheless not a universal definition of what a convention is. Broadly speaking, they are a means by which the hard legal features of a system are able to operate in practice, and by which a polity can develop to keep pace with external circumstances such as social change. But we are not dealing with certainty. For instance, the distinction between conventions of a constitutional nature and mere practice is not always clear.[3] The latter simply involves procedures that tend to be followed at a given point. There is no obligation that they should be adhered to, though they might over time develop into conventions, which by contrast carry with them an expectation of compliance. Because one can morph into the other, there is potential for difficulty in distinguishing between the two. Yet, undoubtedly, the codes considered in this work deal with important conventions, such as those pertaining to the Prime Minister, the Cabinet, and the relationship between the executive and Parliament.

[1] A Blick, 'The Cabinet Manual and the Codification of Conventions' (2014) 67(1) *Parliamentary Affairs* 191.

[2] G Duncan, 'New Zealand's Cabinet Manual: How Does it Shape Constitutional Conventions?' (2015) 68 *Parliamentary Affairs* 737.

[3] R Brazier, 'The Non-legal Constitution: Thoughts on Convention, Practice and Principle' (1992) 43 *Northern Ireland Legal Quarterly* 262.

To give an idea of the way in which codes handle conventions and the issues that can arise, it is useful to consider the approach that *The Cabinet Manual* takes to defining the role of the monarch. The *Manual* is clear about the importance of conventions—which it describes as 'rules of constitutional practice that are regarded as binding in operation but not in law' (paragraph 5)—to the UK constitution. How do they apply to the monarch? The *Manual* describes the UK as in possession of a 'constitutional sovereign as Head of State' (paragraph 1). Conventions are essential to ensuring that the monarch is 'constitutional', and that the legal powers that reside in the head of state are exercised only sparingly. This restraint, founded in convention, is crucial to parliamentary democracy as understood in the UK. Paragraph 6 accordingly refers to a 'convention' that the monarch does not engage visibly 'in the party politics of government'. However, the head of state has a right 'to be informed and consulted, and to advise, encourage and warn ministers'. This list of privileges (repeated in paragraph 1.5 of the *Manual*) draws on an account that Walter Bagehot first published in 1867, but adds to it. The influential description Bagehot offered referred only to 'three rights'—'to be consulted … to encourage … to warn'.[4] He included neither 'informed' nor 'advise'. In using them, the *Manual* could be said to have encouraged change, suggesting an enlargement (if only marginal) in the constitutional role of the monarch. The document goes on to note the existence of a convention that contact between the head of state and members of the government remains secret. The implication appears to be that a monarch can be active in seeking to influence the conduct of government, and that a problem only arises if details of this behaviour reach the public domain, with a responsibility seemingly falling on ministers to ensure that it does not.

Paragraph 6 of the *Manual* then notes that the monarch possesses 'prerogative powers'. These authorities are—again in accordance with 'convention'—under ministerial control, 'save in a few exceptional instances'. The paragraph does not specify what these exemptions are. A stipulation found later on in the *Manual*, in paragraph 3.33, forms part of an account of the sources of ministerial power. In its discussion of the Royal Prerogative, the paragraph notes that it is 'generally exercised by ministers or by the Sovereign on the advice of ministers, particularly the Prime Minister'. Yet it then goes on to emphasise that 'the Sovereign continues to exercise personally some prerogative powers of the Crown', referring to the conferral of the Order of Merit. More intriguingly, the *Manual* then states that the monarch 'reserves the right to exercise others in unusual circumstances'. It does not give us any guide as to what these 'unusual circumstances' might be; and it does not suggest what might be an appropriate use of these reserve powers in such circumstances.

This discussion demonstrates that codification in the UK engages with matters of crucial constitutional significance, and that the outcomes can be complex.

[4] W Bagehot, *The English Constitution* (Oxford, Oxford University Press, 2001) 64.

It might be that there is greater scope for the existence of conventions of pronounced importance in the UK than in other countries, since the lack of a written constitution (that is a discrete text clearly labelled the 'Constitution', with special legal status) leaves more core rules to be dealt with in this way. Yet the 'written' Constitutions of Australia and Canada certainly appear not to have eradicated conventions deemed to be in need of explanation in codes. Furthermore, issues that were once primarily matters of convention in the UK—though they cannot be included in a written Constitution—are arguably increasingly coming to be given a statutory framework. They include the 'Ponsonby Rule', providing for parliamentary oversight of treaty-making by the executive (now dealt with in the Constitutional Reform and Governance Act 2010), and the rules relating to the holding of General Elections within the five-year term limit (now the subject of the Fixed-term Parliaments Act 2011). At the time of writing, the Scotland Bill seeks to enshrine in an Act of Parliament the 'Sewel Convention' regarding the relationship between the UK and Scottish parliaments; and a similar plan is in hand in relation to Wales.

Such Acts may replace convention in the direct areas they affect (though their protection from repeal or amendment by Parliament may rest on convention). Yet they can also create a need for further conventions to help determine the precise way in which they function. Indeed, these rules may themselves become the subject of codes. We can identify an early indication of this possibility with the Fixed-term Parliaments Act 2011. It prescribes how the House of Commons can pass a no-confidence motion, as defined in the Act. But the Act does not explain the precise procedure that should be followed during the two-week period set out in the Act, after which—if no government has won a confidence vote—a General Election takes place. As we shall see, *The Cabinet Manual* provides some basic guidance that the Act does not. Furthermore, some of the codes considered here that defined rules that might be regarded as conventions subsequently gained a statutory basis. Both the *Civil Service Code* (originating in 1996) and the *Code of Conduct for Special Advisers* (first issued in this form in 2001) are now issued under the terms of the Constitutional Reform and Governance Act 2010.

The relationship between codification and convention in the UK, then, has multiple strands. In part, it involves the depiction of key features of the constitution that lack a direct legal grounding. It is at the same time part of a wider process of greater formalisation of the UK constitution. This tendency can entail the publication of official accounts of conventions. But it can also involve statutory intervention to supplant convention. Indeed, codification can be part of this dynamic, with codes appearing and then acquiring a foundation in legislation that they did not previously possess. But conventions are inescapable. Statutes lead on in turn to the emergence of further conventions, which can themselves become the subject of codes, and perhaps one day statute—or at some point in the future, even a UK written Constitution. But even this outcome would prompt the emergence of further conventions still.

I. CODIFICATION AND CONVENTIONS

But what precisely does codification mean for conventions, and our conception of them? I now put forward, and where appropriate expand upon, my previously advanced theories in this area. A first issue requiring consideration is how far it is possible to codify a convention at all. When constitutional commentators began to describe the rules we now know as conventions, they often emphasised the idea that they did not exist in writing. John Stuart Mill, for instance, referred to '[t]he unwritten maxims of the Constitution … these unwritten rules, which limit the use of lawful powers'.[5] In 1872, Edward Freeman described how, 'by the side of our written Law, there has grown up an unwritten or conventional constitution'.[6] Freeman accepted that conventions could be encapsulated in resolutions of Parliament, but that rather than bringing rules into being, they described those that already existed. Sidney Low wrote early in the twentieth century that '[w]e live under a system of tacit understandings'.[7] In the mid-twentieth century, Ivor Jennings noted the practice of documenting conventions involving the interactions between UK and other parts of the Commonwealth. He contrasted this position with conventions that applied within the UK, stating that the external rules had 'thus received a more precise and definite shape than any of the conventions relating to the internal government of the United Kingdom'.[8]

The process of codification that has manifested itself increasingly since the time when Jennings made this observation means that the various accounts referred to in the preceding paragraph would need, as a minimum, to be qualified. Terms such as 'unwritten' or 'tacit' are problematic. Official, publicly available documents now seek to describe a large and growing body of conventions. Furthermore, we need to ask how far it is actually possible for these texts to perform the task they seek achieve, namely, the transposition of conventions into written form. Conventions are difficult to define. A first issue is that their very existence may be subject to uncertainty. For instance, for many decades following the final departure of Lord Salisbury from the premiership in 1902, it was not entirely clear whether a principle had developed that the Prime Minister should be based in the House of Commons and not the House of Lords. Secondly, there may be conflicting versions of what the relevant convention is in a given situation. For instance, some might hold that, following an inconclusive General Election, if a Prime Minister has decided to resign, the decision about when to do so is purely a matter for the personal judgement of the premier concerned; while others could assert the view that in the interests of stability, the incumbent has a duty to take into account the need for a successor arrangement to be ready before she or he leaves. Thirdly,

[5] JS Mill, *Three Essays: On Liberty, Representative Government, The Subjection of Women* (London, Oxford University Press, 1975).

[6] E Freeman, *The Growth of the English Constitution from the Earliest Times* (London, Macmillan, 1872).

[7] S Low, *The Governance of England* (London, T Fisher Unwin, 1914).

[8] I Jennings, *The Law and the Constitution* (London, University of London Press, 1959).

there can be an absence of clarity regarding the specific way in which conventions apply at a particular point. What, for example, does ministers being responsible for executive agencies within their remit mean in practice? Fourthly, it is not always clear when a convention has and does not have force. For instance, under the so-called 'Sewel Convention' (though it may soon be enshrined in statute), the UK Parliament is not supposed 'normally' to legislate for devolved matters without the agreement of the Scottish Parliament. But what does 'normally' mean, and when, therefore, is it appropriate for the Westminster Parliament not to follow the Sewel requirement? Fifthly, a common conception of constitutional conventions is that they are prone to change over time. A rule such as the 'Salisbury-Addison' doctrine—if we accept that it is a convention—has altered since it first appeared in 1945. It meant that the House of Lords would not seek to block a government bill implementing a manifesto policy. Initially it applied only to bills introduced in the Commons; but it subsequently seems to have come to have force with respect to government manifesto bills that begin their legislative progress in either House. As conventions morph in this way, defining them at any given moment is difficult.

Efforts at the codification of conventions must contend with these various manifestations of amorphousness. One possible response is to describe arrangements at such a level of generality as to minimise the contribution of the account. Paragraph 3.3 of *The Cabinet Manual* states that 'The Prime Minister has few statutory functions but will usually take the lead on significant matters of state.' Yet we are not informed of the meaning in this context of the words 'usually', 'take the lead' or 'significant matters of state'. Another means of handling doubt is to acknowledge disagreement. Paragraph 2.10 of the *Manual* accepts that there is not a single accepted view regarding the issue of when precisely it is appropriate for a Prime Minister to resign, discussed above. Yet over another controversial matter, the *Manual* takes a side and does not even recognise the existence of another view. It relates to the procedure to be followed after the resignation of the Prime Minister. One view of the appropriate practice, advanced by Robert Blackburn, is that, when prime ministers resign and their government falls with them, the leader of the largest Opposition party should be the successor.[9] But the *Manual* does not note the existence of this interpretation. The more open-ended formulation it advances is that 'the Sovereign will invite the person who appears most likely to command the confidence of the House to serve as Prime Minister and to form a government' (paragraph 2.8). Codifying conventions as they are is, at best, a challenging task. The difficulties involved in the codification of conventions are further illustrated by the experience of the process leading to *The Cabinet Manual*. Three different accounts appeared of the rules surrounding how to handle inconclusive General Elections. Yet none of them successfully commanded consensus among academic observers.[10] The codification of conventions, then, is a conceptually problematic

[9] R Blackburn, 'Monarchy and the Personal Prerogatives' [2004] *Public Law* 3.
[10] Blick, above n 1, 6.

task. But codification nonetheless takes place. These observations lead us to consider what the consequences are for conventions themselves.

II. CODIFICATION AND CHANGE

It is a characteristic of codification that the documents involved depict themselves neither as bringing about change, nor as having legal effect. They tend also to resist the idea that they actually create rather than simply describe rules. In his Preface to *The Cabinet Manual* in 2011, Gus O'Donnell, at the time Cabinet Secretary and Head of the Home Civil Service, stressed that the purpose of the document was 'recording the current position rather than driving change'. It was 'not intended to be legally binding or to set issues in stone'. Moreover the *Manual* was 'not intended to be the source of any rule'.[11] But what is the reality of such claims? In answering this question, it is necessary to take into account the exceptional extent to which conventions, among constitutional sources, rest upon perception. Their existence depends on their being accepted by those directly engaged in the functioning of the constitution, or who have influence upon it. Moreover, it seems that a major reason that players in political processes choose to act in accordance with conventions—other than their own belief that they are real and ought to be abided by—is that to behave differently would be to court political problems.[12] The threat of such difficulties rests on other political participants' asserting the existence of supposedly violated conventions, which in turn rests in their perceptions. It is therefore clear that codes, if they influence the way in which conventions are understood, can have significant consequences for the conventions themselves, whatever the authors of these texts may claim. It is equally plain that the documents under consideration in this work are intended to impact upon the perception of conventions, and that they are successful in doing so. These texts are drafted and published specifically for the purpose of informing their readerships—whether within a particular institution, or more widely—of certain rules. In other words, bringing about certain perceptions is key to their purpose.

This impact upon conventions can take a variety of forms. First, codification can strengthen conventions. It can lead to a heightened awareness among practitioners and observers of the rules of which it provides accounts, increasing the chances of their being followed. The costs of non-compliance can rise. Criticism of violation of conventions is easier to mount if there is a specific text, setting out the rule in question, that it is possible to cite. As we have seen (Chapter 2, section II.A.), ministerial tenures have ended in the wake of criticism that included in it references to supposed violation of the *Ministerial Code*. It is also possible for

[11] Cabinet Office, *The Cabinet Manual: A guide to the laws, conventions and rules on the operation of government*, 1st edn (London, Cabinet Office, 2011) iv.

[12] Lord Wilson of Dinton, 'The Robustness of Conventions in a Time of Modernisation and Change' [2004] *Public Law* 407.

politicians under pressure to defend themselves by invoking a text, if they feel it provides validation for their actions. Potentially, inclusion of a convention in a code can establish more certainty regarding its exact character (though these documents may not always be successful in this regard), making adherence to it more plausible. Codification might also strengthen a convention through helping to establish the fundamental purpose underpinning it. For instance, rules restricting the party political activities of civil servants (including special advisers) might be presented within the general context of the principle of impartiality. More generally, codification might promote greater public knowledge of the concept of conventions, perhaps enhancing their efficacy as constitutional instruments.

Secondly, codification can impact upon a convention about which there is disagreement if it advances a particular version of it. As an official document, a code's version of the rules is likely to be regarded as authoritative and accepted as definitive, therefore potentially marginalising other views.

Thirdly, codification of conventions could serve to inhibit their potential to develop over time. For instance, paragraph 3.1 of *The Cabinet Manual* states that 'By modern convention, the Prime Minister always sits in the House of Commons.' If, one day, the UK acquired an elected second chamber, it is conceivable that the idea of a premier based in it, rather than in the Commons, might become more acceptable. But the statement contained in the *Manual* to the contrary, if retained, might act as a brake upon this movement.

Fourthly, while a code, as already noted, might strengthen those conventions it includes, it could also undermine the relative importance of those rules that it omits.[13] For this reason, the House of Commons Political and Constitutional Reform Committee in 2011 pressed for the first edition of *The Cabinet Manual* to contain an account of the principle of obtaining, whenever appropriate, express approval from the House of Commons in advance of engaging in armed combat.[14] The draft of the text had not included this rule, but the Committee was successful and the full version did contain a reference to it.

Fifthly, a text can help to bring into being a new convention. A combined outcome of the various drafts of *The Cabinet Manual* was to help facilitate the use of civil servants, with prime ministerial approval, to support—to a limited extent—coalition negotiations in May 2010, and then record that they had taken place. Potentially, with the assistance of the *Manual*, the permissibility of this practice might acquire the status of a convention.[15] Yet there are limits on the potential of codification to press for the emergence of conventions. The initial complete draft of *The Cabinet Manual* that appeared in December 2010 claimed the existence of a principle that, following an inconclusive General Election, the sitting premier

[13] C Sampford, '"Recognize and Declare": An Australian Experiment in Codifying Constitutional Conventions' (1987) 7.3 *OJLS* 369.

[14] House of Commons Political and Constitutional Reform Committee, *Constitutional Implications of the Cabinet Manual* (London, Stationery Office, 2011).

[15] Blick, above n 1, 10.

should not give up the office until it was clear that there was a successor who could secure the necessary support in the House of Commons, and that the monarch had been informed about this position. Possibly the stipulation was a reaction to the way in which Gordon Brown had resigned in 2010, insisting on leaving while the Conservatives and Liberal Democrats were still finalising their arrangement. Following recommendations from the House of Lords Select Committee on the Constitution and the Commons Political and Constitutional Reform Committee, the completed first edition of the *Manual* expressly recorded that the view it had previously advanced was not a fully accepted convention.

This outcome shows that codification is not a means of achieving complete control over conventions. Rather it is a way of impacting upon the general landscape within which conventions form and operate. If the drafters of codes promote ideas that are insufficiently compatible with existing conceptions, they will fail. In 2013 a report from the House of Lords Select Committee on the Constitution contained a discussion demonstrating parliamentary resistance to efforts on the part of the executive unilaterally to assert the existence of conventions.[16] The specific issue involved the ability of the executive to pre-empt Parliament, acting over issues before it had received full statutory authorisation to do so. The Committee stated:

> The word 'convention' is, in constitutional parlance, a term of art. Although there is no universally accepted definition of the term, the feature common to all definitions is that, whilst a convention is not justiciable, it is nevertheless regarded by all relevant parties as binding. (paragraph 25)

It is possible for texts successfully to help bring about change if they do not press the boundaries of acceptability too far. Some of the principles expressed in the devolution *Memorandum of Understanding*, discussed in Chapter 10, were new at the time it stated them, and in this sense an important departure, and perhaps have made progress towards becoming full conventions. In the case of this document, a strength enabling it effectively to perform the task it did was that it rested in an agreement between the different parties to it, rather than on unilateral action.

The sixth and last means through which a code might make a difference to conventions is through facilitating judicial review. As we have seen, O'Donnell expressed the view from within the executive that the *Manual* would not be 'legally binding'.[17] Conventions lack direct legal force. But courts can take them into account in the course of their deliberations. Certainly, the Government thought that *Questions of Procedure for Ministers* (QPM) could be used in support of its case over the Crossman diaries (1975)—though it would clearly be less comfortable with having the words of a code turned against it in similar circumstances. This case features in legal textbooks as a point at which a court, though it did not directly enforce a convention (in this instance, collective responsibility), took its

[16] House of Lords Select Committee on the Constitution, *The pre-emption of Parliament* (HL 2012–13, 165).

[17] Cabinet Office, above n 11, iv.

existence into consideration as part of its wider deliberations. Then in the GCHQ case in 1985, the House of Lords found that government could be required to meet a 'legitimate expectation' regarding adherence to established procedures.[18] It is plausible that codes could figure increasingly in judicial review proceedings, especially if it was being argued that a minister had failed to follow a procedure set out in a particular document.[19] Indeed, it may be that the inclusion of a convention in a code makes its being used by a court more likely than it otherwise would be. Codification can draw attention to the existence of a convention, and might make it easier for the party to a proceeding to claim that it exists, and to pinpoint its precise nature.

A valuable discussion of the relationship between convention, codification and law in the UK context appears in the work of Nicholas Barber.[20] An important—and I believe correct—part of his thesis is to challenge more conventional distinctions between convention and law. He holds:

> The difference between law and convention is one of degree: laws and conventions can be placed upon a spectrum of types of social rules, a spectrum gradated in terms of the formalization of rules. Laws lie at the most formalized end of this spectrum, but there is no single, definable, point at which rules shift from being conventions into being laws.[21]

As Barber notes, a court can recognise that which it chooses in helping it to reach a conclusion, including a convention. It might use a dictionary to help it to interpret a statute, or if 'adjudicating on the reasonable use of a hedge-trimmer in an action for negligence might look at the guidance for safe use contained in the instruction manual'.[22] The observations Barber makes are crucial to an understanding of the possible implications of codification of conventions. Given the potential for a court to take into account a convention as part of its deliberations, by extension it presumably can use codes to help it do so. If a hedge-trimmer manual, why not *The Cabinet Manual*?

These types of enforcement, Barber reminds us, would be secondary. The court would be using a convention, perhaps as described in a text, to help it reach certain conclusions. It might, for instance, employ it to assist in understanding a statute, or when carrying out judicial review of ministerial actions to decide whether they were reasonable or had met the reasonable expectations of a complainant. Could some of the documents setting out proper Cabinet procedure be deployed in support of an argument that a particular decision was taken in a defective fashion? Or might the arrangements for consultation set out in the devolution *Memorandum of Understanding* be used for a similar purpose? A further, and more dramatic, form of enforcement would be direct, with a convention upheld in its own right

[18] AW Bradley, A and KD Ewing, *Constitutional and Administrative Law*, 15th edn, (Harlow, Longman, 2011) 29.

[19] R Rawlings, 'Concordats of the Constitution' (2000) 116 *LQR* 257.

[20] See NW Barber, *The Constitutional State* (Oxford, Oxford University Press, 2010) Chs 5–7.

[21] ibid, 89.

[22] ibid, 90.

rather than as part of a supportive background for 'a pre-existing legal right'.[23] If using the words of a code expressly to help it reach conclusions, a court would be aware that it was to some extent innovating. But if seeking more directly to impose a convention—in particular through refusing to recognise an Act of Parliament—it might be going further, and entering into an area of major controversy. This outcome is less plausible, though perhaps a court might find itself marginally more justified in pursuing such a course if it could draw attention to an official text in support of its actions.

Barber offers a further thesis in addition to his view of there being a spectrum of social rules, on which law lies at an extreme end. It is possible, he holds, for conventions to 'become laws through judicial intervention', and that they 'can "crystallize" into laws over time by becoming increasingly formalized'.[24] Under this model, a court does not specifically decide to give a convention legal force; the convention acquires this status incrementally. Barber specifically cites the historic development of QPM/the *Ministerial Code* as providing evidence of how this process can take place. It has, in this account, generated movement from convention towards law through gathering together previously discrete and informal rules into a single, written document. Over time it has entered the public domain, gaining political force—figuring in political discussion regarding the conduct of particular ministers—and limited enforcement procedures have appeared. One possible limitation on this pattern of development is that code describes itself as subordinate to UK law. So do many other codes considered here, such as *The Cabinet Manual*. A further extension of the codification process may be worth considering in this context. The various codes applying to civil servants (and special advisers) began as attempts supposedly to set down existing rules (or perhaps create some new ones). They are now issued under statute, the Constitutional Reform and Governance Act 2010.

The debate about the impact of codification on conventions has now taken on an international comparative dimension. In an article published in 2014, Grant Duncan considered some of my theories in this area from the perspective of the New Zealand *Cabinet Manual*.[25] Duncan noted that New Zealand (like the UK) lacked a written Constitution. While arguing that the *Manual* to some extent compensated for this absence and the potential for abuse it created, he stressed that it was not a full written Constitution. One of the characteristics of the unwritten New Zealand system was that it was subject to relatively casual alteration. With this malleability in mind, Duncan concluded that it was important to consider the possibility that the *Manual* itself had 'facilitated, reshaped or even impeded the

[23] ibid, 90. See also TRS Allen, 'Law, Convention, Prerogative: Reflections Prompted by the Canadian Constitutional Case' (1986) 45.02 *CLJ* 305; M Elliott, 'Parliamentary Sovereignty and the New Constitutional Order: legislative freedom, political reality and convention' (2002) 22.3 *Legal Studies* 340.

[24] See Barber, above n 20, 89.

[25] Duncan, above n 2.

exercise or development of conventions in New Zealand'.[26] Duncan considers in turn the different ways I have identified in which a code *might* bring about change to convention. He asks in each case how far the New Zealand *Manual* actually has had an impact in practice.

Duncan concludes that the text has served to make the definition of conventions more clear, and reinforce them, especially with respect to caretaker periods and the formation of governments. Possibly, he holds, the *Manual* has provided added credibility to certain interpretations of conventions, and downgraded those versions of conventions that it does not include. An area in which the *Manual* might have had this latter effect, Duncan finds, is that of the reserve powers wielded by the Governor-General. He draws attention to the failure of the *Manual* to deal with the issue of the Governor-General's possibly denying a request for a dissolution of Parliament. The omission of reference to such a circumstance could undermine a Governor-General who was contemplating this course of action. Duncan identifies no evidence that the *Manual* has frozen conventions, discouraging development, noting the ease with which it is possible to alter the *Manual*. Duncan contrasts arrangements under that text with those associated with a written Constitution, alterations to which involve a more demanding process. However, it should be noted that it is in the nature of this particular form of potential influence that it is difficult to establish definitively when it is at work. It involves developments that might *not* be taking place because of a code. Negatives can be difficult to prove. But they still can be real. Duncan identifies as a minimum one new convention the *Manual* has helped bring into being: that newly formed governments should approve the *Manual* itself.

III. PROCESS AND OWNERSHIP

In conjunction with the impact it might have upon conventions, codification raises a further set of issues connected with the process used to bring it about and the ownership of the texts. In many instances it is the UK executive that controls production, such as in the case of the *Ministerial Code*. With *The Cabinet Manual*, the Government issued drafts on which it sought views from Parliament and the public. It issued responses to the views it received, and in some cases amended the text accordingly. In the case of documents such as the Osmotherly Rules, spontaneous outside pressure has encouraged the executive to bring about changes to its codes. But for these texts, it is the executive that makes the ultimate decisions about the content of the documents, even if it takes into account the views of others. The exact means by which it arrives at its conclusions and the internal procedures may remain closed, or at least fairly obscure. There might, however, be a trend towards greater clarity around how these texts are actually written.

[26] ibid, 2.

The Cabinet Office *Guide to Making Legislation* describes the different teams that worked on it in its opening paragraph.[27]

Who owns these texts and how they go about drafting them is important. As we have seen, codes can potentially have an impact on conventions. Those who draft these texts have the chance to take the initiative in shaping the constitutional environment within which they operate, perhaps in ways that suit their particular institutional interests. The entirety of *The Cabinet Manual*, which ranged widely across the constitution, avowedly expressed 'the view of the Executive'.[28] In other words, it was open about being partial. From a constitutional perspective, this practice could be problematic if players are able to influence the constraints applicable to them. The *Ministerial Code*, for instance, contains stipulations regarding the nature of ministerial accountability to Parliament, a core feature of the system of limited government as it operates in the UK. The executive may be at a particular advantage here, since it seems to be configured in such a way as to dispose it towards the production of codes, with entities within it, such as the Cabinet Office and Treasury, prolific in this regard. While issuing single statements of principle is a familiar activity within Whitehall, institutions such as Parliament are arguably less suited to establishing fixed public positions in this way. Perhaps also, to speculate, a document issued by the executive with a foreword by a senior government member such as the Prime Minister is more able to attract attention and be treated as significant than a text issued by a different constitutional branch. The executive may therefore be in a position of structural pre-eminence over other governmental institutions. It has certainly heavily exploited its ability to introduce codes.

However, as we have seen, other players have entered the game, with the judiciary and Parliament also creating texts. In some cases—most notably the devolution *Memorandum of Understanding*—ownership and production of a document is shared between more than one institution. Furthermore, it is possible to challenge the validity of claims made in executive texts, or request other changes to them, including the introduction of new provisions. While the executive may be dominant in the codification field, this position does not necessarily equate directly with its possession of constitutional hegemony. As noted, the practice of introducing these texts came about under various pressures, including media scrutiny, an associated tendency towards public criticism of standards and parliamentary pressure. The existence of these documents is partly reflective of weakness. Moreover, when the executive alters them, it often does so in response to difficulties, such as particular scandals. For instance, in April 2009, Damian McBride, a special adviser to the Prime Minister, Gordon Brown, resigned after e-mails reached the public domain suggesting that he was covertly seeking to taint the reputation of

[27] Cabinet Office, *Guide to Making Legislation* (Cabinet Office, London, 2014) para 1.1.

[28] Cabinet Office, above n 11, iv.

Opposition politicians. In response the Government inserted a new requirement into the *Code of Conduct for Special Advisers*, stating that

> the preparation or dissemination of inappropriate material or personal attacks has no part to play in the job of being a special adviser as it has no part to play in the conduct of public life. Any special adviser ever found to be disseminating inappropriate material will automatically be dismissed by their appointing Minister.[29]

Interestingly, however, in 2015, the newly elected single party Conservative Government clawed the position back slightly, removing the word 'ever' from this passage in paragraph 11 of the new *Code of Conduct for Special Advisers*, and stating that an offending special adviser would 'be subject to a disciplinary process that may include dismissal'—removal from office was no longer depicted as inevitable. But whatever the niceties of drafting, a special adviser involved in a scandal of the type that surrounded McBride would be difficult to retain.

Once publicly issued, codes can become a basis for criticism of a government, as has happened with the *Ministerial Code*. Moreover, the codification of conventions could be seen as serving to reduce the overall level of flexibility available to governments. In some cases, they apply to the internal operation of the executive, for instance ensuring that there is proper consultation between departments and ministers over decisions. In others—and perhaps even more sensitive, constitutionally speaking—they involve the relationship between the UK executive and other institutions, in particular the Westminster Parliament, the judiciary and the devolved governments. A text such as *Guide to Making Legislation*[30] demonstrates how expansive the coverage of codification has become. The *Guide* consists of 312 pages of stipulations regarding the role of government in the law-making process. It describes itself as setting out

> the procedures to be followed in preparing primary legislation and taking it through Parliament, setting out what is required of bill teams at each stage of the process, from bidding for a slot in the legislative programme to gaining Royal Assent. We hope it is comprehensive and answers the most commonly-asked questions, but it should not be regarded as an authoritative statement of parliamentary practice. (paragraph 1.2)

Despite its self-proclaimed limitations, the *Guide* provides in a single place an account of how the executive is expected to operate through every phase of a constitutional activity of the highest importance: law-making (though admittedly, while available online, it is primarily for internal use and has not received the degree of public attention paid to a publication such as the *Ministerial Code*).

In prescribing how it is supposed to operate, even if codes are sometimes drafted to suit the requirements of the executive and contain numerous qualifications insisting that they do not consist of precise, absolute, legally binding

[29] L Maer and E Faulkner, *Special Advisers* (London, House of Commons Library, 2015). For the 2015 *Code*, see Cabinet Office, *Code of Conduct for Special Advisers* (London, Cabinet Office, 2015).

[30] Cabinet Office, above n 27.

obligations, they potentially reduce the discretion available to the executive. To make this observation is not to claim that the executive could behave in an entirely arbitrary fashion without codification. But the existence of rules in written form can make a perceptual difference, with the potential impacts discussed above. Even if the distinction is only marginal, it is at the margins that crucial changes can often occur.

Having assessed the potential types of difference codes can make to the operation of the constitution, it is now appropriate to begin to consider their substantive content.

Part Two

The Content of Codes

5

The Office of Prime Minister

THE MOST PROMINENT figure in UK politics is the Prime Minister. The individual who holds this post sits at the centre of an institution, the premiership, or office of Prime Minister. The office developed gradually and informally from the early eighteenth century. Originally, the idea of there being a single pre-eminent individual within government was considered a constitutional affront, imported from France. All ministers were supposedly equal before the king. But by the early nineteenth century a gradual acceptance of the existence of a chief minister was beginning to pervade. Nonetheless, official recognition of this practical reality was slow to arrive, beginning from the late nineteenth century. To this day, the statutory basis for the office of Prime Minister is slight compared to many other senior Cabinet posts. Codification is therefore important in this respect, since it provides official accounts of the institution that are otherwise lacking.[1]

I. AUTHORITY AND APPOINTMENT

The fullest account of the premiership comes in *The Cabinet Manual*,[2] the publication of which was therefore a breakthrough in this area. An early reference is at the beginning of Chapter One, on the 'The Sovereign', in the opening paragraph (1.1) headed 'Ceremonial and constitutional duties'. It both explains how an individual formally comes to the premiership and depicts one of the major powers attached to the role, with the statement that the monarch 'appoints the Prime Minister and, on his or her advice, other ministers'. The main substance of the description the *Manual* provides of the premiership then comes in Chapter Three, 'The Executive—the Prime Minister, ministers and the structure of government'. 'The Prime Minister' occupies a section in its own right, running from paragraph 3.1 to paragraph 3.6.

Beginning in the first sentence of paragraph 3.1, the *Manual* tells us that the premier 'is the head of the Government'. This statement is reasonable, but it does

[1] A Blick and G Jones, *Premiership: the development, nature and power of the office of the British Prime Minister* (Exeter, Imprint Academic, 2010).
[2] Cabinet Office, *The Cabinet Manual: A guide to the laws, conventions and rules on the operation of government*, 1st edn (London, Cabinet Office, 2011).

not use an official title held by the Prime Minister. While prime ministers are the most senior members of the government, they are not executive heads in the sense normally understood. They do not sit at the summit of a strict legal hierarchy. At times, some prime ministers may have behaved as though they were in such a position, and may have been led to believe that they were or should be so. But the ability to operate in this way, if a particular Prime Minister so wishes, is contingent upon matters such as personality and political circumstances. Therefore the label 'head of government' is applicable, and is used by the present author, but with the caveats discussed above. It is perhaps best viewed as diplomatic shorthand that establishes the rank of the holder relative to other roughly equivalent figures from other countries internationally.

The opening sentence of paragraph 3.1 of *The Cabinet Manual* continues by describing how the Prime Minister, as head of government, 'holds that position by virtue of his or her ability to command the confidence of the House of Commons, which in turn commands the confidence of the electorate, as expressed through a general election'. This statement, too, requires close analysis. Under the present system, prime ministers strictly speaking hold their office—or perhaps that should be, first come to it—because the monarch has appointed them to it, in the belief that they can form a ministry in possession of the confidence of the Commons. But it is then the governments they form, not the Prime Minister, that have to 'command' the necessary support in the elected chamber. The problematic suggestion that the Prime Minister has a direct mandate from the Commons is compounded in the second sentence of paragraph 3.1. It states that 'The Prime Minister's unique position of authority also comes from support in the House of Commons.' Once again, this wording could create the misleading impression that the Prime Minister has a personal endorsement from the Commons providing the office holder directly with a special power.

A further problem arises with the assertion that the Commons 'in turn commands the confidence of the electorate, as expressed through a general election'. The term 'confidence' has a number of meanings. In the sense of the UK constitution, as used earlier in the same sentence, it applies specifically to the relationship between a government and the Commons (though it is possible to debate, as we shall see, the precise details of this type of 'confidence'). To then use the same word, in the same sentence, to describe the relationship between electorate and the Commons is once again to court confusion.

The depiction of the source of prime-ministerial authority, as well as being flawed, creates a potential conflict with the principle, set out elsewhere in the *Manual* (see, for example, paragraph 13), that the supremacy within UK government belongs not to an individual but to a collective body: the Cabinet. Ever since the premiership began to emerge early in the eighteenth century,[3] there were regular complaints about a single politician supposedly becoming a dominant

[3] For a classic account of the history of the Cabinet, see JP Mackintosh, *The British Cabinet* (London, Methuen, 1968) Chs 2–5.

figure. But as the office of Prime Minister developed, so too did the Cabinet, a committee of senior ministers deliberating together about the most important official business. During the course of the nineteenth century, a principle of collective responsibility took hold, discussed in more detail in Chapter 6 of this book. Within this framework the Prime Minister had an important position as the chair of the Cabinet, and with it a responsibility for decisions about who should be appointed to the Government and the Cabinet and what their posts should be. But it was not for a premier to make key policy decisions alone and simply issue orders. A requirement existed—though not formally defined until the commencement of the codification era—to proceed by discussion at regular Cabinet meetings. Whenever allegations appear that prime ministers are wielding excessive authority within government, and perhaps are becoming increasingly prone to do so, one possible counterclaim is to refer to the position of the Cabinet as overriding the individual authority of the Prime Minister, and to hold that it mitigates against such a tendency.[4] However, the wording of paragraph 3.1, with its suggestion of personal prime-ministerial authority derived directly from the Commons, seems to contradict this response.

The exceptionally important paragraph 3.1 then moves on to the position of the Prime Minister within Parliament. It states, '[b]y modern convention, the Prime Minister always sits in the House of Commons'. Perhaps this 'convention' contributed to the confusion earlier in the paragraph, which seems to equate a need for the Prime Minister to sit in the Commons with the premier's having received a personal endorsement from it. The actual position seems to be that, while the Commons has not directly invested the premier, it is widely judged necessary from the perspective of democratic accountability that the senior figure within the Government sits in and is therefore able to answer directly to the elected chamber. This position does not amount to a personal mandate.

The 'convention' to which the *Manual* refers had a long gestation. Even in an era before democratic principles took hold, there were good reasons why a premier might sit in the Commons. By the time Walpole made his important early contribution to the development of the office of Prime Minister in the early eighteenth century, its important responsibilities—particularly its pre-eminence in the area of finance—made close oversight of the Commons crucial to the organisation of government. He opted to remain within the Commons throughout his premiership, and not to move to a theoretically more senior position in the Lords. But it would be centuries before a clear precept emerged that the Prime Minister should be based in the Commons. Footnote 1 to paragraph 3.1 of the *Manual* notes, 'Prime Ministers in previous centuries have sat in the House of Lords, for example the Marquess of Salisbury who was a member of the House of Lords and was Prime Minister for periods in the late 19th century and early 20th century.' Salisbury was the last person to be appointed premier from, and remain within, the Lords. However, when he left the office in 1902, it was not necessarily clear that

[4] See Blick and Jones, above n 1, especially Ch 2.

his departure was the end of an epoch. As we have seen in Chapter 2, the drafters of the *Precedent Book* in the immediate post-Second World War period were not certain on this issue, though they seem to have had suspicions that the era of premiers based in the Lords was over.

The point at which it became more clearly apparent that holding the premiership required membership of the Commons was in October 1963, when Alec Douglas-Home had to make renouncement of his peerage a condition for the taking up of the highest office. However, he was first appointed while still a member of the Lords, though he promptly left it and secured election to the Commons.[5] This episode demonstrates the close relationship between statutory change and the development of conventions: it was possible for Home to disclaim his title because of the recently-passed Peerage Act 1963. That someone felt obliged to leave the Lords, having become premier, established the convention more definitively than a member of the Lords being passed over could have done.

The *Manual* does not cite the Home example, though it is probably the decisive precedent supporting what it calls a 'modern convention'. If it had referred to this case, it might have induced slight uncertainty. Would it today be acceptable for a peer to be appointed as Prime Minister, if she agreed promptly to renounce the peerage? Would such a practice conform to the words and the spirit of the 'modern convention' identified by the *Manual*, that '[b]y modern convention, the Prime Minister always sits in the House of Commons'? Or would an individual have to be present in the Commons already before attaining the premiership? What would happen if, having become Prime Minister, an individual who had renounced a peerage was unsuccessful in a by-election? At what point would that individual have to step down?

Paragraph 3.1 closes by stating that the premier 'will normally be the accepted leader of a political party that commands the majority of the House of Commons'. This statement is significant, partly because it demonstrates the constitutional role of political parties which, though organisations that developed outside of the immediate sphere of government, have become enmeshed within official institutions and their operational rules and procedures: they are in practice part of the working constitution. This wording clearly allows for the possibility that no single party will hold a majority of seats in the House of Commons, as happened following the 2010 General Election and many times previously, especially before the Second World War (see further Chapter 9, sections II. and IV.). Indeed, past evidence suggests that a government party can lose its majority during the course of a Parliament, without the Prime Minister's necessarily having to leave office.

Yet while asserting the importance of party, the wording seems to leave open the possibility that, though not 'normally' the case, the Prime Minister might in certain circumstances conceivably not be 'the accepted leader of a political party'. In May 1940, for instance, at a time of the greatest possible peril for the UK, Winston Churchill succeeded Neville Chamberlain as Prime Minister, but not as leader of

[5] DR Thorpe, *Alec Douglas-Home* (London, Methuen, 2007) 312–15.

the Conservative Party, Chamberlain staying on in the latter role until not long before his death later in the year. Before the Conservative Party adopted rules for electing its leader, when there was a changeover at No 10 during a period of Conservative government, the process of choosing a new leader was difficult to disentangle from that of selecting the next Prime Minister. This blurring of functions was a potential source of problems if the decision was controversial and linked the monarchy and its personal prerogatives to party politics. During 1995, John Major temporarily ceased to be Conservative leader, after resigning from this post to force a contest, but continued as Prime Minister.

Could it still be possible that in a time of political deadlock, perhaps combining with some other form of crisis—maybe involving the economy, security or the environment, or a combination thereof—it would be judged necessary to swiftly choose a Prime Minister who was not at that point the leader of a party? Possibly not holding such a role would be part of the appeal of the individual concerned, or there simply may not be time to hold an internal election, or the person concerned may not wholly be accepted by her or his party. This discussion takes us to an area of opacity at the core of the UK constitution. The *Manual* seeks to define (and in some cases change) certain principles and procedures in this field. But in doing so it draws attention to—and does not resolve—significant uncertainties.

Paragraph 3.2 takes the reader into a closed ceremony in which the premier 'accepts office at a private audience with the Sovereign'. There is no equivalent to the public swearing-in of the US President—or for the coronation of the monarch in the UK. The *Manual* offers no detail as to what is said by either party at this ceremony or what is done, or who is present other than the two individuals directly involved. Here once again the curious form of transparency associated with codification is at play: in describing a particular arrangement, the *Manual* can draw attention to our lack of knowledge about how it actually operates.

II. PORTFOLIO AND FUNCTIONS

Paragraph 3.2 of *The Cabinet Manual* states another important rule when it describes how '[t]he Prime Minister is, by tradition, the First Lord of the Treasury'. It is in this capacity that the premier 'takes oaths of office under the Promissory Oaths Act 1868' (the relevant section of the 1868 Act is section 3). Nearly every individual identified as a premier in UK history has held the post of First Lord of the Treasury. Politicians such as Walpole established themselves as the dominant figure within their governments through their deployment of the First Lord role. In this early phase the First Lord of the Treasury had direct and ongoing responsibility for the Treasury, and if the individual concerned sat in the Commons he combined the role with that of the Chancellor of the Exchequer. From the mid-nineteenth century, however, the post of Chancellor began to separate from that of First Lord, with the former taking control of the Treasury. From the late nineteenth century the post of Prime Minister began to receive formal recognition, though it still retains an amorphous quality, and to this day, as the *Manual* recognises, premiers hold the title First Lord of the Treasury, on which basis they occupy No 10 Downing Street. The First Lord is, then, technically the senior member of the Treasury Board. However, the *Manual* states, the 'Commissioners of the Treasury', comprising the First Lord, the Chancellor and the Junior Lords of the Treasury, 'do not meet in that capacity' (paragraph 3.29). Yet—as footnote 18 to paragraph 3.29 reminds us—the Interpretation Act 1978 defines the Treasury in Schedule 1 as 'the Commissioners of Her Majesty's Treasury'. The *Manual* goes on to explain, in the same paragraph, another equally important convention of UK government, that 'In practice, the Treasury is headed by the Chancellor of the Exchequer', with the assistance of 'the Chief Secretary to the Treasury and other junior Treasury ministers.'

Though paragraph 3.2 of the *Manual* is important in establishing the historically accumulated conventions surrounding the office of Prime Minister, it does not explain the nature of the role itself. Paragraph 3.3 seeks to provide some clarity in this area, but manages at the same to time to raise more questions. 'The Prime Minister', it reads, 'has few statutory functions but will usually take the lead on significant matters of state.' Much rests on the precise meaning attached to words or phrases such as 'usually', 'take the lead' and 'significant matters of state'. How often and when exactly will it be appropriate for Prime Minister to 'take the lead'; and what does assuming 'the lead' actually mean—seeking to force a decision upon colleagues, or to ensure that Cabinet members reach as consensual a conclusion as possible? Lastly, what is the threshold for a 'significant' issue, calling on the Prime Minister to take on this particular function? These questions are best answered through reference to the flexibility of the premiership, with much hinging on the personalities involved and the political circumstances.

Paragraph 3.3 then describes how premiers have 'certain prerogatives'. They include 'recommending the appointment of ministers and determining the membership of Cabinet and Cabinet committees'. These long-established, non-statutory powers demonstrate that the strength of the premier is derived chiefly from the connection to the Cabinet, and not through acting separately from it. The *Manual* is careful to note that 'in some circumstances the Prime Minister may agree to consult with others before exercising those prerogatives'. It alludes here to the coalition arrangement reached between David Cameron and Nick Clegg in 2010 on shared responsibility for appointments[6]—though the way it was drafted could create the impression, perhaps intentionally, that such an agreement was less novel than it seems in truth to have been. This approach is repeated subsequently in the text (see below).

A premier is technically the most senior of the monarch's ministers. The *Manual* tells us that the Prime Minister holds 'regular meetings with the Sovereign', at which the premier 'informs him or her of the general business of government'

[6] Cabinet Office, *Coalition agreement for stability and reform* (London, Cabinet Office, 2010), section one: 'Composition of the Government'.

(paragraph 3.5). The Prime Minister also recommends 'a number of appointments to the Sovereign'. Among them are senior positions in the Church of England, top judges and 'certain civil appointments … appointments to several public boards and institutions' and a number of 'Royal and statutory commissions'. The *Manual* does not describe any practices or conventions that apply to the exercise of these powers. For instance, since 2007 the Prime Minister now receives a preferred name and second acceptable choice from the Crown Nominations Commission for the appointment of the Archbishop of Canterbury. The established arrangement is that the premier passes on the name of the favoured person, unless a change of circumstances necessitates taking the reserve option.[7]

In Paragraph 3.6 the *Manual* describes some of the clearer policy portfolios attached to the Prime Minister. The first is that of Minister for the Civil Service, which—as the *Manual* notes—is a post the premier has held since its creation in 1968. In this 'capacity' the Prime Minister has 'overall responsibility for the management of most of the Civil Service'. The *Manual* does not note here the standard practice for the Prime Minister to devolve this function upon another minister.[8] It then goes on to inform the reader that the Prime Minister is 'responsible for National Security and matters affecting the Secret Intelligence Service, Security Service and GCHQ collectively'. This statement is uncontroversial, but at the same time the precise role of the premier is difficult to establish since, as the *Manual* records, it is the Home Secretary, Foreign Secretary and Secretary of State for Northern Ireland who have statutory responsibilities for these agencies. The section on the Prime Minister closes with the statement in paragraph 3.6 that the premier is 'sworn as a member of the Privy Council'. In practice it seems unlikely that someone who became premier would not already be a member of the Privy Council, as Leader of the Opposition or a senior minister.

Further on in the *Manual*, more descriptions of the function of the office of Prime Minister appear. For instance, it reminds the reader that, when dealing with European Union-related matters, the premier 'represents the UK at the European Council, which is made up of heads of state and government and generally meets quarterly to set the EU's agenda priorities' (paragraph 9.8). More space, in the *Manual* and in a further subject-specific document, is given to an activity introduced in paragraph 3.48. It states that the premier 'is responsible for the overall organisation of the Government and the allocation of functions between ministers'. Again, this authority can be an important source of power. Yet the *Manual* suggests that it brings with it certain obligations, claiming 'It is a fundamental part of the Prime Minister's role to ensure that Cabinet and the Government are structured in the most effective way.' The text, however, offers no guidance as to assessing performance in this regard. Effectiveness can take different forms. A politically

[7] 'Outline of procedures for the appointment of an Archbishop of Canterbury', website of Rowan Williams, former Archbishop of Canterbury, 16 March 2012, available at <http://rowanwilliams.archbishopofcanterbury.org/articles.php/2403/outline-of-procedures-for-the-appointment-of-an-archbishop-of-canterbury>.

[8] Under the Civil Service (Management Functions) Act 1992.

effective decision—for instance, providing a politician with a brief that matches that individual's personal standing but not that person's abilities—might not be effective from the point of view of administrative effectiveness, and vice versa.

The *Manual* states that premiers are responsible 'for machinery of government changes', and cites a Cabinet Office text from 2010 that is itself called *Machinery of government changes* (paragraph 3.55 and footnote 31). The *Manual* provides a list of circumstances in which it is necessary for ministers to obtain 'written approval' from the Prime Minister before the displacement of functions within Whitehall. They are: (i) significant transfers from one Secretary of State or the equivalent to another; (ii) a transfer 'within the field of ministerial responsibility of one minister', if 'likely to be politically sensitive or to raise wider issues of policy or organisation'; (iii) a shifting of responsibilities from one junior minister to another, if it entails 'a change in ministerial titles' (paragraph 3.55). Paragraph 3.56 describes how the agreement of the Prime Minister is needed for the attaching of responsibilities to an individual minister if they are in the general field of more than one senior minister, or if there is a lack of precise agreement about what their present allocation is: a dispute-resolving function. This permission from the premier is also required for decisions about the roles of junior ministers, and of 'courtesy titles' provided for them (paragraph 3.57).

In the account it provides of these recalibrations of Whitehall, then, the *Manual* affords the Prime Minister a position of pre-eminence. However, the power that the premier wields is subject to legal and practical limitations, though they may not be particularly stringent. *The Cabinet Manual* notes that 'major changes involving ministerial departments' will probably require a 'transfer of functions order', that is an Order in Council issued under the authority of the Ministers of the Crown Act 1975.[9] Yet in circumstances where there is merely a shift from one individual acting as Secretary of State to another, the change can take place before the issue of the order has occurred (paragraph 3.57). Paragraph 3.59 suggests further constraints. While iterating that the attaching of particular responsibilities to individual ministers is the business of the Prime Minister, it notes that 'the Government informs Parliament of significant machinery of government changes'. The form that this announcement takes, the *Manual* recounts, is online publication by the Cabinet Office of 'an explanatory document about major changes … placed in the libraries of both Houses'. The purpose of this publicity is to facilitate an account to parliamentarians and to the general public of 'the Prime Minister's reasoning for making the changes'. While in this account the premier is at the centre of the decision, paragraph 3.59 of the *Manual* states that it is ministers who 'usually make themselves available to any relevant select committee that wishes to examine the implementation of such changes'.

[9] For an assessment of parliamentary control of machinery of government changes, see House of Commons Public Administration Select Committee, *Machinery of Government Changes* (HC 2006–07, 672).

The Cabinet Office text referred to in the *Manual—Machinery of government changes: Best practice handbook*[10]—suggests in its 35 pages that further conditions apply to the use of this largely prime-ministerial authority. As usual, describing itself as '*guidance* [emphasis in original]', the document stresses that it 'is intended to record best practice, not to establish any legal obligations'. Regardless of its precise legal status, the document could be seen as helping to create expectations that might in practice serve to bind a Prime Minister. Moreover, while it states that it is intended 'primarily for use by the civil service' ('Overview', p 3), it has nonetheless been made available online to those—such as the present author—who wish to look for it. This availability serves potentially to widen awareness both of its existence and of the principles it promotes, and perhaps to strengthen them further in the process.

The guidance notes that 'responsibility for the allocation of functions between ministers is a fundamental part of the Prime Minister's role' in making sure that Cabinet and government as a whole 'are structured in the best way', enabling them to react to contemporary 'challenges, thereby ensuring a constant focus on the key issues'. If a premier is to attain this objective, she must have the capacity for swift action. 'However', the guidance cautions, 'changes are not made lightly, nor in a vacuum' (Part One, p 4). As noted in the *Manual* as well, in nearly every case, a modification will necessitate a 'transfer of functions order'. It may also require primary legislative action. Beyond this legal facilitation, the guidance proposes 'key principles' it holds to be 'applicable to considerations of machinery of government change', though not necessarily 'possible to follow' on every occasion (Part One, p 5):

1. Changes in the machinery of government are the business of the Prime Minister, acting 'on the advice of the Cabinet Secretary'.
2. Given the expense and potentially prolonged disruption that is entailed for the departments, a necessity exists for 'a clear explanation' as to why a given change offers the 'the best solution to current challenges'. A possible reading of this point is that alterations should take place on a basis of rational administrative requirements, as a means of better achieving policy objectives. The reality is that it is difficult fully to eliminate party political and personal considerations from decisions over the precise division of responsibilities within Whitehall. They may take place, for instance, partly out of a desire on the part of a government to be seen to act over a given issue; or to reward (or demean) a particular politician.
3. Full 'information' is needed for decisions, and civil servants working in those departments involved in a particular change should cooperate in providing it. Perhaps the drafters of the text had in mind past instances of barriers to change arising from the actions or inactions of officials, whether they intended to create problems or not.

[10] Cabinet Office, *Machinery of government changes: Best practice handbook* (London, Cabinet Office, undated).

4. A specific 'transition team' is needed for the more substantial transfers.
5. 'Communication', both within and outside the Government, is essential.
6. A newly formed department, or one taking on a transferred function, should be provided with the level of resources it needs for its tasks.
7. There is normally a movement of officials along with the role being shifted, 'subject to the receiving Permanent Secretary's judgement' regarding what is needed. Once again the text, drafted by career officials, bolsters the position of senior civil servants, to the point of their seeming to have an authority distinct from that of ministers.
8. Historic record keeping should not be damaged by a transfer (Part One, pp 5–6). This focus on continuity and institutional memory is a recurring feature of codes, providing a further insight into the priorities of the staff who took a lead in their production (though that is not to dismiss this concern as petty).[11]

Returning to *The Cabinet Manual* account of the premiership, it reiterates in paragraph 4.5 that the Prime Minister is the chair of the Cabinet. This proposition is as close to uncontroversial and as well established as it is possible for a convention to be, but simply seeing it in writing in an official document, since the emergence of the rule took place in an informal fashion, serves to remind the reader of the nature and importance of codification as a constitutional tendency. Further on, paragraph 4.38 deals with the procedure applying when the Prime Minister cannot come to Cabinet. The 'next most senior minister should take the chair', in accordance with 'the order of precedence as determined by the Prime Minister'. This approach also applies when the chair of a Cabinet committee—and deputy chair, if there is one—is not able to come to the committee. But there is a series of broader related issues with which the *Manual* does not deal specifically, and which involve the possible reason for a premier missing a Cabinet. They can range from the less to the more serious. At the latter end of the scale, if a Prime Minister becomes incapacitated, is it possible for someone to act as premier in a more general sense than simply chairing the Cabinet? And if the inability of the incumbent to perform becomes prolonged and her resignation cannot be obtained, at what point does it become legitimate to deploy the Royal Prerogative to unseat her? Does the temporary Prime Minister, if there is one, then become the permanent one, or should a fuller selection process take place? Similar questions can be raised about the circumstances of a premier's dying in office.

Paragraph 4.5 of the *Manual* then states that the Prime Minister 'also determines' the 'membership' of Cabinet. This concept became more complicated in the circumstances of the coalition that operated from 2010–15. In footnote 4 to paragraph 4.5, it is stated that 'Ministerial selection may be subject to consultation in the event of a coalition government.' This wording could create the impression that, at the time of the drafting of the *Manual*, this kind of arrangement

[11] For an investigation into machinery of government changes, see T Gash, *Reshaping Government: strengthening Whitehall's top level structures and processes* (London, Institute for Government, 2015).

was relatively familiar. In fact, there was no coalition between 1945 and 2010, and though the sharing of power between parties was a common event in earlier eras, there was no public formal commitment equivalent to that issued in 2010 to provide the Deputy Prime Minister with a role in decisions.[12]

Paragraph 3.9 informs us that the premier 'determines who forms Cabinet' (again, presumably potentially subject to an agreement such as that which formed part of the coalition from 2010–15). The *Manual* asserts a well-established and lasting limitation on the discretion of the Prime Minister, in that the Cabinet 'will always include the Chancellor of the Exchequer, the Lord Chancellor and the secretaries of state'. Here the *Manual* is going further than simply stating that the Cabinet has in practice included these individuals; it is claiming that it is a rule or a convention. It does not offer any authority for this claim. While it may seem entirely reasonable, some explanation would have been helpful. Past premiers have formed inner Cabinets that have not necessarily included these named individuals. The most celebrated examples of this practice came in the First and Second World Wars, which saw the formation of formal War Cabinets that supplanted the position of the regular Cabinet as the supreme committee of executive deliberation. The first Lloyd George War Cabinet, formed in December 1916, comprising the premier and four other members, excluded all Secretaries of State and the Lord Chancellor, though it included the Chancellor of the Exchequer. In May 1940, Churchill formed his first War Cabinet (Chamberlain preceding him also had such a body), comprising the same number of members as the first Lloyd George War Cabinet. Though it included one Secretary of State (the Foreign Secretary), neither the Lord Chancellor nor the Chancellor of the Exchequer was chosen. Unfortunately, the *Manual* does not refer to the possibility of the formation of war cabinets, whether on the model used in the World Wars or in later limited conflicts (though see the discussions both of 'Ad hoc or miscellaneous committees', and of the 'COBR' committee in Chapter 6, section III.).

The Cabinet Manual then stipulates that the setting of the 'overall structure of the Cabinet committee system' is a prime-ministerial matter, 'with the advice of the Cabinet Secretary'. Once again, with the reference to the Cabinet Secretary, the *Manual* has served to emphasise the position of a senior civil servant. The premier, the reader is informed, chooses committee chairs (paragraph 4.10). Such decisions are of great significance, since they can determine who is the focal point for the formulation of important policy. Therefore, while the ability to shape the Cabinet committee framework is an important authority for premiers, the system of sub-bodies itself does not necessarily increase their direct influence over decision-making. Removing part of the process from the larger body, full Cabinet, can concentrate decisions in a smaller group, and in that sense shift the balance away from the collective. But it does not follow automatically that the Prime Minister is the only beneficiary of this tendency, or indeed is necessarily a beneficiary at all. If the premier has chosen, or felt obliged, to make a powerful rival chair of a

[12] Cabinet Office, above n 6.

committee, then it is that person, not the Prime Minister, who may well be wielding great personal influence at the expense of wider group decision-taking. Paragraph 4.10 of *The Cabinet Manual* stipulates that the Prime Minister also selects (again with advice from the Cabinet Secretary) deputy chairs of select committees, if such appointments are made. It then refers in footnote 7 to the *Coalition Agreement for Stability and Reform*, paragraph 3.1, and notes that 'Ministerial selection may be subject to consultation in the event of a coalition government.' A reader of this sentence who was unaware of the circumstances lying behind it would probably be surprised to learn that, seemingly, the only clear instance of such a practice in UK constitutional history dated to the year before the *Manual* was published. Once again the *Manual* was attempting to incorporate this dramatic recent change in long-established practice arising from the coalition as if it were a general rule that did not challenge the underlying principles: an attempt at instant tradition-making.

Aside from *The Cabinet Manual*, another text containing significant material on the Prime Minister, with a history long pre-dating the *Manual*, is the *Ministerial Code.*[13] It describes various rights possessed by the premier. For instance, the Code requires that the premier be 'consulted in good time' over the forming of Royal Commissions and important public inquiries (paragraph 4.10). It provides an important role for No 10 as an institution, when stating that, to achieve 'the effective coordination of Cabinet business, the policy content and timing of all major announcements, speeches, press releases and new policy initiatives should be cleared in draft with the No 10 Press and Private Offices at least 24 hours in advance'. Furthermore, the Code insists that it is necessary to clear 'All major interviews and media appearances' with the Press Office at No 10 (paragraph 8.2). If wishing to take up a matter with the Press Complaints Commission or the Broadcasting Complaints Commission, ministers are required by the Code to obtain the approval of the Chief Press Secretary in No 10 (paragraph 8.13). This role in the handling of public relations is crucial to the premiership, since acting as the outward face of government has always been an important part of the role of the Prime Minister. The stipulations contained in the Code represent an attempt to impose discipline across Whitehall in fulfilment of this function. It is a burden, but presumably can provide a basis for engaging not only in the presentational aspects of a given policy, but also in its substance.

The *Ministerial Code* demonstrates how codification has itself created a role for the premier, and is in a sense a vehicle for prime-ministerial authority. Premiers draft the text (in conjunction with the Cabinet Secretary), and it depicts them as the ultimate arbiters of whether it has been adhered to, and what to do if it has not. Yet successive prime ministers have in practice retained most of the Code as inherited from their predecessors. Changes to the text can generate controversy, as occurred in October 2015 with the removal of the references to international

[13] Cabinet Office, *Ministerial Code* (Cabinet Office, London, 2015).

law. Furthermore, the Code amounts to a large body of rules—however vague they may be in places—against which members of their governments can publicly be judged. Possession of the power to decide how to respond to controversy involving the contents of the Code can generate problems for a Prime Minister if she is criticised for not using it appropriately, for instance through failing to remove a minister held to have transgressed the rules. The Code will not quietly go away. There is a strong convention that premiers will continue to issue new editions. It would be politically difficult for a Prime Minister, in the hope of lessening constraints upon government, to avoid publishing a revised version following a General Election, or after taking office mid-term. Moreover, abolishing or failing to renew the *Ministerial Code* would not in itself end all the conventions, practices and principles that the existing editions to date have served to promote, of which they would survive as a reminder, even if the *Code* failed to receive the customary update.

III. CONCLUSION

That the passages from *The Cabinet Manual* comprise the fullest available official account of the office of UK Prime Minister helps demonstrate the significance of the *Manual* and the codification trend of which it is a part. Yet that this relatively short collection of material should be such a breakthrough for official exposition of the subject matter also underlines how opaque the premiership has tended to be. There is potential for a more comprehensive description. Nonetheless, the following quibbles are made subject to recognition that the *Manual* is a substantial achievement in this area, on which it is possible to build further. A significant omission involves the mechanisms that exist for supporting the Prime Minister.[14] The *Manual* could have described the role of the Private Office—the traditional core of the prime-ministerial team—the private secretaries who work within it and the way they have tended to divide work between them. It might provide an account of the different units that have emerged to provide additional support to premiers through history, and which bodies were operative at the moment the new edition appeared, while stressing that there was no set pattern that every Prime Minister had to follow. It could depict the different roles played by permanent civil servants and outside appointments such as special advisers on the prime-ministerial staff, and the nature of interaction between them. A list of some of the key posts—that again stressed it was not prescribing future structures—would be useful.

Another valuable addition could be an account of the role of ministers such as parliamentary private secretaries and Ministers of State with special functions in supporting the Prime Minister. The *Manual* could note that that the Prime Minister does not have a full department. It does provide descriptions of the role of the

[14] A Blick and G Jones, *At Power's Elbow: aides to the Prime Minister from Robert Walpole to David Cameron* (London, Biteback, 2013).

Cabinet Secretary and the Cabinet secretariat. However, it could have given a fuller account of the connection between the Prime Minister and the Cabinet Office, and the nature of the assistance that the latter provides to the former. To do so would be to deal with the system of collective government that lies at the heart of traditional interpretations of the UK constitution, the subject of the next chapter. As we shall see, as it has done with the premiership, *The Cabinet Manual*—in conjunction with other texts—has proved effective once more in stimulating debate about the core features of the UK system of democratic governance.

6

The Cabinet and Collective Government

'CABINET', ACCORDING TO paragraph 1.14 of *The Cabinet Manual*,[1] 'is the executive committee of the Privy Council'. In fact, in its origins in the late seventeenth century, Cabinet was a rival body to the Privy Council.[2] The emergent Cabinet of this period provided monarchs and their most senior advisers with a means of short-circuiting the larger, more cumbersome Privy Council. Cabinet as we understand it today grew out of a smaller still sub-group of this early Cabinet or 'Cabinet Council'. But it is now easier to define the Cabinet as a committee of the Privy Council. Like the Privy Council, the Cabinet is a decision-taking body; but unlike the Privy Council, it cannot issue legislation, and it has none of the judicial functions of the Judicial Committee of the Privy Council. As we have seen in Chapter 1, section I, members of Cabinet are required to be Privy Counsellors (as it is spelt in *The Cabinet Manual*), swearing an oath that places them under a confidentiality requirement.

The position of the Cabinet became firm during the nineteenth century. It has over time passed through significant changes, such as the introduction of a War Cabinet secretariat, charged with taking and distributing minutes of meetings, from late 1916. This institutional transformation encouraged the codification process that is the subject of this work. As a consequence of this trend, the work of the Cabinet, once far more informal in its approach, has become more regulated, albeit by rules lacking the full force of law. Moreover, codification has brought the Cabinet system more into the open than it previously was. Secrecy has always been crucial to the Cabinet: the actual proceedings remain confidential. Paragraph 4.5 of the *Manual* notes that since all Cabinet members are Privy Counsellors, they are subject to the Oath of the Privy Council (paragraph 4.5; see Chapter 1, section II.). But at least some of the rules and structures are now public. This chapter considers the documents that have made the Cabinet an increasingly defined and public entity.

[1] Cabinet Office, *The Cabinet Manual: A guide to the laws, conventions and rules on the operation of government*, 1st edn (London, Cabinet Office, 2011).

[2] For the history of the Cabinet, see JP Mackintosh, *The British Cabinet* (London, Methuen, 1968) Chs 2–5.

I. CABINET AND THE *MINISTERIAL CODE*

Before the appearance of *The Cabinet Manual*, the main official published source on the Cabinet was the *Ministerial Code*.[3] It continues to be treated as the prime authority in the areas it covers, with *The Cabinet Manual* citing it. The Code describes the 'general principle' of collective responsibility as being that ministers ought to 'be able to express their views frankly in the expectation that they can argue freely in private while maintaining a united front when decisions have been reached'. Consequently it is necessary for the views offered, orally or in writing, to be confidential (paragraph 2.1). This account of collective responsibility does not state expressly that a key component of this concept is that ministers should have the opportunity to contribute to deliberation, and that it should be a collective process. Instead it focuses on the status of the discussions, stressing that the participants should have the confidence that they can express their views, but not making clear that the purpose of their being able to do so is to facilitate inclusive decision-taking. *The Cabinet Manual*, as we shall see in section II. below, has a different emphasis.

The *Ministerial Code* sets out core features of the Cabinet system that are replicated across other texts such as the *Manual*. It tells us that 'Cabinet and Ministerial Committees' deal with matters that involve collective responsibility because of their importance to policy or to the public; or over which a dispute has arisen among different departments, in need of resolution (paragraph 2.2). The Code insists that the precise means through which a conclusion was reached—that is, whether it went to a Cabinet Committee or full Cabinet—should remain private. Regardless of the level at which it was settled, a decision is 'binding on all members of the Government'—in other words, within and outside the Cabinet. Generally ministers present the decision as their own, though on some limited occasions 'it may be desirable to emphasise the importance of a decision by stating specifically that it is the decision of Her Majesty's Government' (paragraph 2.3). A further rule is that ministers are required to see to it that the conclusions of the Cabinet and its committees are put into force (paragraph 2.3). An issue that is purely within the remit of an individual minister does not have to be taken to Cabinet or a 'Ministerial Committee'. However, paragraph 2.4 of the Code notes that 'No definitive criteria can be given for issues which engage collective responsibility.' Cabinet secretariats can provide advice on this matter, with the premier having the last word. Before a disputed issue is taken to full Cabinet, all other methods of mediation have to be attempted. It falls to a department instigating a policy to ensure that it has engaged other parts of government that are likely to want an input. These interactions should be reflected in the paper produced on the proposal (paragraph 2.4). The Code stipulates that the duty for ministers to attend the Cabinet and Cabinet committees takes priority over all their other activities

[3] Cabinet Office, *Ministerial Code* (London, Cabinet Office, 2015).

except the Privy Council. There are, however, possible exceptions involving foreign or parliamentary functions. Junior ministers may attend Cabinet committees instead of their senior minister (paragraph 2.5). White and green papers should be subject to the appropriate form of collective approval before they are issued (paragraph 2.6).

II. CABINET AND *THE CABINET MANUAL*

While the *Ministerial Code* retains an important status, a possibly even more informative text on the workings of Cabinet is *The Cabinet Manual*, particularly in its Chapter Four, 'Collective Cabinet decision-making'. The introduction to this chapter explains that the scale and complexity of the government necessitates 'formal and informal mechanisms for discussing issues, building consensus, resolving disputes, taking decisions and monitoring progress'. It goes on to state that the Cabinet and its committees, operating on the basis of convention, 'take decisions which are binding on members of the Government'. The members of these bodies are ministers in the Government, 'who are then accountable to Parliament for any collective decisions made'. The principle of collective responsibility makes it possible for those taking part in deliberations 'to express their views frankly'. While internal dissent is possible, the principle of collective responsibility requires those who are party to it to coalesce outwardly around the decision reached. Adherence to this set of values has often been strained and involved a degree of tension. But at the time of the publication of the *Manual* they were facing a greater, more sustained challenge than ever before, associated with the reappearance of coalition government in the UK.

Paragraph 4.1 enunciates the crucial constitutional principle that 'Cabinet is the ultimate decision-making body of government.' It explains that the purpose of Cabinet and its network of committees is to establish 'a framework for ministers to consider and make collective decisions on policy issues'. The overall system is founded in convention, with any government responsible for the precise way in which it works in practice. Yet though loose, the convention is powerful, and can even overlay the operation of Acts of Parliament. An early paragraph of the *Manual* (paragraph 3.30) describes how, while statutes may vest particular powers in a specific minister, 'in practice the exercise of those powers is normally subject to collective agreement'.

Paragraph 4.2 then introduces the concept of collective responsibility. It begins by stressing that it applies to ministers, 'save where it is explicitly set aside'. This qualification arose specifically from the needs of the coalition, and it is likely that a future edition, if it appears during a time of single-party government, would omit it. Ministers, paragraph 4.2 goes on, bear 'joint responsibility' for the conclusions they reach and the actions they initiate. The principle applies, the *Manual* tells us, to 'all members of the Government, regardless of whether they were present when the decision was taken or their personal views'. They must, in other words, subordinate themselves to the group for the purposes of public cohesion. But for collective responsibility to be viable, it must mean more than a simple demand of loyalty from participants in the administration. Senior members—that is, Cabinet ministers—must have the opportunity to discuss decisions (though they cannot all have the chance to participate every time, for instance if an issue is dealt with in a committee of which they are not a member). Consequently, it is important that paragraph 4.3 of the *Manual* states 'Before a decision is made, ministers are given the opportunity to debate the issue, with a view to reaching an agreed position.' Ultimately, '[i]t is for the Prime Minister, as chair of Cabinet, or the relevant Cabinet committee chair to summarise what the collective decision is'. The *Manual* offers no guidance has to how the Prime Minister or other chair should discern the 'collective decision'. If discussion is confused or divided, the premier presumably possesses flexibility as to defining the outcome, within the bounds of the politically acceptable. The Cabinet Secretariat takes a minute of the decision (paragraph 4.3).

International comparisons are illuminating regarding the role of the Prime Minister as summariser of the views of the Cabinet. The Australian *Cabinet Handbook* suggests a more commanding position for the Prime Minister with the statement that in circumstances of Cabinet discord, 'the Prime Minister's view is authoritative' (paragraph 8; see Chapter 3, section I.). In Canada, *Accountable Government* does not depict as firm a role as the Australian text, but it does state in paragraph D1 that in Cabinet, '[d]ecision making is *led* by the Prime Minister' (emphasis in original). Moreover, in paragraph F2, the same text states that once the Cabinet has agreed a particular legislative initiative, the premier makes the final decision over whether to introduce it into Parliament (see Chapter 3, section II.). Paragraph 5.23 of the New Zealand *Cabinet Manual* refers to the possibility of votes taking place in Cabinet, though stressing that they are an exceptional event (see Chapter 3, section III.). Such a procedure would appear to deny the Prime Minister the right to interpret the will of the Cabinet, and seemingly presents the possibility that the view of the premier may achieve only minority support and not prevail.

Who makes up the Cabinet? The UK *Manual* tells us, vaguely, that the Cabinet 'will usually comprise senior ministers' (paragraph 4.5). While the premier makes the decisions about composition, the Secretaries of State, the Lord Chancellor and the Chancellor of the Exchequer are automatically members (paragraph 3.9). A premier can also invite ministers who are not members of Cabinet to come to its meetings. Some may take part on specific occasions—for instance, when the Attorney-General provides legal advice. Others may be non-members but come regularly (paragraph 4.5). Paragraph 3.10 gives an idea of who are the '[o]ther ministers who are often invited by the Prime Minister to be a member of, or attend, Cabinet'. Among them are the Parliamentary Secretary to the Treasury—that is the Chief Whip in the Commons, the holder of which post is responsible for the discipline of Members of Parliament in the party to which she or he belongs—the Lord President of the Council, the Chancellor of the Duchy of Lancaster, the Chief Secretary to the Treasury and the Lord Privy Seal. Ministers of State, furthermore, 'may … sometimes' join the Cabinet, or at least go to its meetings.

The *Manual* records in paragraph 3.9 that no official cap exists on the size of the Cabinet, though restrictions exist on how many ministers there can be on the public payroll, including those in the upper bracket appropriate to Cabinet membership. The *Manual* does not explain whether the occasional or regular attendees who are not actual members of the Cabinet are able to take part fully in discussions as equals, and whether their views play a part in forming the final view, as interpreted by the chair.

The *Manual* then emphasises the informality and fluidity of the Cabinet. It 'is established by convention and does not have specific terms of reference or powers laid down in legislation' (paragraph 4.7). The existence of a text like the *Manual*, providing at least some kind of official guidance, is consequently important. It is the Prime Minister who 'determines and regulates the procedures of Cabinet, including when and where meetings take place'. At present, the full Cabinet meets at No 10 Downing Street, in the Cabinet Room (at the back of the building). The holding of Cabinet meetings in this room dates from the eighteenth century, though it has occurred elsewhere at various points. The *Manual* then notes that 'Regional Cabinets can also take place'—a case of mixing a long-established activity with a recent novelty, without seeking to distinguish the two. At present, the *Manual* informs the reader, Cabinet meetings are held on Tuesday mornings when Parliament is in session. Regular items on the agenda are 'Parliamentary business, domestic and foreign affairs, and topical issues'. The predictable reinforcement of the role of the Civil Service, and in particular Cabinet Office staff, grinds on as the *Manual* reminds us that the Cabinet Secretariat records the meetings of the Cabinet and its committees (paragraph 4.7). The Prime Minister may also facilitate a 'political Cabinet'. These events, held in the Cabinet Room, 'are not attended by officials and the conclusions of the discussion are not recorded in minutes' (paragraph 4.8). There is no account given of the membership, purpose or possible procedures of the political Cabinet. Nonetheless, in referring to this entity the *Manual* has provided it with more of an official status than it previously possessed.

The *Manual* does not discuss the possibility, during coalition government, of the individual parties holding caucus meetings in advance of full Cabinet, a practice that appears to have developed during 2010–15. Another absence from the *Manual* and the other codes is the possibility that a Prime Minister may hold bilateral or multilateral meetings that are not within the formal remit of the Cabinet or its committees, and which are designed in practice to guide the outcomes of the more official meetings. A controversial example of such a practice occurred during the premiership of Tony Blair, during the lead-up to the Iraq War of 2003.[4] The Blair example represented the use of a structure parallel to that of Cabinet. But there are other less developed cases of relationships and alliances between different members of the Cabinet that have an impact on its dynamics. Could a code in fact deal with this issue? It would not be possible to end such interactions

[4] Butler Review Team, *Review of Intelligence on Weapons of Mass Destruction* (London, Stationery Office, 2004) paras 606–11.

altogether, and it would probably be wrong to try. They are an inevitable component of political processes. However, a code could include a stipulation that the purpose of Cabinet discussion is to consider issues arising on their merits in an open manner, rather than to advance courses of action previously determined outside of Cabinet.

III. CABINET COMMITTEES

The function of Cabinet committees, according to the *Manual*, is to reduce the burden of work on the Cabinet and enable more effectiveness in the handling of business. Furthermore, they underpin collective responsibility, enabling decisions to be subject to proper scrutiny even though not considered at full Cabinet level. Crucially, as the *Manual* states, 'Cabinet committee decisions have the same authority as Cabinet decisions' (paragraph 4.9). This practice differs from the arrangements described in the equivalent text in New Zealand. According to paragraph 5.8 of this latter document, Cabinet committees usually do not have the right to take decisions that have the full force of Cabinet, and they can only pass them on to the full body, which may amend them, return them to the committee for further work or agree to them (see Chapter 3, section III.).

How is the network of UK Cabinet committees configured, and what issues do they deal with? As the *Manual* states, '[t]he Committee structure varies depending on the requirements of the incumbent government' (paragraph 4.12). It is for the Prime Minister, yet again with assistance from the Cabinet Secretary, to decide exactly how to express the needs of the Government in committee form (paragraph 4.10). But in practice the canvas is not blank, and though a premier may innovate in some areas, there are certain practices that are likely to some extent to survive. No doubt the Cabinet Secretary as adviser can contribute to continuity in this area, as well as making change, when the premier wants it, more manageable. The *Manual* suggests that it is standard practice to set up committees to address subject specific areas, 'such as home or domestic affairs, or national security'. Sub-committees may focus on 'detailed issues' on behalf of a Cabinet committee (paragraph 4.11). The *Manual* contains an account of a Cabinet committee that is different from others, and by implication is a less of an optional part of the Cabinet system. It describes a committee 'that is responsible for Parliamentary business and legislation'. Plans for legislation, after the appropriate specialist committee has agreed them, require approval from this committee too (paragraph 4.20). Rather than settling on particular packages, this committee is responsible for coordinating the overall legislative business of the Government (paragraph 4.21).

A Prime Minister can set up '[a]d hoc or miscellaneous committees … to carry out a particular task'. Much history lies behind this bland, passing reference. Prime ministers have pursued fateful and controversial courses of action using this practice, as did Anthony Eden with his Egypt Committee at the time of the Suez crisis of 1956.[5] The *Manual* tentatively proposes a norm, stating that '[a]d hoc or miscellaneous committees' operate 'usually over a limited timescale'. It then, slightly confusingly given this reference to the supposed likely ephemeral nature of such bodies, gives the example of the National Security Council. Formed in 2010, supported by a set of sub-committees, it has a wide brief for security coordination, covering such issues as 'terrorism, other security threats, hazards, resilience, intelligence policy' (paragraph 4.11). While it is an exemplar of how a Prime Minister, supported by the Civil Service, can innovate in a useful way in the Cabinet committee system, far from being a fleeting idea, it soon seemed well-established.

Whatever the particular decisions taken about the composition and areas of interest of Cabinet committees, there is now a strong convention regarding openness in this regard. The *Manual* states that '[d]etails are usually announced biannually in a written ministerial statement in Parliament' (paragraph 4.11). Paragraph 4.12 adds, 'A list of current committees, their terms of reference and the ministers who sit on them is available from the Cabinet Office website.' In this case a code, which itself emerged partly as a manifestation of the tendency towards greater openness in government, is acting as a guarantor of this same principle, helping to strengthen an assumption of public announcement.

This openness stretches to take in the machinery in place to handle exceptionally sensitive matters. Following its description of Cabinet committees, under the heading 'National emergencies', the *Manual* provides an account of the 'Cabinet Office Briefing Room [or Rooms]' or 'COBR'. When a meeting is held at COBR, it is 'in effect' a Cabinet committee meeting. But the personnel making up this body is not fixed as it is for regular Cabinet committees, and it can meet in 'ministerial' or 'official' form, according to the particular matter being addressed. Normally, the Secretary of State whose department has a primary role in the relevant field sits in the chair. The purpose of COBR is to form an official response to serious incidents impacting across multiple regions in the UK, the UK as a whole or on an international scale (paragraph 4.13).

An 80-page Cabinet Office document dated March 2010, *Responding to Emergencies*, contains further information on this subject in a section on 'The Role and Organisation of the Cabinet Office Briefing Rooms (COBR)'.[6] If an emergency reaches what is classed as level 2 or level 3, the required intervention from the UK Government takes place with the assistance of COBR. (Level 1 is a 'significant emergency', not serious enough to require coordination from COBR; level 2 is a 'serious emergency'; and level 3 a 'catastrophic emergency'.) As we have seen, the title COBR derives from the 'Cabinet Office Briefing Rooms', the place ('usually in Westminster') from which the response is driven. Attaching the COBR label to the committee is an example of how the name of a physical space or object

[5] J Pearson, *Sir Anthony Eden and the Suez Crisis: Reluctant Gamble* (Basingstoke, Palgrave Macmillan, 2003) 27.

[6] Cabinet Office, *Responding to Emergencies: The UK Central Government Response, Concept of Operations* (London, Cabinet Office, 2010) Section 3, 21–43.

can become associated with a more abstract institution, as has happened many times in the past. Sometimes the artefact or place can become an official term, or it may remain a colloquialism: the 'Crown' was a word describing a piece of royal headwear that came to serve as the closest equivalent to the 'state' in English law; a cabinet was a piece of furniture, but came to refer to the highest committee of UK government; Whitehall is a highway, once the location of a royal palace, now a synonym for the Civil Service and its central departments; 'No 10' is part of an address in Downing Street being the official residence of the First Lord of the Treasury, and is now a phrase used to describe the institution of the premiership. In media and other accounts, COBR now refers to a committee, rather than to a room, a label that is also codified.

The committee known as COBR has a loose membership determined by the specific requirements of a given emergency. It comprises the 'appropriate' ministers and senior officials, as well as individuals drawn from 'other organisations as necessary'. The combined purpose of the participants is to attain 'a common appreciation of the situation and to facilitate effective and timely decision making' (paragraph 3.1). The internal structure is for a 'senior decision making body' with a set of supporting 'cells' and 'blocks of activities' (paragraph 3.2). The document anticipates that it will be necessary to deploy the full apparatus 'only in the most complex emergencies', such as certain kinds of terrorist strikes (paragraph 3.3). The 'key decision-making body', with the Prime Minister in the chair, is known as the Strategy Group. It can also convene as a body of officials. The text notes that 'conventions on collective ministerial responsibility apply'; the conclusions that COBR reaches are 'binding on departments' (paragraph 3.6). This stipulation appears to imply that government can be subject to the decisions of a committee including within it people who are not members of Cabinet, or not even ministers, as though it were the Cabinet or a Cabinet committee.

Below COBR a 'Situation Cell' is formed, with the Cabinet Office at the head, working with the 'Lead Government Department' dealing with the particular problem that has arisen. The role of the Situation Cell is to provide a clear, instant and accurate picture of the position to those responsible for directing the response (paragraph 3.9). One of its tasks is to produce a 'Common Recognised Information Picture (CRIP)' that is 'summarised on display boards' in COBR (paragraph 3.10). In circumstances including terrorist emergencies an 'Intelligence Cell' is to be formed. It will draw its personnel from the various intelligence and security agencies and staffs, and possibly from other sources. With the Chief of the Assessments Staff serving as its director, it handles various intelligence briefing tasks for COBR (paragraphs 3.16, 3.17). There may also be an Impact Management Group (IMG) (paragraphs 3.27–3.33) and a Recovery Group (RG) (paragraphs 3.34–3.39). A News Co-ordination Cell (NCC) will form to manage public information, if required (paragraphs 3.40–3.42). Further scientific, technical and legal advice may be obtained as necessary (paragraphs 3.44–3.47).

IV. THE WORK OF THE CABINET SYSTEM

The configuration of the Cabinet and its committees is important, but what do they actually do? The basic task is to take group decisions. 'Collective agreement', the *Manual* tells us, can be obtained through one of two routes. The first takes place at a Cabinet or Cabinet committee gathering, the second through ministers signing off circulated letters (paragraph 4.16). The former is the better-known part of the process of collective government. But much business is resolved through the latter route—and it clearly cannot involve the discussion that the former method makes possible. But when is a decision important enough to need Cabinet approval of some form? The principle of collective responsibility is central to the conduct of government in the UK, but, like the *Ministerial Code*, *The Cabinet Manual* notes that 'definitive criteria' for those matters that require it to be obtained are lacking. In this instance the *Manual* provides an example of the process of codification serving to provide greater certainty about the very absence of clarity. Having established the presence of indeterminacy, it predictably promotes the role of a particular group based in the Cabinet Office as able to offer guidance: 'the Cabinet Secretariat can advise where departments are unsure' (paragraph 4.17). The *Manual* then identifies issues demanding attention by Cabinet committee, which it emphasises apply '[a]t present'—that is, they are not firmly fixed. The first, clearly a current concern when the *Manual* was in its final stages of production, involves measures that implemented or had implications for the programme of the then coalition. Second is a matter it is anticipated will generate outside interest or controversy. Third is a proposal the scope of which engages two or more Whitehall departments. Fourth is an issue over which departments are in disagreement (paragraph 4.17).

Once again, uncertainty surrounds exactly what full Cabinet, rather than a Cabinet committee, should consider. 'There are', the *Manual* states 'no set rules … it is ultimately for the Prime Minister to decide the agenda'. As ever, the *Manual* is careful to stipulate that the premier carries out this important task, crucial to the armoury of prime-ministerial power, 'on the advice of the Cabinet Secretary'. Regardless of the level at which they are reached, that is in Cabinet committee or full Cabinet, conclusions have equal status as 'collective decisions'. The precise level at which they were taken should remain confidential. The *Manual* then provides an indicative list of matters it would be reasonable to expect might reach full Cabinet:

1. entry into armed combat;
2. the contents of the Queen's Speech, which describes the programme for government legislation each year;
3. constitutional matters, such as alterations to arrangements for devolution, changes to Parliament and issues involving the monarchy;
4. major domestic affairs;
5. European or international issues of substantial importance;

6. subjects of such importance that they have implications for all the members of the Cabinet; and
7. emergencies such as terrorism (paragraph 4.18).

The *Manual* suggests flexibility about the precise point in the development of a particular measure when agreement from the full Cabinet is required. It is possible, subject to approval from the premier, for a Secretary of State to initiate discussion of an important policy at a formative stage, prior to carrying out more detailed work. Another option is to take it to Cabinet at a later stage, when it is nearly ready for public unveiling, 'normally' following consideration and agreement at a Cabinet committee (paragraph 4.19). Arguably the former option affords greater authority to the full collective, enabling it to encourage and shape—or veto—an idea when it is forming. The latter scenario could suggest the idea of accepting a policy as a predetermined outcome, both as a general idea and in the particulars of its design. The word 'normally' creates the possibility of a major initiative only being presented for collective approval of any kind after its design is complete. Yet as ever, to follow such a course of action could produce negative consequences for those who pursued it within the Cabinet.

Paragraphs 4.23–4.25 of the *Manual* are headed 'Areas outside Cabinet collective decision-making'. The *Manual* sets out certain areas that are not within the remit of collective responsibility. First, in paragraph 4.23, it describes how the Budget and associated announcements are only made available to the Cabinet when it convenes on they day they are announced to the House of Commons. However, the *Manual* allows that 'the content of the proposal will have been discussed with relevant ministers in advance of the meeting'. It does not specify how these earlier talks should take place, or who the 'relevant ministers' are. Suggesting an important principle that strengthens in particular the hand of the Chancellor of the Exchequer, the *Manual* states that '[t]he expectation is that the proposals will be accepted by Cabinet without amendment'. Nonetheless, it goes on to say, 'the Chancellor may, if necessary, make amendments'. There is no explanation of when the 'expectation' of approval of the Budget does not apply and when changes might be 'necessary', and how, precisely, these circumstances differ from the more regular process of Cabinet discussion.

Paragraph 4.24 describes the 'quasi-judicial functions' some ministers carry out without being subject to Cabinet approval. They include decisions in such disparate areas as the granting of mercy and the provision of planning permission. The *Manual* also refers to a procedure concerning whether or not public prosecutions should take place, known as a 'Shawcross exercise'. It takes its name from the Labour Attorney-General, Sir Hartley Shawcross, who explained the principles involved to Parliament in 1951. Decisions about whether or not to mount prosecutions in particular cases ultimately fall to the particular authority involved. However, under the 'Shawcross' practice, in certain circumstances, 'the Attorney General may write to relevant ministerial colleagues seeking any information that should be considered by a prosecuting authority when weighing the public interest in a prosecution'. The example the *Manual* offers of such a circumstance is the existence of 'a risk that a prosecution may endanger national security, international relations or the safety of the Armed Forces abroad' (paragraph 4.25). The implication is that if ministers judge a prospective court case as likely to cause difficulties in the relationship with a foreign state, or to bring information to light that the Government feels would in some way be a threat if placed in the open, then political pressure can be applied to the relevant authorities not to continue with it. No mention is made of the broad principles that should apply, or whether the need to maintain the rule of law should remain an overriding concern at all times.

V. CABINET PROCEDURE

The *Manual* sets out a number of rules regarding Cabinet procedure. Paragraph 4.26 tells us that agendas are fixed for every meeting of the Cabinet and of Cabinet committees. The Prime Minister arranges the agenda of the full Cabinet; and individual chairs do the same for Cabinet committees. It is possible, according to paragraph 4.27, for ministers to inform the Cabinet Secretariat that they would like 'to raise business orally … and, where agreed, this is included as an item on the agenda'. The *Manual* attributes to the Cabinet Secretariat an important role as guarantor of 'standards for the form and content of papers and presentations' (paragraph 4.28). The standard practice is for the 'lead minister, or ministers' concerned to produce a paper for each item on the agenda. Yet 'any member of the committee and the Cabinet Secretary' can also produce an additional paper on the subject (paragraph 4.29). Paragraph 4.30 sets out requirements for the material reaching Cabinet and its committees, in pursuit of the principle that it should 'include any information that is needed for ministers to make an informed decision'. It is important for it to be 'concise' and for it to present the 'benefits, disadvantages and risks' linked to the intended course of action it presents. The paper should be 'clear' about the decisions ministers must reach; and it must give an account of the 'public expenditure implications'. The *Manual* states that the Cabinet Secretariat can decline a paper that fails to meet the 'appropriate standard', or it can produce a replacement paper of its own or create a 'cover sheet … highlighting the key issues for ministerial consideration'. The intended impact of these rules, then, is to ensure adherence to a set of standards facilitating meaningful and effective collective discussion, with the Cabinet Secretariat having an important role as the upholder of integrity.

According to paragraph 4.32 of *The Cabinet Manual*, it is necessary to obtain approval from 'other departments' for a measure that engages them prior to trying to obtain 'collective agreement'. In cases of plans with 'public expenditure implications, the Treasury should be consulted before they are submitted for collective agreement'. This requirement would presumably apply to a wide range of possible policies, since most significant proposals must have 'public expenditure implications'. If it is not possible to secure the approval of the Treasury, the material presented to ministers must contain an account of the view of the Treasury in a way that the Treasury approves. The *Manual* then appears to state that ultimately the Treasury has a veto, at least at Cabinet committee level. It recounts that 'Policy proposals with public expenditure implications will not be agreed unless Treasury ministers are content.' In a circumstance where the Treasury opposes a plan put forward by a department, the *Manual* explains, it is possible to pass the matter to the Prime Minister, who seemingly can resolve it personally or choose to submit it to the full Cabinet for arbitration. This arrangement suggests that the Treasury—or perhaps it is better to say the Chancellor of the Exchequer—and the Prime Minister can between them veto an idea on grounds of cost, and prevent their decision from being considered and possibly overturned at the full Cabinet. In theory, other members of the Cabinet could insist on discussing a proposal, and threaten serious consequences if they were not allowed to do so. Nonetheless, the *Manual* suggests that an important authority is attached to the Chancellor and Prime Minister combined—but to neither one of them individually. Equally, the premier could in theory overrule the Treasury; and could also resolve a dispute in a Cabinet committee individually without involving the full Cabinet. Yet both courses of action might carry great political costs.

These realisations are important. They suggest, first, that an important source of prime-ministerial authority derives from the premier's being a mediator of disputes as opposed to instigator of proposals. Secondly, a premier and a Chancellor of the Exchequer acting in concert are a powerful force. Yet this authority arises in the first instance, at least as depicted in the *Manual*, from their ability to block proposals. If they wish to initiate a policy, it may be that they can achieve this outcome not so much through a positive power to impose themselves but through a trade-off, agreeing to permit other proposals it is within their scope to veto in return for collective consent over a particular issue in which they have an interest. This model is compatible with that promoted by core executive theorists, according to whom policy formation arises from interaction between different players in central government, trading resources such as authority and information in return for the attainment of particular goals. In this account, power is not a solid object held at the centre but a dispersed, fluid entity. No one individual wields it over others; it is deployed through negotiation between different participants.[7] Another important consequence of the potential power of a Prime Minister and Chancellor of the Exchequer acting in concert is that their personal relationship is vital. If they are close, they can achieve much, though they may in the process minimise the part played by the wider collective, a potential problem. If a Prime Minister and Chancellor of the Exchequer clash, on the other hand, dysfunction is likely.

[7] M Smith, *The Core Executive in Britain* (Basingstoke, Palgrave Macmillan, 1999).

Another crucial part of the Cabinet system, especially since 1916 and the formation of a War Cabinet with the support of a secretariat, has been the production of written records of the meetings. Paragraph 4.34 states, 'Minutes are taken for each Cabinet and Cabinet committee meeting, forming part of the historic record of government.' These minutes, the *Manual* explains, 'record the main points made in discussion and the Cabinet or Cabinet committee or Cabinet committee conclusions as summed up by the chair'. This task is not necessarily as straightforward as it might seem, since a discussion may be confused and a Prime Minister may summarise it in a vague way, perhaps deliberately so in relation to an issue that proves controversial. The skill of the minute-taker is important. The *Manual* offers little guidance on the standards or practices required. What level of detail, for instance, is appropriate? How far should an account be focused on the outcome of the discussion, rather than on the different streams of thought connected to it? The *Manual* simply states that 'To help preserve the principle of collective responsibility, most contributions by ministers are unattributed.' As is often the case with the *Manual*, the wording—in this case the use of 'most'—deliberately preserves flexibility. It goes on, 'points made by the minister introducing the item and the chair's summing-up are generally attributed'. An internal document giving a clearer idea of the task seems to exist but is not publicly available.

The *Manual* provides the vague but nonetheless significant guidance that '[a]ttendance of officials … at Cabinet and Cabinet committee meetings is kept to a minimum'. This restraint is justified on the grounds that it permits 'ministers to have a free and frank discussion of the issues'. The Cabinet Secretariat, however, has its place at meetings protected, further demonstrating its privileging in the arrangements depicted in the *Manual* (paragraph 4.39). The staff of the Prime Minister also have special rights. Paragraph 4.40 of the *Manual* describes 'a standing invitation for a member of the Prime Minister's office to attend any Cabinet committee meeting'. Chairs of committees also 'may be accompanied by a private secretary'. Dealing with the particulars of the time in which it appeared, the *Manual* states 'This invitation also currently extends to the Deputy Prime Minister's office.' Having sought to restrict attendance at meetings, the *Manual* then crowds them even more. It states, again vaguely, 'Where necessary, other officials may be invited to attend Cabinet committee meetings as set out in the terms of reference.' However, it goes on to note that '[r]estrictions are in place regarding the attendance of other officials'—though it does not give any details about what they are. Once again the *Manual* casts the Cabinet Secretariat in an important role with respect to application of the rules: 'the Cabinet Secretariat must be consulted in advance should officials need to attend' (paragraph 4.41).

Neither the Cabinet nor its committees have a 'set quorum'. By way of contrast, as previously noted, according to the New Zealand *Cabinet Manual*, the Cabinet has a quorum of 'half the full membership … plus one'. Yet at risk of undermining the previous statement, the New Zealand text then tells us that '[t]he chair of a Cabinet meeting may vary the quorum requirements, if necessary' (paragraph 5.60; see Chapter 3, section III.). The final decision in the UK on whether to proceed also rests with the chair, 'on the advice of the Cabinet Secretariat' (paragraph 4.42). Both the New Zealand and UK arrangements seem to leave open the possibility that a poorly attended meeting could take a controversial decision, the legitimacy of which other members who were not present might subsequently challenge. As we have seen, this type of incident was at the centre of the collapse of a coalition in New Zealand (see Chapter 3, section III.). But however taken, decisions of the Cabinet are not only (normally) binding but require positive action. As paragraph 4.43 of the UK *Cabinet Manual* iterates, 'Ministers are responsible for ensuring that their departments take whatever action is necessary to implement decisions made by Cabinet or Cabinet committees, and for reporting back to colleagues on progress if needed.' This paragraph makes an important connection between the two main strands of ministerial responsibility, both its collective and individual components. It suggests that though particular ministers may take on implementation (and will be directly answerable to Parliament in this regard), the collective retains ownership of it and a legitimate interest in how it is put into practice.

Paragraphs 4.44–4.48 of the *Manual* contain the section 'Cabinet committee correspondence'. This informs the reader that the majority of matters that necessitate the approval of the collective need not be discussed at an actual Cabinet committee meeting but can be dealt with using written exchanges (paragraph 4.44). The *Manual* describes a process whereby the chair of a Cabinet committee, or less often the chair of the full Cabinet (that is, the Prime Minister), writes to the ministers involved with a specific proposition, 'normally' permitting them 'at least six working days' to reply (paragraph 4.45). No mention is made of whether e-mail can be used, or if traditional hard copy is required. All the responses are circulated to the Prime Minister, Deputy Prime Minister (though there may not always be one), members of the relevant committee and the Cabinet Secretary. First Parliamentary Counsel receives copies if the particular matter is relevant to legislative drafting (paragraph 4.46). The chair then writes back 'to the minister'—presumably meaning every minister concerned—'confirming whether collective agreement has been reached or not, and setting out any conditions to that agreement'. The *Manual* does not make it clear how to decide if the necessary agreement has been attained. Does it, for instance, require unanimity among correspondents? However, the text does, once again, emphasise the importance of the Cabinet Secretariat to the process, stating that the chair acts 'on advice from' this entity. The phrase 'on advice' could appear firmer than 'with advice' (paragraph 4.47). In the event a conclusion cannot be reached through correspondence, the chair may convene a physical meeting (paragraph 4.48).

In a section entitled 'The Cabinet Secretariat', the *Manual* states that this body 'exists to support the Prime Minister, and currently the Deputy Prime Minister, and the chairs of Cabinet committees' in the task of 'ensuring that government business is conducted in an effective and timely way and that proper collective consideration takes place'. It is, the *Manual* notes, 'non-departmental' and comprises staff 'based in the Cabinet Office but drawn from across government' (paragraph 4.51). The Secretariat reports to the Prime Minister, the Deputy Prime

Minister and the chairs of Cabinet committees. It 'prepares the agenda of Cabinet committee meetings, with the agreement of the chair', and it also supplies 'them with advice and support in their functions as chair'. Lastly, it 'issues the minutes of the committees' (paragraph 4.52).

Another assertion of the institutional importance of the Cabinet Office and the Civil Service more broadly comes when the *Manual* describes in paragraph 4.14 the role of 'Official committees' that 'can be established to support Cabinet committees'. It states that the Cabinet Secretariat provides the chairs of these bodies. Who should sit on them is not 'fixed', but the general principle is that civil servants will come from the departments of the ministers who take part in the Cabinet committee that the official committee supports (paragraph 4.14). Paragraph 4.15 describes how they operate. It states that official committees can form for diverse reasons, but that they frequently have a shared feature that they 'would normally meet in advance of a Cabinet committee'. This assertion suggests that the purpose is something more than simply receiving and implementing instructions from the ministerial committee that the official committee shadows. The paragraph goes on to state that convening before rather than after the Cabinet committee allows official committees 'to consider the issues that would need to be covered in Cabinet committee papers and to help the Cabinet Secretariat identify points that are likely to be raised so that it can brief the chair of the Cabinet committee effectively'. The language is flat, but on further consideration it contains much potential. It allows for a body of officials from different departments to work towards a group agreement on what ministers at a Cabinet committee should discuss, the information made available to them and how the chair should handle proceedings. Some of the essentials of the approach found in the *Precedent Book* compiled in the time of Norman Brook, the Cabinet Secretary in the immediate post-Second World War era, have persisted. Yet on the other hand, as ever, there are limitations on the amount of manipulation that can take place, and officials must always work within parameters set for them by ministers and the wider political environment.

Codification of Cabinet extends beyond the *Ministerial Code* and *The Cabinet Manual*. A 26-page Cabinet Office document, *Guidance on the collective agreement process*, dated March 2013, is intended to help inform officials in departments on whether a particular decision requires collective agreement, in what form and how they should go about seeking it.[8] Yet it stresses that 'there are no definitive rules' and that 'the final decision' rests with the Cabinet Secretariat ('Introduction'). A further Cabinet Office text, *Guide to Cabinet and Cabinet Committees*, provides in its 24 pages detailed information on the operation of the system.[9] The version consulted for this book is dated 2012, but it contains some references that were already out of date by this point, suggesting it may be one or two years older. The 'Introduction to Cabinet and Cabinet Committees' explains that the scale

[8] Cabinet Office, *Guidance on the collective agreement process* (London, Cabinet Office, 2013).
[9] Cabinet Office, *Guide to Cabinet and Cabinet Committees* (London, Cabinet Office, 2012).

and complexity of the business of government is such that there is a need for both 'formal and informal' means of 'discussing issues, building consensus, taking decisions, resolving disputes and chasing progress'. The Cabinet and its committees fit into this picture as the only entities 'formally empowered to take binding decisions' for the Government. The text explains that collective responsibility is a means by which ministers are able to put forward their honest opinions in debate, while being able to unify publicly behind whatever conclusions are reached.

While some of it repeats material available elsewhere, particularly in *The Cabinet Manual*, the *Guide* provides some valuable procedural detail. In a section on 'Requests for clearance through correspondence', it explains that when collective agreement is sought in written form rather than at a meeting, there should be a minimum of six full working days allowed for responses—and nine days during parliamentary recess. Further time still should be allowed 'for finalising clearance'. Departure from this rule is possible only in exceptional circumstances. The section headed 'Deciding policy through committee meetings' tells the reader that papers for Cabinet committee meetings should be 'clear … concise—no more than three pages (with detail, if necessary, in an annex)' and 'available **48 hours** [emphasis in original] before a meeting takes place'. A department that is producing a paper should provide a draft for the Cabinet Secretariat a minimum of five working days before the committee meeting. If the paper fails to meet the standards required of it, or is not circulated soon enough, the chair of the committee can, 'on the advice of the Cabinet Secretariat', cancel the meeting. As we have seen, the Cabinet Secretariat can 'refuse the paper, substitute their own note, or produce a cover sheet to the paper'. A section headed 'Clearing policy through Cabinet' explains that, for full Cabinet meetings, the office of the Cabinet Secretary should receive presentations and papers 'on Friday before the Cabinet meeting', allowing circulation to ministers in advance of the weekend. Exceptionally, it is possible to supply a paper by midday on the Monday before the Cabinet meeting.

VI. CONCLUSION

The subject matter of this chapter is important from the perspective of a number of the key themes of this work. It shows how far the process of codification has come, with a range of matters that were once probably not written down at all now dealt with in texts available immediately to anyone with unrestricted Internet access. In some ways, these documents have confirmed the existence of practices and rules that were already widely known through less formal sources, such as the basic operational procedures of the Cabinet. In others, they have revealed fascinating details, such as the workings of COBR, that might not otherwise be accessible—and the revealing of which would once have been unthinkable. In further cases still, codification has both provided some clarity but also retained uncertainty, for instance over what issues, precisely, require collective agreement in some form. The texts provide an insight into the jostling for and around power that takes place at the summit of government. Broadly speaking, a range of senior figures must be engaged in important decisions, and the processes used must successfully bind the whole of government. This constraint applies to all involved. Within this overall framework, the codes considered here attribute special roles to certain figures—most notably the Prime Minister and then the Chancellor of the Exchequer. They also provide a continual reminder of the part played by Cabinet Office officials in the facilitation of the processes involved, reflecting the institutional affiliation of those who draft the documents.

A last observation is possible. A continual subject of speculation among constitutional observers is whether the Cabinet has in some way declined in importance within government. Some hold, or have held, that it has become largely redundant, replaced, perhaps, with an informal presidential form of government.[10] If this theory is correct, somebody forgot to tell the codifiers. During the very period when—in some accounts—Cabinet was becoming irrelevant, it was being defined in writing to an increasingly meticulous extent. The documents issued suggested that though certain posts were more prominent than others, it was not possible simply to ignore the collective. Moreover, it might be asked, why did politicians and officials—those who had first-hand experience of the system and how it was developing—go to so much trouble to codify something if it was an anachronism?

We now turn our attention to the ministers who make up the government, and the structures and personnel that play a part in supporting decision-taking processes and ensuring their outcomes are implemented.

[10] For an overview of the literature in this area, see A Blick and G Jones, *Premiership: the development, nature and power of the office of the British Prime Minister* (Exeter, Imprint Academic, 2010), Chs 1 and 2.

7

The Executive: Ministers, Departments and the Civil Service

IN THE PREVIOUS two chapters we considered the codification of two entities—the premiership and the Cabinet—found at the political and administrative summit of the executive. This chapter provides a wider view of the executive machine, taking in ministers, official staff and administrative structures. The Cabinet and the office of the Prime Minister stand out for the extent to which they lack a statutory basis, resting largely in convention. Codification therefore has a particularly important task to perform in defining them. There is a greater role for Acts of Parliament in the posts and institutions considered here (and some codes pertaining to the Civil Service now have a statutory footing). Nonetheless, there are important gaps that codes—with or without a grounding in an Act of Parliament—can help to fill. Moreover, the interaction between direct legal enactment and practice and convention can provide material for these documents; and the limitations on the capacity of statute to prescribe for every possible form of constitutional activity are highlighted when they are considered in this wide perspective. We begin with a consideration of ministers and the departments to which they are attached.

I. MINISTERS AND DEPARTMENTS

The key document dealing with the conduct of ministers is the *Ministerial Code*.[1] The current, 31-page, edition dates from October 2015. Each of the 10 sections opens with a general principle upon which it then elaborates. All ministers, including parliamentary private secretaries, are subject to the Code (paragraph 1.4). Section 1, 'Ministers of the Crown', begins by stating that 'Ministers of the Crown are expected to behave in a way that upholds the highest standards of propriety' (paragraph 1.1). It then stresses the need to consider the Code 'against the background of the overarching duty on Ministers to comply with the law and to protect the integrity of public life'. (This passage, as discussed in the Introduction to this book, generated controversy when published because of the omission of

[1] Cabinet Office, *Ministerial Code* (Cabinet Office, London, 2015).

words that appeared in the previous version of the Code referring to the need to maintain international law, adhere to requirements created by treaties and support the administration of justice.) The text then goes on to state that ministers 'are expected to observe The *seven principles of public life*' (included as the sole annex, Annex A, to the Code; see Chapter 2, section II.). It lists a further 10 'principles' that it stipulates ministers must 'observe'. They are:

> The principle of collective responsibility applies to all Government Ministers …
>
> Ministers have a duty to Parliament to account, and be held to account, for the policies, decisions and actions of their departments and agencies …
>
> It is of paramount importance that Ministers give accurate and truthful information to Parliament, correcting any inadvertent error at the earliest opportunity. Ministers who knowingly mislead Parliament will be expected to offer their resignation to the Prime Minister …
>
> Ministers should be as open as possible with Parliament and the public, refusing to provide information only when disclosure would not be in the public interest …
>
> Ministers should … require civil servants who give evidence before Parliamentary Committees on their behalf and under their direction to be as helpful as possible in providing accurate, truthful and full information …
>
> Ministers must ensure that no conflict arises, or appears to arise, between their public duties and their private interests …
>
> Ministers should not accept any gift or hospitality which might, or might reasonably appear to, compromise their judgement or place them under an improper obligation …
>
> Ministers in the House of Commons must keep separate their roles as Minister and constituency Member …
>
> Ministers must not use government resources for Party political purposes …
>
> Ministers must uphold the political impartiality of the Civil Service … (paragraph 1.2)

One observation on this list is that it contains a mixture of types of rule. Some lean more clearly towards straightforward propriety and integrity issues, such as not accepting inappropriate gifts, and would be recognised (though not necessarily adhered to) anywhere in the world. Others relate more to the particular and even peculiar nature of the UK constitution. They do not necessarily engage ethical concerns in the abstract, but involve more the specific ways in which objectives such as accountable government can be attained within the specific UK context. The use of different methods in these cases would not necessarily amount to a lack of integrity, but could just be part of a different approach intended to achieve similar underlying goals. Falling within this category are the requirements to maintain an impartial Civil Service, and to adhere to collective responsibility.

What force do these varied rules have, and who is responsible for upholding them? The *Ministerial Code* states that the Cabinet Secretary and other officials are not responsible for ensuring compliance. Following a claim regarding supposed violation of the Code, the Prime Minister can decide, 'having consulted the Cabinet Secretary', to involve the 'independent adviser on Ministers' interests' (paragraph 1.3)—or, by implication, choose not to do so. The text holds that it falls to ministers individually to choose how they should go about adhering to the Code and explaining themselves to the public and to Parliament. But if they lose the backing of the Prime Minister they will fall. It is the premier who is 'the ultimate judge of the standards of behaviour expected of a Minister and the appropriate consequences of a breach of those standards' (paragraph 1.5).

As already discussed in previous chapters, a preoccupation of many codes is the handling of official papers. Indeed, to the outsider this subject may appear to receive an inordinate degree of attention. Yet from the perspective of the officials who draft these texts, they are of substantial importance, explaining their prominence in codes. The *Ministerial Code* explains that departing ministers are supposed to return 'Cabinet documents and/or other departmental papers' (paragraph 2.7). When a new administration takes office, 'the Cabinet Secretary on behalf of the outgoing Prime Minister, issues special instructions about the disposal of Cabinet papers' (paragraph 2.8). The Code then refers to a 'convention' that, subject to the approval of the Government, 'former Ministers are allowed reasonable access to the papers of the period when they were in office'. However, other than in the case of 'former Prime Ministers, access is limited to former Ministers personally' (paragraph 2.9), presumably meaning not research assistants working for them.

While the *Ministerial Code* chiefly deals with how ministers should conduct themselves, *The Cabinet Manual* expands into structural and organisational areas. It depicts a fourfold distinction between types of minister: junior ministers, senior ministers, Law Officers and whips. It suggests that while it is possible for the Prime Minister to 'agree' that ministers can have a 'courtesy title' according with any particular tasks given to them, such as 'Minister for Europe', these labels have 'no legal or constitutional significance' (paragraph 3.7). The *Manual* then deals with a principle that is critical to the UK constitution, yet which has seemingly not previously received this type of official expression, and is easier to comprehend as a shared, tacit understanding than it is to set out in writing. It states:

> There is a convention that an individual will be a minister only if they are a Member of the House of Commons or the House of Lords, with most being Members of the House of Commons. However, there are examples of individuals being appointed as a minister in anticipation of their becoming a Member of one of the Houses and of continuing to hold office for a short period after ceasing to be Members of the House of Commons. (paragraph 3.8)

The statement that 'most' ministers sit in the Commons is not controversial but it is vague. If only slightly over half of ministers were Members of Parliament, would this arrangement be acceptable? Moreover, there is a qualitative as well as quantitative issue. The *Manual* does not identify any post other than that of Prime Minister that must be held by members of the Commons. Could, for instance, a member of the Lords be Home Secretary? By the same token, until recently, it would have been considered necessary for the Lord Chancellor to sit in the Lords, given the special functions attached to that office as Speaker in the upper chamber and head of the judiciary.

Footnote 7 to paragraph 3.8 refers to the Patrick Gordon Walker precedent. Harold Wilson made Gordon Walker Foreign Secretary in 1964, despite his having been defeated at the General Election of that month. (In the same footnote, the *Manual* also recounts that, prior to the introduction of devolution, the Solicitor-General for Scotland frequently sat in neither House.) Gordon Walker continued in this ministerial post while he sought re-entry to Parliament, but he resigned after he lost a by-election in January 1965. The Gordon Walker issue was charged because it involved an anti-immigration campaign. Were a sitting Member of Parliament defeated at a General Election in less controversial circumstances, a Prime Minister might not choose, and might feel less able, to take the stance Wilson did with Gordon Walker. Much could depend, therefore, on political circumstance. A possibility the *Manual* does not expressly exclude, but which it does not positively allow for either, and which could prove controversial, is that a minister in a position analogous to that of Gordon Walker after his second reverse could then be created a peer and operate from the House of Lords. Would such a decision be seen as a democratic affront? It is only as recently as 1926 that the practice of Members of Parliament being appointed to high ministerial office having to recontest their seats was completely abolished, so the idea that an individual constituency rather than the electorate as a whole should be able to approve or veto a ministerial appointment was once a part of our constitutional arrangements.

Paragraph 3.26 of *The Cabinet Manual* contains a reminder of some of the archaic quality of the UK constitution, and the understandings that have been layered upon it to allow it to continue to function. It notes that statutes generally vest responsibilities in 'the Secretary of State'. While there are in practice many Secretaries of State, Acts of Parliament do not recognise this position. There is a 'doctrine that there is only one office of Secretary of State, even though it is the well-established practice to appoint more than one person to carry out the functions of the office'. The *Manual* here exposes some of the smoke and mirrors at the heart of the UK constitution. The great offices of state, with leading politicians at their summit, with their buildings around Whitehall, St James's and Victoria, thousands of staff, budgets in the billions of pounds, the accumulation of functions and in some cases long histories, when viewed from another perspective, barely exist beyond being the product of the subdivision of a post with its origins in the personal assistant to the monarch of medieval times. In paragraph 3.27 the *Manual* describes a 'well-established practice for each secretary of state to be allocated responsibility by the Prime Minister for a particular department'. It gives the examples of Defence, Education, Foreign Affairs, Health and Transport. Once allotted their role by the premier, they 'in practice … exercise only those functions that are within that department'. Some strengthening of the existence of secretaries of state comes in the next paragraph, with the reference to most of their being 'incorporated as "corporations sole"' (paragraph 3.28).

The *Manual* devotes a paragraph (3.11) to the 'Deputy Prime Minister'. It tells us that this title 'is sometimes given to a senior minister in the Government'. In providing examples of who might become Deputy Prime Minister, it states that such an individual might be 'the deputy leader of the party in government or the leader of the smaller party in a coalition'. At the time the *Manual* appeared, Nick Clegg, Leader of the Liberal Democrats, was Deputy Prime Minister; the previous holder of this title was John Prescott (1997–2007), Deputy Prime Minister under Tony Blair and Deputy Leader of the Labour Party. However, as the *Manual* allows but does not expand upon, there have been other Deputy Prime Ministers who fitted neither category, such as Rab Butler (1962–63) and Michael Heseltine (1995–97).

While instances of granting a person the title Deputy Prime Minister are possibly in the process of becoming more frequent, it is not a clearly identifiable role. It is harder to imagine a government that did not have someone performing the role of 'Minister for Europe' (even—or perhaps especially—if the UK left the EU) than it is to envisage the absence of a 'Deputy Prime Minister'. While being called Minister for Europe may not denote a formal office, it clearly identifies a specific function. The label 'Deputy Prime Minister' does not. Perhaps the two-party coalition that existed when the first edition of the *Manual* was being completed created a strong reason to use the Deputy Prime Minister title, and in such circumstances senior officials and others may encourage the view that this model is appropriate. Yet this outcome should not be seen as inevitable (and in a coalition of more than two parties, the attraction of having a Deputy Prime Minister could weaken, depending on the balance of forces and assuming there is only one Deputy Prime Minister). On entering a coalition, a party leader who was not becoming Prime Minister might be better advised to seek an established office of state, such as Foreign Secretary, as opposed to a title that is flattering but in itself empty. As paragraph 3.11 of the *Manual* notes, 'The role of the Deputy Prime Minister is sometimes combined with other roles, but responsibilities will vary according to the circumstances.' It cites the example of Clegg's simultaneously taking on the post of Lord President of the Council, and having 'responsibility for political and constitutional reform'. The title does not carry with it any specific task or formal power, afforded either by statute or by convention. Unlike that of Vice President in the US, the holder has no succession rights. As the *Manual* iterates carefully at the close of paragraph 3.11, 'The fact that a person has the title of Deputy Prime Minister does not constrain the Sovereign's power to appoint a successor to a Prime Minister.'

It may be that eventually the post 'Deputy Prime Minister' will become a more fixed part of the system, with tangible functions attached to it in its own right—but that moment has certainly not arrived yet. At present there would be some justice in characterising it as a political bauble designed to signify importance without in itself conceding substance, to secure cooperation from the individual to which it is granted. Deputy prime ministers are likely to be important figures within government, but not primarily because they are deputy prime ministers. The *Manual* has presented the title of 'Deputy Prime Minister' in a way that suggests it has a more prominent constitutional role than is actually the case. The motive for doing so was presumably the existence of a Deputy Prime Minister at the time it was finalised and published. A similar case of present arrangements having a distorting impact upon representations of the established practices comes in the following paragraph (3.12), which is a section entitled 'The First Secretary of State'. At the time, William Hague, the Foreign Secretary and a senior Conservative member of the coalition, held this title. The *Manual* tells us, 'A minister may be appointed First Secretary of State to indicate seniority. The appointment may be held with another office. The responsibilities of the First Secretary of State will vary according to the circumstances.'

This account only illuminates in that it reveals that the significant feature of the First Secretary of State post is that it signifies 'seniority' and, in itself, little else, though positioning in the order of precedence has certain procedural consequences that may be practically useful. It is conceivable that there would have been some reference to the concept of the Deputy Prime Minister if no one held the title at the time of the *Manual*, though it would probably not have received the same degree of prominence. However, it is reasonable to question whether, were it not for the position of Hague in the Government at the time, there would have been any perceived need to refer to the First Secretary of State at all. Just as the granting of the Deputy Prime Minister and First Secretary of State titles are about managing political and personal sensitivities, so too was the way in which the *Manual* dealt with them. To have left them out, or not made them seem important, would have been impolitic. The consequence for the *Manual* is that in these sections it appears more ephemeral and trivial, and less a statement of more fundamental, lasting principles.

Another case of bland statement comes in paragraph 3.13, which describes how junior ministers are 'generally' parliamentary secretaries, parliamentary under secretaries of state and Ministers of State. It explains that '[t]ypically' these appointments operate within a government department and that they 'support and assist' the minister in overall charge. No reference is made as to whether the 'senior minister' in question should have any informal input into who is appointed to such roles. Citing the *Ministerial Code*, paragraph 3.21 of the *Manual* describes how members of the Cabinet and Ministers of State 'may appoint Parliamentary private secretaries'. The *Manual* presents the initiative as coming from the appointing minister, but subject to 'prior written approval' from the premier and consultation with the Chief Whip. Parliamentary private secretaries, while subject to collective responsibility, 'are not members of the government' (paragraph 3.22). They are, therefore, part of the block of support on which a government can expect to rely in Parliament, but their appointment does not engage the statutory limits on numbers of paid ministers. The *Manual* offers no guidance on how many Parliamentary private secretaries ministers are permitted individually, or as a group, to recruit. Indeed it arguably incites exploitation of this loophole. In paragraph 3.23, the *Manual* describes the caps imposed under the Ministerial and other Salaries Act 1975 (a total of 109 ministers on the public payroll in Parliament in total) and the House of Commons Disqualification Act 1975 (an upper limit of 95 ministers in the House of Commons, whether or not they receive remuneration). In the next sentence it then expressly remarks. 'Parliamentary private secretaries do not count towards the limit on House of Commons ministers or the limits on salaries', without suggesting any need for restraint.

Paragraph 3.20 is headed 'Resignation of ministers'. It attempts to offer some reasons as to why they might go. The first is that they 'are not able to continue to accept collective responsibility'. This statement is core to the UK constitution—at least as traditionally understood. The experience of the Coalition Government of 2010–15 was that many senior government members saw a rejection of collective responsibility (even aside from those cases where it was expressly suspended) as entirely compatible with continuing to hold their office.[2] Other possible reasons for exit the *Manual* proposes are 'issues relating to their conduct in office, or due to a personal or private matter'. It does not refer specifically to the issue of knowingly misleading Parliament as necessitating resignation. This motive for departing government is, unlike some of the other reasons that the *Manual* does address, arguably a constitutional convention, referred to in paragraph 1.2 of the *Ministerial Code*, as we have seen. Apart from the assertion of collective responsibility, the potential reasons the text deals with are flexible matters of personal judgement for the individual minister concerned and the Prime Minister, based on estimations of the political position. It is not clear that they should be in the *Manual*.

II. THE CIVIL SERVICE

The importance to codification of the Civil Service and those who work within it is a primary theme of this work. Officials have been important instigators of the process, and have been charged with the drafting. Understandably, given the perspective of this group and its importance to these texts, the Civil Service itself has been a prominent concern within this body of documents. This tendency manifests itself in many ways, some of which have already been highlighted in this work. An example of the Civil Service perspective comes in paragraphs 4.53 and 4.54 of *The Cabinet Manual*, which comprise an account of a senior official, 'The Cabinet Secretary'.

Paragraph 4.53 opens by stating that 'The Cabinet Secretary is the head of the Cabinet Secretariat.' Next it asserts that Cabinet Secretaries are chosen 'by the Prime Minister on the advice of the retiring Cabinet Secretary and the First Civil Service Commission'. It offers no supporting evidence for this view. Nor does it

[2] A Blick, *Beyond Magna Carta: a constitution for the United Kingdom* (Oxford, Hart Publishing, 2015) 157–61.

explain what is meant by 'advice' and what a Prime Minister who does not like the 'advice' provided can do. Premiers have sought other opinions in the past, and it is right they should be able to do so.[3] Perhaps 'advice' is meant to imply the product of a sounding process of some kind, to which others can add their views—but the overall impression is of a desire to place the Cabinet Secretary and the Civil Service Commission at the centre of events, framing the overall consideration that takes place, and that anyone else who has influence must do so through them, and not through some other route or direct intervention with the Prime Minister. This account is probably more an aspiration expressed by those directly involved in the drafting of the *Manual* than an account of precisely what happens in practice. Footnote 32 to paragraph 4.53 describes how, since 1983, the same person held both this post and that of Head of the Home Civil Service. It then refers to an announcement of 11 October 2011—shortly before the appearance of the first edition of *The Cabinet Manual*—that, starting in January 2012, the two offices would be separated, each held by a different person. However, it offers no further account of how this division might work in practice. Subsequently, the two titles have been recombined.

Paragraph 4.54 recounts that the Cabinet Secretary is present at every Cabinet meeting, 'unless unavoidably absent'. The holder of the post 'is responsible for the smooth running of Cabinet meetings and for preparing records of its discussions and decisions'. This role includes 'responsibility for advising the Prime Minister on all questions connected with the appointment and organisation of Cabinet committees, including membership and terms of reference'. This statement is a firm assertion not only of the need for the Cabinet Secretary to support the Prime Minister in the organisation of the Cabinet system, but also of the need for the premier to involve the Cabinet Secretary in every aspect of this business.

These passages from *The Cabinet Manual* concern a particular post. Codification has also encompassed wider systemic regulation of the official machine, as far back as the time of *Estacode* (see Chapter 1, section II.). The *Ministerial Code*, as we have seen, requires ministers to 'uphold the impartiality of the Civil Service'. They must not ask officials to carry out actions that would violate the *Civil Service Code* (discussed below) or the Constitutional Reform and Governance Act 2010 (paragraph 5.1). Though ultimately ministers make their own choices, and officials are not given a monopoly on providing advice, ministers are required to take the views of civil servants seriously. Paragraph 5.2 of the *Ministerial Code* refers to an obligation upon ministers 'to give fair consideration and due weight to informed and impartial advice from civil servants' alongside 'other considerations and advice in reaching policy decisions'. Ministers, the Code stipulates, should also take into account a text called *Principles of Scientific Advice to Government*. These

[3] For an account of efforts of aides to Tony Blair to have an input into the decision early in the twentieth century, and the tension that arose with the then outgoing Cabinet Secretary, see J Powell, *The New Machiavelli: wielding power in the modern world* (London, The Bodley Head, 2010) 76–77.

requirements are constitutionally important, but assessing whether they have been adhered to is a difficult task.

The *Ministerial Code* goes on, in paragraph 5.3, to set out the principles surrounding Accounting Officers. It notes that official departmental heads and chief executives of executive agencies are appointed to these posts. The role entails 'a personal responsibility for propriety and regularity of the public finances' within the remit of the individual concerned. The specific concerns involved are 'keeping proper accounts … avoidance of waste and extravagance' and 'the efficient and effective use of resources'. In what is an important exception to the general principle of Civil Service responsibility to ministers, 'Accounting Officers answer personally to the Committee of Public Accounts' over these issues, though in the overall context of 'Ministerial accountability to Parliament for the policies, actions and conduct of their departments.' Paragraph 5.4 explains that Accounting Officers have a duty to ensure that 'appropriate advice is tendered to Ministers on all matters of financial propriety and regularity and more broadly as to all considerations of prudent and economical administration, efficiency and effectiveness and value for money'. Referencing a document to which we shall return, *Managing Public Money*, the *Code* deals with the possibility that a minister at the head of a department might intend to carry out an 'action which would involve a transaction which the Accounting Officer considers would breach the requirements of propriety or regularity' (see Chapter 8, section IV.; see also Chapter 1, section V.). In such circumstances Accounting Officers explain their concerns in writing. If the minister is determined to continue regardless, paragraph 5.5 stipulates, then Accounting Officers 'seek a written instruction to take the action in question'. This practice is an insurance policy for the officials involved, placing on the record that they were acting on orders over which they had personal reservations. It applies not only over issues of propriety, but also over supposed failure to secure value for money. By insisting on this 'notification process', Accounting Officers are able to demonstrate to the Committee of Public Accounts that they do 'not bear personal responsibility for the action concerned'.

Central to the codification of the Civil Service, and demonstrating the potential power of brevity, the *Civil Service Code*[4] is two pages long. Unlike many of the documents discussed here, the basis for which is the Royal Prerogative, in its current edition it is now issued under statutory authority, provided by the Constitutional Reform and Governance Act 2010 (Part 1). Paragraph 20 of the text explains that the *Code* forms 'part of the contractual relationship between' civil servants and their employer (paragraph 20). It applies to civil servants working in the domestic departments in Whitehall, as well as to civil servants employed in Wales, Scotland and England (but not Northern Ireland) and in 'Non Ministerial Departments'. Excluded from its coverage are officials attached to the Scottish and

[4] Civil Service, *The Civil Service Code* (London, Civil Service, 2010).

Welsh devolved governments and associated Agencies, which have codes of their own, as do the Civil Service of Northern Ireland and the UK Diplomatic Service (footnote 1 to paragraph 2).

The *Civil Service Code* describes the Civil Service as 'an integral and key part of the government of the United Kingdom', the function of which is to support the 'Government of the day in developing and implementing its policies, and in delivering public services'. This account makes it clear that the Whitehall machine is expected to do more than perform the role that was once most closely associated with the senior Civil Service, that is produce well-written papers for ministers considering policy options. The reference to 'Government of the day' is significant too, for reasons discussed below. The *Civil Service Code* goes on to iterate the core constitutional principle: that civil servants 'are accountable to Ministers, who in turn are accountable to Parliament' (paragraph 2). This reporting line can potentially create a conflict if a minister is—contrary to fundamental principles stated elsewhere—misleading Parliament and is enlisting a civil servant in this endeavour. Which rule should take precedence: Civil Service responsibility to the minister, or the requirement on ministers and civil servants to be open and truthful with Parliament? The *Civil Service Code* alludes to this tension, though only in a footnote, and not in a way that resolves it, with its statement that officials who provide advice to ministers 'should be aware of the constitutional significance of Parliament, and of the conventions governing the relationship between Parliament and Government' (footnote 3). The footnote does not explain what the 'constitutional significance of Parliament' or these 'conventions' are, nor does it explain whether they have priority over the principle of Civil Service accountability to ministers. At this point, brevity may be a fault. The *Civil Service Code* records another qualification in footnote 2 to paragraph 2, explaining that civil servants can be accountable not to a minister but to 'the office holder in charge of their organisation', something that is stated in their contract.

A key principle of the Civil Service, of complex provenance but often linked to the so-called Northcote-Trevelyan Report of 1854, is that its personnel are recruited on 'merit' and through 'fair and open competition'. After asserting this tenet the *Civil Service Code* goes on to describe an expectation that civil servants will perform their functions with a 'commitment to the Civil Service and its core values'. These 'core values' are 'integrity, honesty, objectivity and impartiality'. Integrity entails prioritising 'public service' above personal gain. Honesty means 'being truthful and open'; while objectivity involves founding 'advice and decisions' on 'rigorous analysis of the evidence'. Lastly, impartiality requires civil servants to act 'solely according to the merits of the case' and to serve different governments 'equally well' regardless of their party complexion (paragraph 3). Paragraph 4 of the *Civil Service Code* then iterates that adherence to the 'core values' helps ensure the maintenance of 'good government' and the quality of performance among officials, and as a consequence enables the Civil Service 'to gain and retain the respect of Ministers, Parliament, the public and its customers'. The Code does not explain who 'customers' are in this context, or how they differ from, for instance, ministers or the public, and how they fit into the accountability relationship explained elsewhere in the text.

The *Civil Service Code* then goes on to expand upon the meaning of these 'core values', engaging some important constitutional points in the process. Integrity includes handling public money in a fashion that is both appropriate and efficient; and maintaining 'accurate official records' and managing information in a way that is as open as can be managed 'within the legal framework'. Civil servants are required to adhere to the law and 'uphold the administration of justice' (paragraph 6). Integrity means also that civil servants should not abuse their office to further their private interests or those of their associates. They must not 'disclose official information without authority', a requirement that remains in force even when they are no longer employed in Whitehall (paragraph 7).

An important part of the 'Honesty' value is that officials 'must not … deceive or knowingly mislead Ministers, Parliament or others'. The Code once again fails to explain here how civil servants should deal with a circumstance in which a minister wants them to mislead Parliament, the public or those fitting into the mysterious category of 'others'. 'Objectivity' includes within it basing decisions and advice on evidence and expert counsel, and not overlooking 'inconvenient facts or relevant considerations' (paragraph 10). A clear implication is that officials must bring information to the attention of ministers, even if it appears to call into question particular courses of action towards which ministers may be predisposed. A stated corollary to this requirement is that if a decision has been made then civil servants must loyally implement it and not block it in any way (paragraph 11). In its 'Political Impartiality' category, the *Civil Service Code* stresses that the personal political orientation of officials should not impact upon their performance of their role. They should behave in a fashion that merits and sustains 'the confidence of Ministers' yet simultaneously guarantees that they will be able to form an equivalent attachment to possible future ministers. They should not allow their private affiliations to determine their actions, the use of public resources or the counsel they provide (paragraph 15).

If they feel they 'are being required to act in a way which conflicts with' the Code, there is a procedure that civil servants can follow, though it does not create a means by which people outside Whitehall can highlight any concerns they may have in this regard. Officials can in the first instance raise an issue with their 'line manager or someone else in [their] line management chain'. If civil servants do not want to follow this path, there are individuals designated within departments whom they can approach (paragraph 17). The same procedure applies if an official believes others are involved in inappropriate behaviour, though if they suspect that the law is being violated, they must report it to law enforcement agencies (paragraph 18). Having exhausted this route, if still unsatisfied, officials can address the Civil Service Commission, a body that can also potentially deal with issues immediately without the other procedures having been followed. Ultimately, if civil servants do not achieve an outcome with which they are content and decide 'they cannot carry out the instructions [they] have been given', they are required to 'resign' (paragraph 19). This account demonstrates that civil servants are not, as is sometimes claimed, independent. They cannot, ultimately, refuse to carry out a particular instruction if within the law and their formal objections are quashed. The procedure described suggests an answer to the question regarding what course of action an official asked to mislead Parliament by a minister can follow. That official can complain, and if she does not achieve the conclusion she wants, leave her post.

Also issued under the Constitutional Reform and Governance Act 2010, a longer document than the *Civil Service Code* is the *Civil Service Management Code* (CSMC; 91 pages).[5] It covers a wider ranger of issues, some of a more technical nature, alongside constitutionally significant material. The CSMC has chapters on the taking up of appointments by civil servants; equal opportunities policy; health and safety; then—perhaps most significant for this work—'Conduct and Discipline'; 'The Senior Civil Service'; 'Management and Development'; 'Pay and Allowances'; 'Expenses'; working hours and leave; the moving around of staff; departure from the Civil Service; and, lastly, support from public sources for legal representation and appeals procedures.

As we have seen, competitive recruitment on merit is a core feature of the impartial Civil Service of the UK. Paragraph 1.5.3 of the CSMC describes how the process for those seeking entry into the Graduate Fast Stream works. The first stage takes place on-line. Initially, candidates take part in an 'online self-assessment of suitability'. They then complete 'Verbal and Numerical Reasoning' and 'Competency' questionnaires. Those who meet the necessary standard in these last two tests then attend 'an electronic in-tray test (the e-Tray)', arranged at a number of locations across the country. The most successful candidates at e-Tray can then attend the 'Fast Stream Assessment Centre (FSAC)', which measures their 'potential' across a set of different 'key competencies'. If they pass through FSAC they can then secure employment in the 'Central Departments'—the new name for the Home Civil Service. If seeking a place in other parts of the Civil Service, such as the Diplomatic Service, they have to complete one last stage, the 'Final Selection Board'. Paragraph 1.5.6 deals with the academic qualifications required of applicants. Those seeking to enter via the 'open competition' need, 'usually', to have as a minimum 'a Second Class Honours Degree or equivalent'. There is no reference to a requirement for relevance in choice of subject, or for a preference for having attended certain academic institutions over others. For other fast streams—Statistician and Science and Engineering—'the degree must be in a relevant subject'. For the Economist Fast Stream, entrants need to have a 2:1 either in economics, or in 'a joint or mixed degree of which at least half the courses are core economics'. For those seeking to enter the 'Technology in Business' programme, a 2:1 'in a specified discipline' is necessary. Paragraph 1.5.9 states that 'Most posts in the Fast Stream are open to EU and Commonwealth citizens.'

[5] Cabinet Office, *Civil Service Management Code* (Cabinet Office, London, 2015).

In Chapter 4, entitled 'Conduct and Discipline', CSMC reiterates some of the core constitutional principles contained in the *Civil Service Code*. It explains:

> Civil servants are servants of the Crown and owe a duty of loyal service to the Crown as their employer. Since constitutionally the Crown acts on the advice of Ministers who are answerable for their departments and agencies in Parliament, that duty is, subject to the provisions of the Civil Service Code ... owed to the duly constituted Government. (paragraph 4.1.1)

In expanding upon the various stipulations contained in the *Civil Service Code*, one particular reference CSMC makes is to 'Leaked Select Committee Reports'. If civil servants receive such documents, CSMC prohibits them from using them or passing them on to others. Interestingly, given their constitutional position, officials are required, CSMC notes, to 'return the report without delay to the Clerk of the relevant Committee'—an official, rather than a politician such as the chair or other member of the committee. With the report safely back with the clerk, CSMC goes on, 'only then' may civil servants 'inform their Ministers or Assembly Secretaries' about the unauthorised release. The same rules apply at devolved level (paragraph 4.2.10). Their purpose seems to be to protect Parliament against pre-emption by the executive, possibly involving collusion between a member of a select committee from a party of government and a minister. Such a prospect presents a clear example of the duty to the minister clashing with other constitutional principles, and CSMC—in stating that the civil servant should act first and inform the minister afterwards—seems to lean towards the latter.

Chapter 4 of CSMC includes within it 'The Business Appointment Rules for Civil Servants' (4.3 Annex A). While other parts of the Code are concerned with how people join the Civil Service and how they should conduct themselves while within it, these rules cover what they do upon leaving its employ. The twin principles the rules seek to promote are (i) that there is a 'public interest' in individuals who have worked in the Civil Service being able to transfer their experience to other areas, but (ii) that when doing so, 'there should be no cause for justified public concern, criticism, or misinterpretation' (4.3 Annex A, paragraph 2). The word 'justified' is an important qualification. All civil servants, including special advisers, are subject to the rules (4.3 Annex A, paragraph 4). Their purpose is to prevent 'any reasonable concerns' of three types. The first is that officials might, while going about their work, 'be influenced' by the prospect of obtaining an appointment outside the Civil Service at a later stage. The second is that someone, having moved on from the Civil Service, might seek 'improperly' to use personal connections or knowledge obtained while within it. The third concern is that an individual outside employer could obtain inappropriate benefit through recruiting a former civil servant who has knowledge about possible future policies or rival operations, acquired during the former civil servant's period of public office (4.3 Annex A, paragraph 3). The precise way in which the rules apply varies according to the 'seniority' of the person involved (4.3 Annex A paragraph 7). High-level departures are scrutinised by the 'Advisory Committee on Business Appointments'.

It advises the Prime Minister, with whom the ultimate authority rests (4.3 Annex A paragraph 8). The potential exists to impose various waiting periods and conditions that relate to the lobbying of departments after leaving them.

The documents considered so far are certainly not the only texts applying to civil servants. There is, for instance, a *Competency Framework*[6] that describes a series of 'competencies' expected of officials, grouped into three 'Strategic' clusters: 'Setting Direction', 'Engaging People' and 'Delivering Results'. It would be possible to fill much space considering the content and value of such documentation. However, for practical reasons it is now appropriate to move on to a specific type of civil servant, the regulation of which has important implications for the underlying values of the system.

A. Special Advisers

A significant source of pressure for codification in Whitehall has been the use of special advisers to ministers.[7] On the surface, this category of civil servant has received attention out of all proportion to the numbers involved. Yet tendencies such as their closeness to ministers, and the delicate tasks in which they are often engaged, help explain the interest special advisers have generated. First introduced by the Labour Prime Minister Harold Wilson in 1964, special advisers differ from regular officials in that they are appointed on a basis of patronage, are attached expressly to a particular individual serving as minister, can have open party-political allegiance and are only temporary employees. Their anomalous position has led to a variety of regulations being included across different texts. The *Ministerial Code*, for instance, states that, other than the Prime Minister, 'Cabinet Ministers may each appoint up to two special advisers'. It is possible for the Prime Minister to permit other ministers who go to Cabinet on a regular basis to recruit a single special adviser. If ministers have extra duties then 'additional advisers may be allowed'. Every special adviser appointment is dependent upon the agreement, in writing, in advance, of the premier (paragraph 3.2).

Special advisers, the *Ministerial Code* stipulates, have an obligation to the entire government, rather than solely to the minister who appoints them. While the Prime Minister approves appointments, 'responsibility for the management and conduct of special advisers, including discipline, rests with the Minister' who recruits them. Ministers are 'accountable to the Prime Minister, Parliament and

[6] *Civil Service Competency Framework 2012–2017* (London, Civil Service Human Resources, *c*. 2012).

[7] The following draws on A Blick, *People Who Live in the Dark: the history of the special adviser in British politics* (London, Methuen, 2004). For other work on special advisers, see, eg, R Hazell and B Yong, *Special Advisers: Who they are, what they do and why they matter* (Oxford, Hart Publishing, 2014); and N Hillman, *In Defence of Special Advisers: Lessons from Personal Experience* (London, Institute for Government, 2014).

the public' for the way in which they handle their special advisers. Premiers can also remove special advisers from their posts if they choose (paragraph 3.3). The Code requires the Government to issue to Parliament every year an account of the 'numbers, names and paybands of special advisers, the appointment Minister and the overall paybill' (paragraph 3.4). This stipulation is an illustration of how the tendency towards transparency is self-sustaining. It drives the publication of a document such as the *Ministerial Code*, including within it details about the working and rules of government, as well as a requirement for the regular publication of more information still.

Special advisers have a code specifically devoted to them.[8] The *Code of Conduct for Special Advisers* opens by explaining that '[s]pecial advisers are a critical part of the team supporting Ministers'. Their role is to 'add a political dimension to the advice and assistance available to Ministers'. The value of special advisers to ministers, who naturally have a close interest in party political matters, is plain. But the *Code* then points out a merit connected to special advisers: safeguarding the professional standards of permanent civil servants through carrying out tasks it would be inappropriate for career officials to execute. As the *Code* states, a purpose of special advisers is 'reinforcing the political impartiality of the permanent Civil Service by distinguishing the source of political advice and support' (paragraph 1). It re-emphasises this point in paragraph 2 when noting that special advisers can 'help Ministers on matters where the work of government and the work of the government party overlap and where it would be inappropriate for permanent civil servants to become involved'. Yet there are limits even to how far special advisers are supposed to engage in party politics; and sometimes they need protection. For instance, there were complaints that Conservative special advisers had been inappropriately pressurised into taking part in the 2014 Rochester and Strood by-election campaign.

Though special advisers are unlike regular officials in the way they are recruited, their tenure and the rules governing their operation, they are nonetheless categorised as a type of civil servant. Moreover, it is imperative to their effectiveness that they work within the machine, rather than at a remove from it. Hence the emphasis in paragraph 2 of the Code on special advisers being 'fully integrated into the functioning of government'. It describes them as 'part of the team working closely alongside civil servants to deliver Ministers' priorities'. This passage raises an important issue involving the impact of the special adviser. The UK has never formally adopted a *cabinet* system of the type associated with government on the European Continental mainland, under which ministers construct their own inner teams, mixing seconded career officials and outsiders. But when special advisers first came into being in 1964, this bureaucratic model was in vogue. Their introduction assimilated some of the features of the *cabinet* system into the UK constitution, though it stopped short of a full adoption of the *cabinet*. Many

[8] Cabinet Office, *Code of Conduct for Special Advisers* (Cabinet Office, London, 2015).

members of the core team can remain in post when a new minister takes office, even if there has been a change in the party or parties of government. But special advisers represent the potential for discontinuity.

Special advisers are chosen and appointed by a particular minister (subject to prime-ministerial approval), for whom they work directly. The fortunes of aide and employing politician are closely connected. If the latter prospers, the former is likely to also. Equally, if the minister loses office, the future of the special adviser is uncertain. A successor, even if of the same political party, may not keep on that same special adviser. Often special advisers are already personally connected to ministers before they start working for them, and they are frequently members of their innermost groups of personal and political allies. For all these reasons it can at times appear that special advisers prioritise personal loyalty to the minister over all else. Potentially this tendency can become destabilising, with rival camps within the administration battling against each other. Seeking to anticipate and discourage this problem, paragraph 2 of the *Code of Conduct for Special Advisers* cautions that special advisers 'are appointed to serve the Prime Minister and the Government as a whole, not just their appointing Minister'. The point appears again in paragraph 10, with its statement that special advisers 'are employed to serve the objectives of the Prime Minister, the Government and the Minister(s) for whom they work'. This statement seems to imply that the 'objectives' of all three are always the same. Yet if they were, there would be no need for such an exhortation. The Code offers no guidance as to what should happen if and when 'objectives' do diverge.

Paragraph 3 refers again to the need for the effective integration of special advisers, insisting that they 'should work closely with the ministerial team and with other civil servants, and establish mutual relationships of confidence and trust'. At times—though certainly not always—over the decades, tensions have developed between special advisers and career officials. The former can regard the latter as obstructing the objectives of the minister and party of government, while the latter can perceive the former as interlopers and a threat to the integrity of their institution and its values. This stipulation about close working, confidence and trust, like that in the previous paragraph requiring support for more than just the appointing minister, is an attempt, based on an observation of past difficulties, to warn against these problems. Such declarations are not necessarily successful. Paragraph 3 then provides examples of some of the tasks special advisers can perform. The unacknowledged origin of this list lies in a speech that Harold Wilson gave in 1975 describing his use of special advisers. It was drawn on for the *Special Adviser Model Contract* issued in 1997, and has been updated subsequently with the issue of each new *Code*. The tasks it sets out include providing 'assistance on any aspect of departmental business'—a potentially expansive category. Special advisers can also carry out 'policy planning', write speeches, 'liaise with the Party, brief party representatives and parliamentarians on issues of government policy', brief the media on the position of the minister on given issues (with ministerial approval) and 'liaise with outside interest groups'.

The *Code* then moves in paragraph 4 to the sensitive area of interactions with permanent officials. It describes how special advisers can operate when 'working with other civil servants'. An important qualifying phrase here is that they do so 'on behalf of their Minister'. They can 'convey' the 'views, instructions and priorities' of Ministers to officials, 'including on issues of presentation'. They can ask civil servants 'to prepare and provide information and data'; and 'hold meetings with officials' to consider advice being submitted to ministers. Lastly, they can 'review and comment on—but not suppress or supplant—advice being prepared for Ministers by civil servants'. The limitations on special advisers when dealing with officials come in paragraph 5. They are not permitted to request that civil servants carry out an action that violates either the *Civil Service Code* or their departmental rules. They cannot 'authorise expenditure of public funds or have responsibility for budgets'; neither can they 'exercise any power in relation to the management of any part of the Civil Service' other than a fellow special adviser. Nor can they wield any other 'statutory or prerogative' authority. Paragraph 6 adds that special advisers 'should not be involved in the line management of civil servants or in matters affecting a civil servant's career'. These 'matters' include 'recruitment, promotion, reward and discipline'. Lastly, special advisers do not 'have access to personnel files of civil servants'.

Most of the paragraph 5 restrictions arise from obligations imposed by the Constitutional Reform and Governance Act 2010. This statute, which requires the Prime Minister to issue a special adviser code, stipulates that certain requirements be included within it (section 8(5)). They are that

> a special adviser may not … authorise the expenditure of public funds … exercise any power in relation to the management of any part of the civil service of the State … otherwise exercise any power conferred by or under … any … Act or any power under Her Majesty's prerogative.

In other words, these rules have to be included in the special adviser code by law. But is it possible that other parts of the text, for which there is no statutory requirement, have the effect of undermining or contradicting the obligatory components? The prohibition relating to 'management' requires close consideration. The *Code* does not specify what 'management' means (and the 2010 Act itself does not provide an entirely clear account). But some of the functions described in paragraph 4 (above) could be seen as having a management character to them.

Qualifying phrases, however, are employed. Special advisers are described only as conveying instructions from ministers, not strictly issuing them themselves; as requesting, not ordering, the production of information; and as discussing or commenting on advice, which they cannot block or replace. Moreover, all of these actions are carried out 'on behalf of their Minister'. The ultimate source of significance for a special adviser is the position as trusted ministerial confidant and envoy. The minister may entrust the aide with express tasks; and the special adviser may also be sufficiently close to the minister to be able to anticipate what the minister's response would be to a particular circumstance without needing to ask. Indeed, this ability is a clear value of special advisers in the high-pressured political environment. The special adviser, then, could be seen as an extension of the minister. On this interpretation, if any of the paragraph 4 functions are managerial, they represent management by the minister, not the special adviser. However, from the point of view of recipients of communications, delivered to them personally by the special adviser, not the minister who is the supposed source of the authority, the distinction may not be entirely clear. It may seem at times that special advisers are using their connection to the minister to arrogate power to themselves. Nonetheless, special advisers who overplay their hand in this regard may eventually find themselves in difficulties, alienating themselves from the department and other parts of government, and potentially undermining the vital personal confidence of the minister.

Aside from these restrictions, the *Code* specifically requires that special advisers should have permanent Civil Service support staff allocated to them to carry out work 'of a non-political nature'. Special advisers are allowed to direct these staff 'in relation to their day-to-day work for them' and feed in to their 'performance appraisals', though these reviews are ultimately written by career officials (paragraph 6). They can, if the minister agrees, see 'all papers submitted to Ministers', subject to their having the correct security clearance, to the rules regarding the 'papers of a previous Administration' and to the bar on their reading personnel material (paragraph 7). While special advisers are bound by the *Civil Service Code* generally, they are not governed by the parts relating to 'impartiality and objectivity', or those rules that require them to be able to command 'the confidence of future governments' (paragraph 8). The idea of complete exemption from being impartial and objective is curious, since these terms have applications that extend beyond concerns about whether or not an individual is politically partisan, involving matters of basic judgement and behaviour. Working to further a particular party should not preclude a fundamental ability to behave in an impartial and objective fashion.

The appointment and retention of special advisers is subject to prime-ministerial approval. Their tenure ceases 'at the end of the Administration … or when the appointing Minister' exits government or changes jobs inside the Government. The appointing minister is responsible for managing them, and for their conduct (paragraph 9). Special advisers should seek to maintain the 'political impartiality of other civil servants' and 'should not use official resources for party political activity' (paragraph 10). The Code forbids them from disclosing 'official information … received in confidence' (paragraph 11). Special advisers are potentially allowed to provide media briefings with a partisan dimension that career officials would not. But 'purely party political matters must be handled by the Party machine'. Special advisers must coordinate on these issues with No 10 (paragraph 12). Any dealings with the media require approval from the minister (paragraph 13); and special advisers are not allowed to 'take public part in political controversy'. The Code obliges them to 'observe discretion and express comment with moderation, avoiding personal attacks'. They 'would not normally speak in public' on behalf of either their department or minister (paragraph 14).

Paragraph 18 i allows for special advisers, with the agreement of the minister and the premier, to 'be publicly identified as a candidate or prospective candidate for the United Kingdom Parliament'. This represents a clear change from the previous, 2010 Code,[9] which stated that 'before a special adviser is publicly identified as a candidate or prospective candidate for Parliament ... either by adoption by a political party or in any other way, he/she must first resign their [*sic*] appointment' (paragraph 20 i). Again the executive was, through this alteration, deploying its role as code-maker to change the rules unilaterally, or at least legitimise changes to them, and it is difficult to view the text purely as a neutral reflection of existing practice. The Code then seeks to confine activities involving 'this new role' for special advisers who become parliamentary candidates to 'their own time'. It stipulates that they should not engage within Whitehall in issues connected to their prospective constituency, and should resign when the 'short campaign period' commences (paragraph 18 i). Special advisers can also take part in local politics, including serving on local authorities. As councillors, however, they are supposed to avoid involvement in public controversy (paragraphs 19 and 20). The Code concludes by describing how the *Business Appointment Rules for Civil Servants* apply to special advisers when exiting official employment (paragraphs 21–22); and describing the practices surrounding the publication of memoirs (paragraphs 23–24).

B. Election Guidance

Further codification arises from the need to regulate conduct during General Election campaigns. They are periods in which partisan conflict intensifies. They present challenges for Civil Service impartiality, given that ministers—to whom officials are accountable—remain in post but as party politicians are closely involved in the struggle for the control of government taking place at that time (see also Chapter 9, section I.).

With this issue in mind, a practice has developed for the Cabinet Office to issue guidance, which now appears publicly online. The most recent edition, *General Election Guidance 2015*, appeared on 30 March of the named year.[10] It is 39 pages long. The Preface sets out the central purpose: to preserve Civil Service 'impartiality' and to be perceived as so doing; as well as to prevent 'any criticism of an inappropriate use of official resources' (paragraph 1). The 'General Principles' of the guidance are that governments have a duty to continue governing, and ministers are still responsible for the departments they head. Crucial activities need to take place; yet ministers must 'observe discretion in initiating any new

[9] Cabinet Office, *Code of Conduct for Special Advisers* (Cabinet Office, London, 2010).

[10] Cabinet Office, *General Election Guidance 2015* (London, Cabinet Office, 2015).

action of a continuing or long-term character'. In areas where a possible different government might have views at variance with the present administration, it is better—if possible—not to select a particular course of action before the poll (paragraph 3). The guidance presents itself as expanding upon the basic values set out in the *Civil Service Code*, which apply to officials continuously, for use in the specific circumstances of a General Election. Civil servants should not engage in actions that might cast doubt upon their being politically impartial, or which might encourage claims that 'public resources' were being diverted towards the ends of a political party. 'Departmental activity', moreover, ought not to create the impression of being in competition for publicity with the General Election campaign itself. Lastly, ministers 'must not' bring about violation of these principles through utilising 'Government resources' for ends that are party political; and they should maintain Civil Service 'political impartiality' (paragraph 5).

The guidance then deals with a succession of specific areas in which issues might arise. An important theme running through it is that officials will need to continue to interact with the outside world, for instance through providing information about government activity, but that they should do so in a way that does not compromise their impartiality or entail the misappropriation, actual or merely perceived, of public resources. There are attempts to distinguish the actions of ministers as public office holders, to whom the Civil Service can properly provide support, from their roles as party politicians. The document also reflects the relatively reduced importance of the UK Parliament, and of the UK tier of governance as a whole, in the changed UK constitutional landscape. Dissolution at Westminster is not directly relevant to the devolved institutions, or to the European Union (alongside a variety of other regional and international organisations): they continue to operate according to their own agendas, taking decisions that may be of immense internal significance to the entire UK, particularly in the case of the European Union. The guidance seeks to accommodate this persistence (see Section M, 'European Union and International Business'; and Section N, 'The Devolved Administrations').

Section F, 'Cabinet and Official Documents', provides for the handling of papers issued to ministers during the campaign. If there is a 'new Government' after the Election, 'all Cabinet and Ministerial Cabinet Committee documents issued to Ministers should be destroyed' (section F, paragraph 3). The guidance does not address the issue of what should happen if there were to be a transition from a coalition government to a different government, but formed wholly or partly by a party that had taken part in the previous coalition. This scenario was fully plausible in 2015 when the guidance was issued, and in fact came to pass, when a single-party Conservative Government succeeded the Conservative-Liberal Democrat coalition. The text also repeats, in a section on 'Government Decisions', the important convention that 'it is customary for Ministers to observe discretion in initiating any action of a continuing or long-term character' (section G, paragraph 2). It would be a serious problem if, during a period when Parliament was dissolved and the electorate was about to determine who might form the next government, those who were ministers for the time being made controversial use of delegated legislative powers vested in them. Section G, paragraph 3 refers to a further document containing guidance on the issuing of statutory instruments.[11]

III. CONCLUSION

The UK executive has lain at the centre of codification. While the process of writing down constitutional arrangements in the documents considered here has now spread beyond Whitehall, it still provides a substantial portion of this body of literature. These texts reveal that the executive is far from homogeneous. It contains within it a variety of different individuals and entities, in possession of their own distinctive principles and operational practices. These diverse groups include individual ministers, departments, civil servants as a whole and special advisers. At times there can be tension between them. For instance, the needs of ministers, who are politicians, may conflict with the impartiality of the Civil Service. Within the Civil Service, there are potential strains between special advisers and regular career officials. Codes are a means of defining the roles of the different groups, and of managing their relationships with each other. While the groups may have diverse perspectives, it is in their shared interest that they should be able to work together, and texts may help them to do so. Another feature of these codes is that they demonstrate the importance of external forces and events in their impact on the executive. They suggest that it is a reactive entity, subject to contingencies, as well as an initiator. Codes display a perceived requirement on the part of the executive to display to outside opinion the pervasiveness of proper practice. The need to deal with institutions such as Parliament manifests itself, for instance in the provisions regarding Accounting Officers. The challenge posed by General Elections to the functioning of Whitehall has necessitated a variety of written provisions for officials, including a document specifically dedicated to this subject. No governmental institution exists in isolation; and when it codifies, the outputs reflect the importance of these outside connections.

Increasingly, the environment without the executive has itself become a subject of codification. The desire to describe the system in writing has spread to other constitutional branches. In some cases the executive has sought to describe its relationship with other entities, such as Parliament and the judiciary. In others, it has made agreements with bodies encapsulating their intended mode of interaction—in particular the devolved administrations. Sometimes it attempts to define processes—such as elections and the formation of governments—that take in multiple arenas at once. And in a number of further cases, institutions other than the executive have codified areas of interest to them. Our first focus beyond the executive is upon Parliament, examined in Chapter 8.

[11] Office of Public Sector Information, *Statutory Instrument Practice* (London, Stationery Office, 2006).

8

Parliament and Executive Accountability

THE FIRST SENTENCE of the opening paragraph of *The Cabinet Manual*[1] begins with the words 'The UK is a parliamentary democracy'. That a text commissioned by a Prime Minister for purposes already set out should commence in this way demonstrates the importance of Parliament to the UK constitution. The *Manual* describes this institution as 'sovereign'—a contestable claim discussed in the Introduction to this book—and 'supreme to all other government institutions'. It then notes that Parliament comprises 'the Sovereign, the House of Commons and the House of Lords'; and that the UK has 'an executive drawn from and accountable to Parliament' (paragraph 1). The description in the following paragraph suggests the complex interplay of forces involved in the concept of parliamentary democracy. It refers to a '[c]onstitutional convention ... that executive power is exercised by the Sovereign's Government, which has a democratic mandate to govern'. The text does not make the point explicitly, but it implies that the 'democratic mandate' to which it refers is derived from Parliament. Presumably it comes about because one of the three components of Parliament, the House of Commons, is elected (the other two, the House of Lords and the monarch, are not). This 'democratic mandate', then, if we accept the concept, is indirect: it is derived from voters but via Parliament. Paragraph 2 goes on to suggest how, precisely, this conferral from Parliament takes place. Government members 'are normally' present either in the Commons or the Lords, 'and the Government is directly accountable to Parliament'. A government, furthermore, 'holds office by virtue of its ability to command the confidence of the House of Commons'. We shall return to the 'confidence' concept, but it suffices to say at this point that there are layers of complexity beneath this statement of the basis for legitimate executive authority in the UK.

The final link in the democratic chain leads on to the public, or at least those members of it who are allowed to vote. In the UK there is no formal concept of popular sovereignty, but in the democratic era it is axiomatic that governmental legitimacy is in some way derived from below. The *Manual* explains that 'Elections'—by which it means General Elections—'are held at least every five years to ensure broad and continued accountability to the people'. The terms 'broad and continued' are not precise; and there is no clear allowance here for 'the

[1] Cabinet Office, *The Cabinet Manual: A guide to the laws, conventions and rules on the operation of government*, 1st edn (London, Cabinet Office, 2011).

people' to participate in democratic processes in between the occasions on which they are allowed to vote for a Member of Parliament (MP). The paragraph closes by referring to entities that in practice play an important part in the operation of the UK constitution, though they are not official governmental organs as such. It states that while '[e]lection candidates can stand independently ... they usually represent political parties'. Moreover, 'party numbers in the House of Commons determine the composition of the Government' (paragraph 2). The *Manual* thereby suggests an embedded status for parties within the UK constitution. As a view of political parties it has an elite slant, treating them as a means of determining the membership of Parliament and the make-up of administrations, rather than providing a route to wider involvement in the system. This outlook, however, fits with the avowed perspective of the *Manual* as from the executive point of view.

The overall account discussed above shows that Parliament sits at the centre of a complex network of relationships that are the essence of UK-level democracy. Moreover, crucial features of this system of parliamentary democracy are founded neither in a written constitution nor in statute. For instance, paragraph 2 of the *Manual* states that the principle of the Government's having executive power by virtue of some kind of 'democratic mandate'—the core of our system—is a '[c]onstitutional convention'. Codes are the closest we get to an official written account of some of the rules. Given the potential importance of codification to conventions, as already considered, any texts dealing with Parliament and parliamentary democracy merit close investigation. This chapter considers the considerable body of documents that already exists.

I. INTERNAL ARRANGEMENTS

Both Houses of Parliament issue codes regulating the conduct of their members, with some significant constitutional components to them.[2] Section II of the House of Commons *Code of Conduct*, 'Duties of Members', is of interest in this regard. It opens with reference to the requirement of loyalty to 'Her Majesty the Queen, her heirs and successors' (paragraph 4), and then the need for MPs to 'uphold the law, including the general law against discrimination' (paragraph 5). Paragraph 6 then raises some interesting constitutional issues. It states that MPs are subject to 'a general duty' that they 'act in the interests of the nation as a whole' as well as having a 'special duty to their constituents'. It does not explain which of these loyalties should come first in the event of a clash. But it does touch upon a perennial tension in the role of the elected representatives, and the extent to which they should make decisions on a basis of their more general judgement, or be guided by the opinions and interests of the locale of their constituency.

[2] House of Commons, *The Code of Conduct together with The Guide to the Rules relating to the Conduct of Members* (London, Stationery Office, 2015, 1076).

The issue of nationhood is of heightened relevance at a time when territorial distinctions within the UK—and even within the Westminster Parliament—are of heightened importance. The 'English Votes for English Laws' mechanism incorporated into the Commons Standing Orders in 2015 accords different voting and participation rights to MPs according to the area in which they were elected, suggesting a lean away from a UK-wide conception of the loyalty of MPs.[3] Moreover, to use the word 'nation' in describing the UK as a whole is probably incorrect.[4] Different MPs will differ in their view as to which 'nation' they represent. Some may not regard themselves as having a duty to any nation. The 'General principles' section of the House of Lords *Code of Conduct* opens with an assertion of the need 'to be faithful and bear true allegiance to' the monarch and those who come after her (paragraph 6).[5] But, unlike the Commons *Code*, it does not then move to a requirement to 'uphold the law'. In describing the duties of members of the Lords, it does not refer to the interests of the nation or—for obvious reasons—of constituents, but deploys the phrase 'public interest' instead (paragraph 7).

Beyond these general duties, both codes subsequently set out a series of stipulations that are focused on ensuring that parliamentarians, in pursuit of financial or other gain, do not allow their integrity to become compromised or appear to be so; and that the reputation of the House in which they sit is not damaged by their behaviour. Critical concepts include that they should not, in their activities within Parliament, be subordinated to an outside interest; and that they should not misuse any special access with which their public office provides them. Both MPs and peers are required to adhere to transparency in registering their outside interests. These stipulations represent responses to a series of scandals with their roots in the 'sleaze' era of the mid-1990s, that recurred intermittently thereafter, and will probably continue to do so, perhaps triggering additions to these documents, and even fresh codification (see Chapter 2, sections II.B. and II.C.).

The Cabinet Manual contains its own account of arrangements within Parliament. Since the executive, responsible for authorship of the *Manual*, is able more readily to rely on the support of the Commons than the Lords, it potentially had an interest in stressing the authority of the former chamber over the latter. Paragraph 5.2 states a critical principle: 'The House of Commons has primacy over the House of Lords. It is the democratically elected institution of the United Kingdom and the Government derives its democratic mandate from its command of the confidence of the Commons.' Paragraph 5.2 goes on to assert that the Houses 'acknowledge various conventions governing the relationship between them, including in relation to the House of Commons, financial privilege and the operation of the Salisbury-Addison convention'. In support of this claim it references

[3] Cabinet Office, *English Votes for English Laws: An Explanatory Guide to Proposals* (Cabinet Office, London, 2015).

[4] For a discussion of these issues see L Colley, *Acts of Union and Disunion: What has Held the UK Together—and What is Dividing It?* (London, Profile, 2014).

[5] House of Lords, *Code of Conduct for Members of the House of Lords/Guide to the Code of Conduct/Code of Conduct for House of Lords Members' Staff* (London, Stationery Office, 2015) 3.

the Joint Committee on Conventions Report of 2006, *Conventions of the UK Parliament* (see Introduction).[6] As well as Salisbury-Addison (see further below), the *Manual* defines this primacy in terms of financial privilege, both of the ancient type and as contained in the Parliament Acts of 1911 and 1949 (paragraph 5.3); the other provisions for Commons legislative superiority provided for under those Acts (paragraph 5.4); and—a recent addition—the monopoly by the Commons of the ability to bring about General Elections before the five-year maximum under the Fixed-term Parliaments Act 2011 (paragraph 5.5).

As we have seen, the *Manual* cites a 2006 Report from the Joint Committee on Conventions as evidence that both Houses had a shared acceptance of the conventions applying to them. This Joint Committee (that is, a committee comprising members from both Houses) was charged with assessing 'the practicality of codifying the key conventions on the relationship between' the Lords and the Commons, while accepting the 'primacy' of the latter chamber over the former. It offered definitions of some key conventions in this area, including the Salisbury-Addison doctrine, which has its origins in an understanding dating from 1945. The purpose of this arrangement was to establish a principle that following a General Election, the Lords should not obstruct programmes that were included in the manifesto of the winning party. It occurred in the circumstances of the Labour victory of 1945, and took its name from Lords Addison and Salisbury (who was then Lord Cranborne), who were respectively the Leader of the House of Lords and the Leader of the Opposition in the Lords. The Joint Committee described the convention as it saw it as having developed by 2006:

> In the House of Lords:
>
> A manifesto Bill is accorded a Second Reading;
>
> A manifesto Bill is not subject to 'wrecking amendments' which change the Government's manifesto intention as proposed in the Bill; and
>
> A manifesto Bill is passed and sent (or returned) to the House of Commons, so that they have the opportunity, in reasonable time, to consider the Bill or any amendments the Lords may wish to propose. (p 32)

The Committee added that there was reason to conclude that lately there had developed 'a practice that the House of Lords will usually give a Second Reading to any government Bill, whether based on the manifesto or not … [T]o reject Bills at Second Reading on a regular basis would be inconsistent with the Lords' role as the revising chamber'. Words such as 'usually' and 'regular' are open to interpretation.

Such codification as exists in the field of relations between the Commons and the Lords failed to prevent a major clash in 2015. On 26 October, 'the Lords withheld agreement to the Tax Credits (Income Thresholds and Determination of

[6] For the report, see House of Lords/House of Commons Joint Committee on Conventions, *Conventions of the UK Parliament* (2005–06, HL 265-I, HC 1212-I).

Rates) (Amendment) Regulations 2015'.[7] As a consequence, the Prime Minister asked Lord Strathclyde to conduct a review of statutory instrument procedure. In his Report Strathclyde found:

> Since 1968, a convention has existed that the House of Lords should not reject statutory instruments (or should do so only rarely), but it has been interpreted in different ways, has not been understood by all members of the House, and has never been accepted by others. The rejection of the Tax Credits Regulations broke new ground. It suggests that the convention is now so flexible that is barely a convention at all. (p 4)

Yet the definition Strathclyde offered for this supposed convention was problematic. The difference between 'not' and 'rarely' rejecting statutory instruments is difficult to overlook, but he allowed for either possibility to apply. Moreover, as Strathclyde conceded, the claimed convention was subject to varying interpretation, lack of comprehension and outright rejection. Perhaps a more appropriate question was whether it had ever existed, rather than whether it had recently disintegrated. Paragraph 5.28 of *The Cabinet Manual* describes parliamentary procedure around statutory instruments, but does not identify a convention along the lines suggested by Strathclyde. In relation to the Lords, the *Manual* simply states that 'in the House of Lords, negative instruments are debated fairly regularly' and that 'Instruments subject to the affirmative Parliamentary procedure must be approved, usually by both Houses, before being made. They must therefore be subject to a debate in each House'. Paragraphs 15.2–15.3 of the *Guide to Making Legislation*, which describe 'Forms of parliamentary scrutiny' of statutory instruments, similarly fail to note a rule restricting the Lords in rejecting them. In his Report, Strathclyde set out a range of three possible courses of action. One was to 'codify the convention'—or rather his version of what the convention ought to be—using a Lords resolution or changes to the Lords Standing Orders. The other two options involved statutory intervention, a device that Strathclyde favoured, perhaps unsurprisingly, given his sense that convention was not working.

II. EXECUTIVE–PARLIAMENT RELATIONS

Interactions between the executive and Parliament are crucial to the UK constitution, in particular because they engage the principle of accountable government. The *Ministerial Code*[8] states that ministers are obliged to 'comply at all times with the requirements which Parliament itself has laid down in relation to the accountability and responsibility of Ministers', including a Commons resolution of March 1997 (paragraph 1.6). We have already seen in Chapter 1, section I. that ministers

[7] *Strathclyde Review: Secondary legislation and the primacy of the House of Commons* (Cm 9177 2015) 3.

[8] Cabinet Office, *Ministerial Code* (Cabinet Office, London, 2015).

who deliberately mislead Parliament are expected to resign, a rule recorded in the *Code*. A further acknowledgement of the importance of Parliament comes with the stipulation in this text that while Parliament is sitting, 'the most important announcements of Government policy should be made in the first instance, in Parliament' (paragraph 9.1).

Yet whatever requirements there are for the executive to show respect to Parliament, government is also determined to impose its will upon the legislature. *The Cabinet Manual* provides an account of those for whom this task is a primary responsibility: the whips (paragraph 3.16) In its description of them the *Manual* states some important and long-standing practices. It describes how the Government has whips in both Houses of Parliament, and that the 'chief whips' in both 'arrange the scheduling of government business, often in consultation with their opposition counterparts'. Together, these representatives of rival parties are, the *Manual* notes, known as 'the usual channels' in relation to the process of 'finding time for a particular item of business'. This passage demonstrates once again the importance of parliamentary parties to the constitution, that they are to some extent institutionalised, and the importance of this latter quality to the functioning of Parliament. At Westminster, notwithstanding recent reforms involving the establishment in 2010 of the Backbench Business Committee, the basic principle remains that the agenda of the Government takes priority in the allocation of parliamentary time. The *Manual* goes on to describe the role of the whips in handling their parties in Parliament. They have an information-giving role and are responsible for 'maintaining the party's voting strength by ensuring the members attend important votes, and passing on to the party leadership the opinions of backbench members'. The text concludes its account of the whips by informing the reader that whips in the Commons 'do not generally speak during Parliamentary debates', but that in the Lords they 'may' (paragraph 3.17).

The *Manual* deals with a specific area of constitutional tension and development in recent years: the role of Parliament in armed combat. Following the controversy of the Iraq War of 2003, pressure built, particularly within Westminster itself, for the provision of a clearer role for Parliament in decisions about the deployment of the armed forces overseas in circumstances that were potentially or actually hostile.[9] The *Manual* records that in the period since 1945, government practice has been to inform the Commons 'of significant military action' through statements, and that there have on occasions been adjournment debates, that is discussions not focused on an explicit policy proposition (paragraph 5.36). However, the *Manual* continues, in the case of operations in Iraq (2003) and Libya (2011), Parliament had the chance for a 'substantive debate'. On the first of the two occasions, there were debates in February and March, immediately before the invasion began (as well as a debate the previous year, 2002, on the approach taken at the United Nations over this issue). The *Manual* then recounts that, over Libya, the

[9] A Blick, 'Emergency Powers and the Withering of the Royal Prerogative' (2014) 18(2) *The International Journal of Human Rights* 195.

Prime Minister, David Cameron, informed the House on 18 March 2011, before the operation commenced. It goes on to state that there 'followed ... a government motion for debate on 21 March' that referred to 'the taking of all necessary measures to protect civilians and civilian-populated areas' (paragraph 5.37).

The *Manual* fails, however, to make clear that the 21 March debate took place after the action in Libya had already begun. This sequence is significant to the following paragraph. Paragraph 5.38 refers to the recognition by the Government in 2011 of the emergence of a 'convention ... that before troops were committed the House of Commons should have an opportunity to debate the matter'. The Government stated 'that it proposed to observe that convention except when there was an emergency and such action would not be appropriate'. As the *Manual* records in footnote 36 to page 44, the then Leader of the House of Commons, Sir George Young, made this undertaking to the Commons on 10 March. The Conservative MP, Edward Leigh, asked him to 'guarantee that if a no-fly zone is to be imposed, there will be a vote in the House of Commons? ... May we definitely have a vote before there is any military action?' A critical word in this instance was 'before'. Young replied that '[a] convention has developed in the House that before troops are committed, the House should have an opportunity to debate the matter'. Young went on:

> We propose to observe that convention except when there is an emergency and such action would not be appropriate. As with the Iraq war and other events, we propose to give the House the opportunity to debate the matter before troops are committed.[10]

On Friday 18 March 2011, the UK announced that it was taking part in the mission to facilitate a 'no-fly zone' above Libya. Not until the following Monday, 21 March, did the House of Commons debate and agree to a substantive motion endorsing this policy. In the course of this session William Hague, then the Foreign Secretary, pledged his Government to introducing a statute that would 'enshrine in law for the future the necessity of consulting Parliament on military action'.[11] Hague's pledge went unfulfilled. However, that he felt the need to make this commitment is perhaps an example of how problems connected to a convention—the Government had failed to live up to the principle of consultation in advance—can create a dynamic in the direction of statutory intervention to better enforce a rule that previously lacked a direct legal basis.

Other executive-produced documents deal with the intersection between executive and Parliament. For instance, a 319-page Cabinet Office text, *Guide to Making Legislation*, sets out the practices to be followed by officials in producing bills and taking them through Parliament.[12] The procedures it describes of necessity frequently relate to Parliament, and to some extent seek to guarantee standards

[10] HC Deb 10 March 2011, vol 524, col 1066.

[11] See House of Lords Select Committee on the Constitution, *Constitutional arrangements for the use of armed force* (HL 2013-14, 46) para 11.

[12] Cabinet Office, *Guide to Making Legislation* (London, Cabinet Office, 2014).

that could enhance Parliament in its effectiveness in processing legislation. For example, it refers to a government preference for issuing a greater number of bills in draft form, enabling parliamentary pre-legislative scrutiny (paragraph 3.18). It describes a 'convention' that when tabling amendments to legislation, the Government ought to seek to do so 'at least one sitting week before they are due to be debated'. The purpose of this rule is to ensure that parliamentarians are able to prepare themselves properly for discussion (p 156). The *Guide* also stipulates that 'Explanatory notes must be published alongside every government bill'. They are subject to the approval of Clerks of Legislation in both the Commons and the Lords (paragraph 3.9). The *Guide* refers to further principles it expressly describes as conventions. There is, it holds, a 'convention' that the Commons Second Reading debate of a bill 'will not usually take place until two weekends have passed following the publication of the bill' (paragraph 3.24). Another 'convention' is that, 'subject to certain exceptions, provisions in bills/Acts should not be commenced before the end of the period of 2 month following Royal Assent, unless Law Officers consent.' For consolidation bills, there is a three-month gap after Royal Assent (paragraph 10.67). The *Guide* also describes the 'Sewel Convention' (p 80), and similar conventions applying to the relations between the UK Parliament and the other devolved legislatures (eg paragraph 14.23; see Chapter 10). They are understood as having the effect of making legislation from Westminster dealing with devolved matters subject to the approval of the devolved legislatures.

The *Guide* recognises more expectations conditioning the behaviour of the executive when it describes the processes involved in taking a bill through Parliament. It states that '[m]ost flagship government measures, in particular those which have major spending implications, are introduced in the House of Commons'. The *Guide* then goes on to set out the 'conventional minimum timetable that can be expected for a bill of reasonable length and complexity' (paragraph 25.2). Whether the term 'conventional' is meant to imply 'subject to constitutional convention' or simply 'usual' is not entirely clear, but the procedures the *Guide* then describes could well be regarded as a clear part of constitutional convention. The same phrasing is applied to the House of Lords (paragraph 33.7). The text refers to a 'convention' that bills beginning their passage in the House of Lords will, when they reach the Commons, 'proceed directly to the public bill committee for a clause-by-clause examination of the bill', with no public evidence sessions taking place (paragraph 25.6). It also acknowledges a 'convention' that a minimum of two weekends should pass between a public bill's being published and receiving its Second Reading (paragraph 29.3). Though it does not use the word 'convention', the *Guide* describes principles applying to bills of constitutional significance. Paragraph 20.21 notes that 'Bills that have major constitutional implications should start in the House of Commons'; and a repeated stipulation in the text (for example, paragraph 25.6) is that 'Bills of major constitutional significance will have all (or some) of their Committee Stage on the floor of the House'. These provisions are sometimes known as the 'first class convention', applying to bills of supposedly 'first class' constitutional significance. We can see them as a substitute—though rather weak—for the amendment procedure that might be found in a country with a written constitution, trying to ensure that a change to the underlying system is subject to special consideration.[13]

Overall, the *Guide* creates an important impression. The executive must devote considerable time and attention to the handling of Parliament as a legislature. Governments are subject to a sophisticated and demanding range of expectations, and recognise that they are. While it is certainly true that the executive has enjoyed special advantages in its relationship with Parliament, it is important to avoid crude characterisations. A term such as 'rubber stamp' would convey neither the complexity of the machinery at work, nor the subtle dynamics of the relationships involved. It is not only procedures that matter, but institutions such as committees in both Houses that emerge from the *Guide* as important players (see, for example, paragraphs 32.12–32.15 on the House of Lords Select Committee on the Constitution). Codification in the *Guide* amounts in part to an acknowledgement of the constraints applying to the Government, and perhaps makes those limitations more firm.

Yet the text also contains at least one assertion that some would hold suggests an inappropriate degree of discretion on the part of the executive and a departure from established convention. It comes in a passage headed 'Powers to incur expenditure (the "Second Reading Convention")' (paragraphs 18.7–18.8). It starts by identifying the basic principle at work, that a department 'should not normally consume resources or incur expenditure on new services until the relevant legislation has Royal Assent and the department has obtained parliamentary authority through the supply estimates process'. But when there is a need to spend 'urgently, it may be possible' to do so after the relevant bill 'has passed Second Reading in the Commons' (paragraph 18.7). As we shall see in section IV. below, the very idea of a 'Second Reading Convention' is disputed.

III. PARLIAMENTARY COMMITTEES AND GOVERNMENT ACCOUNTABILITY

Committees have historically been crucial to the effectiveness of Parliament. But 1979 was a moment of substantive change in their nature. From this year a group of select committees has operated in the House of Commons shadowing specific departments and policy areas.[14] It has come to be a central part of the work of the Commons and Parliament as a whole in holding the Government to account.

The Liaison Committee, a committee including the chairs of the Commons select committees, is responsible for a document known as *Core Tasks for Select*

[13] A Blick, D Howarth and N le Roux, *Distinguishing Constitutional Legislation: a modest proposal* (London, The Constitution Society, 2014); R Hazell, *Time for a New Convention: Parliamentary Scrutiny of Constitutional Bills, 1997–2005* (London, The Constitution Unit, 2006).

[14] G Drewry, *The New Select Committees*, 2nd edn (Oxford, Clarendon Press, 1989); M Jogerst, *Reform in the House of Commons: The Select Committee System* (Lexington, KY, University Press of Kentucky, 1993).

Committees, the development of which was discussed earlier in this book (see Chapter 2, section III.).[15] It presents itself as a set of broad guidance rather than specific instructions. *Core Tasks* describes the general objective of select committees as being, 'To hold Ministers and Departments to account for their policy and decision-making and to support the House in its control of the supply of public money and scrutiny of legislation.' To this end it sets out 10 categories of work or 'Tasks'. Task 1 involves 'Strategy', that is, assessing the strategy of the particular department under examination, including how it has formulated its strategy and whether it is able to attain it. Task 2 is 'Policy', that is, to consider policy initiatives that the department puts forward, policies that are in the process of appearing and cases in which present policy is in some way lacking, 'and make proposals'. This activity has traditionally been one of the central activities of select committee system. So too has Task 3, 'Expenditure and Performance'. *Core Tasks* defines this sphere of work as involving scrutiny of planned expenditure and 'performance of the department and its arm's length bodies', and considering how expenditure matches with the attainment of specific outcomes. Task 4 relates to 'Draft Bills'. In many legislatures, rather than select committees focused on policy, as exist in the Westminster Parliament, there are standing committees primarily charged with considering laws. These bodies can become reservoirs of expertise in their given areas, exercising their judgement on behalf of the plenary. In the UK, legislative scrutiny has tended traditionally to be the work of ad hoc committees, with members drafted on for a particular bill, lacking in this kind of specialism. However, Task 4 alludes to a process whereby select committees, though not specifically legislative bodies, can engage in a process known as 'pre-legislative scrutiny', considering government proposals for new laws at an early stage of development. It is possible for specially convened committees, comprising members from both Houses, to form to carry out pre-legislative scrutiny, but select committees in the Commons may also perform this role. Task 5, 'Bills and Delegated Legislation', puts forward a further legislative role for select committees, supporting the Commons in its work considering full bills, as well as secondary legislation. A further legislative function comes with Task 6, 'Post-Legislative Scrutiny', an activity that involves considering the practical impact of legislation, and assessing 'post-legislative assessments' produced by departments.

Task 7 entails considering 'policy developments at the European level' and legislation emanating from the European Union. Task 8 involves the consideration of significant appointments that the department may make and the holding of pre-appointment hearings. Task 9 is 'Support for the House', that is, publishing reports to feed into its debates, whether in the main Chamber, or Westminster Hall or 'debating committees', and considering petitions. Lastly, with Task 10 comes another concern that has become more prominent within Parliament in recent years: the idea that the wider public is somehow disconnected from its work. This

[15] Contained in House of Commons Liaison Committee, *Select committee effectiveness, resources and powers* (HC 2012–13, 697).

issue is connected to wider social trends, whereby some of the traditional modes of engagement with representative democracy, such as voting and party membership, have declined. The specific task is for select committees to support the Commons in 'better engaging with the public' through making Commons' activities 'accessible to the public'.

But what are the rules applying to officials when appearing before increasingly assertive Commons select committees? Chapter 2, section I.C. of this book discussed the historic appearance and development of the so-called 'Osmotherly Rules'. This text now appears under the formal title *Giving Evidence to Select Committees: Guidance for Civil Servants.*[16] The latest, 28-page edition dates from October 2014. The 'Introduction' reminds us that select committees are crucial to the role of Parliament in holding government to account, and that ministers should require officials, when giving evidence for them to these bodies, to 'be as forthcoming and helpful' as possible. In particular they should not deny information that would be released if applied for under the Freedom of Information Act 2000 (paragraph 1).

However, when civil servants take part in a select committee hearing, they do so on behalf of the minister, not in their own right. The text reminds us of the stipulation set out in the *Civil Service Code* that 'civil servants are accountable to Ministers who are in turn accountable to Parliament' (paragraph 4). Paragraph 9 adds that civil servants provide evidence to select committees not only 'on behalf' of 'their Ministers', but also 'under their directions'. Officials can provide a description of government programmes and the thinking that lies behind them, but they should do so in a way that facilitates the accountability of ministers, and not provide their own individual perspectives. To do otherwise would be a threat to the political impartiality of the person concerned (paragraph 5). Civil servants may discuss the reasons for a policy and how far it achieved what was hoped for it, and 'administrative factors' that may have impacted upon the selection of a course of action and the way in which it was put into practice. However, they should seek not to engage in consideration of 'the merits of alternative policies, including their advice to Ministers'. If a committee tries to force the issue, an official should remind it of the constraints that exist in this regard, referring the committee to the minister. The text asserts, '[s]elect Committees should respect this position'—an example of an attempt by an executive code to extend beyond its own remit and seek to induce another institution to behave in a certain way (paragraph 33). The document also insists that select committees are not supposed to perform the function of 'disciplinary tribunals' for officials. These matters are, according to the text, to be handled internally (paragraph 35).

The document then introduces two exceptions to the general rules it has set out. The first is the Accounting Officer, encountered in Chapter 7 as described in the *Ministerial Code*. The Accounting Officer 'is accountable to Parliament for the

[16] Cabinet Office, *Giving Evidence to Select Committees: Guidance for Civil Servants* (London, Cabinet Office, 2014).

stewardship for the department's resources'. Those who perform this role 'have a personal responsibility to account to Parliament', via the House of Commons Public Accounts Committee (paragraph 6). The text now allows for former Accounting Officers to appear before the Committee (paragraphs 23–24). There are also individuals, known as 'Senior Responsible Owners', from whom Parliament can seek an 'account' of 'the implementation and delivery of major projects for which they are responsible' (paragraph 7). Aside from these limited exemptions, the principle is that if a select committee wishes a 'particular named official, including special advisers', to attend a hearing, there is a 'presumption … that Ministers will seek to agree to such a request'. Nonetheless, ultimately the minister chooses who will be sent to the committee (paragraph 12).

The text concedes that if a committee wished, and if it secured the agreement of the whole House to this course of action, it could force the attendance of a particular official, just as it would be able to do with anyone else. Yet the document insists that in such circumstances, the civil servant 'would remain subject to Ministerial instruction and the Civil Service Code'. The text adds, '[t]his would be a very exceptional action' (paragraph 13). As regards 'the powers of Select Committees to send for "persons, papers and records"', the document recognises their 'unqualified' nature, but refers to 'certain long-standing conventions on the provision of information which have been observed in practice by successive administrations on grounds of public policy' (paragraph 39). While stressing the desire to be 'as open and as helpful as possible', it sets out the procedures by which such information might be withheld. Potentially the Government can provide confidential access to 'sensitive information, including that carrying a protective security marking … on the basis that it will not be published' (paragraph 47).

IV. PARLIAMENT AND PUBLIC MONEY

Control of finance is historically, and remains, central to the accountability of the executive to Parliament; and within Whitehall, the Treasury is crucial to this relationship. A Treasury document, *Managing Public Money*, sets out some of the core principles, from the executive perspective.[17] It is 217 pages in total, and seems first to have appeared in 2007, with an update in 2013. *Managing Public Money* divides into a 'main text', which the Foreword refers to as describing 'timeless' principles, while its annexes contain information that may at times require updating. Chapter 1 deals with 'Responsibilities'. It notes that 'much of this document is about meeting the expectations of parliament' (paragraph 1.1.3). Some of it is directly relevant only to England, because of devolution (paragraph 1.1.3). The text notes that, '[i]n the absence of a written constitution', the authority to utilise public money rests in a combination of 'common law, primary and secondary legislation, parliamentary

[17] HM Treasury, *Managing Public Money* (London, HM Treasury, 2013, rev'd 2015).

procedure, the duties of ministers, and other long-standing practices' (paragraph 1.2.1). It makes a variety of important constitutional statements. They include the principle that ministers alone (presumably as opposed to other parliamentarians) are able to introduce to Parliament bills intended to 'raise public revenue through taxation, or to use public funds to pursue their policy objectives'. Furthermore, allowing a 'private sector' body to 'raise taxes' or disburse the money acquired by this means 'is not normally acceptable' (paragraph 1.2.6). In a section entitled 'The Treasury', the document states that 'Parliament looks to the Treasury to make sure that … departments use their powers only as it has intended; and … revenue is raised, and the resources so raised spent, only within the agreed limits' (paragraph 1.4.1). Consequently, the text holds, it is the responsibility of the Treasury to establish the basic rules for the handling of public money, and to 'account to Parliament for doing so' (paragraph 1.4.2).

Managing Public Money describes a set of principles to which the Treasury must adhere in meeting the requirements of Parliament. They are 'regularity, propriety, value for money and feasibility'. The document notes that the Treasury 'may also work through the Cabinet Office' in applying 'certain standards … across central government' (paragraph 1.4.3). Paragraph 1.5.1 introduces the Accounting Officer, a figure we have already encountered in this chapter and the last, who is responsible within the particular department to which she is attached for ensuring financial compliance, and accounting for it. 'Accounting Officers' are the subject of Chapter 3 of the document. It explains how they may 'ask for a formal written direction' from a minister who is insistent upon proceeding with an activity that the Accounting Officer has counselled against (paragraph 3.4.2). The document also explains the unusual position of Accounting Officers with respect to Parliament, as previously discussed. It notes that when attending hearings with the House of Commons Public Accounts Committee, an Accounting Officer 'should take responsibility for the organisation's business, even if it was delegated or if the events in question happened before he or she was appointed accounting officer'. This arrangement potentially raises problems for the House of Common Public Accounts Committee in its investigations. Consequently, if it or another select committee so asks, 'previous accounting officers may also attend … relevant hearings'. However, it is not automatic that a committee will obtain access to an earlier Accounting Officer. One condition that the document suggests should apply is that the matter under consideration should be 'fairly recent' (paragraph 3.5.3).

The Treasury text deals with a further sensitive and controversial area when describing the basis on which departmental expenditure takes place. It explains that 'Parliament usually authorises spending on a specific policy or service by approving bespoke legislation setting out in some detail how it should work' (paragraph 2.5.1). Simply relying on a Supply and Appropriation Act is not generally sufficient. The text then sets out the limited exceptions to this general rule. They include 'routine administration costs … lease agreements … contractual obligations … [and] expenditure using prerogative powers such as defence of the realm and international treaty obligations' (Box 2.5). Another possible exception involves circumstances in which 'ministers want to start early on a new policy which is intended to continue but whose enabling legislation has not yet secured royal assent'. Possibly they can do so to a small extent, drawing on the Contingencies Fund, subject to permission from the Treasury (paragraph 2.6.2). However, the text explains, there are certain tests that must be passed before pursuing this course of action. The intended outlay must be 'urgent' as well as 'in the public interest'. That is to say, the gains must be great enough to 'outweigh the convention of awaiting parliamentary authority'. The mere existence of a 'political imperative' is insufficient. The Bill the minister is waiting to pass into law 'must have successfully passed second reading in the House of Commons'. That it will become law shortly (normally inside the financial year), and not be subject to significant alteration, should be 'certain, or virtually certain'. This judgement involves making predictions that, however well informed they may be, rest on the behaviour of an institution, Parliament, not under the formal control of the executive. The government department seeking to begin spending early has to provide an account of what it is doing and a justification of its actions to Parliament, and set out when the special arrangement will cease (Box 2.7). As we shall see, the practice described and the interpretations placed upon it are highly controversial, involving as they do the pre-emption of Parliament as the body responsible for authorising and holding to account government expenditure.

A document referenced in *Managing Public Money*, and which itself in turn references *Managing Public Money*, also with a bearing on the nature of parliamentary control of public finance, is *Corporate governance in central government departments: Code of good practice 2011*.[18] Issued jointly by the Treasury and the Cabinet Office, it is 35 pages long. It first appeared in 2005. The purpose of the Code, as described in the 'Foreword', is to 'promote good corporate governance in central government departments'. A section on 'Parliamentary accountability' states the basic principle that '[t]he minister in charge of the department is responsible and answerable to Parliament for the exercise of the powers on which the administration of that department depends' (paragraph 1.1). It goes on to enumerate a series of 'Supporting provisions', within which a description of the Accounting Officer is prominent. This section includes the claim that 'Parliament grants resources to departments for specified purposes. HM Treasury administers these resources on behalf of parliament and appoints the AOs [Accounting Officers] who are charged with ensuring resources are used as parliament intends' (paragraph 1.7). This statement appears not to allow for the possibility of expenditure not for 'specified purposes' already agreed by Parliament, yet exceptions, discussed in *Managing Public Money*, exist. Moreover, its description of the Treasury as acting 'on behalf of parliament' is contentious.

Parliament does not always share with the executive an identical view of the proper approach to the handling of public money. Some of the documents

[18] HM Treasury/Cabinet Office, *Corporate governance in central government departments: Code of good practice 2011* (London, HM Treasury/Cabinet Office, 2011).

considered in this work—and concepts depicted within them—provide a focus for this controversy. In May 2013, the House of Lords Select Committee on the Constitution issued a report, *The pre-emption of Parliament.*[19] It noted that while the basic constitutional precept was that ministers executed laws that Parliament had produced, there were times when it was necessary for the executive to engage in activity in relation to particular legislation in advance of its being passed. The Committee noted the existence of apprehensions about the scale on which pre-emption took place, and an absence of clarity around the practice. The report concluded that there was not a serious problem with the extent or nature of pre-emption. Nonetheless, it made a series of recommendations the Committee felt were needed to regulate the activity. It was important, the report found, that pre-emption, whenever it occurred, should be subject to particular standards, among them parliamentary oversight and the rule of law. The Committee held that while the Treasury was important within government in decisions about pre-emption, it did not have constitutional authority. It called upon the Government to notify Parliament whenever it carried out a pre-emption, clarify the particular authority under which it had done so and explain why the action was appropriate. In response the Government agreed that it should make all plans for pre-emption clear to Parliament.

For the Committee, *The Cabinet Manual* was—as presently drafted—symptomatic of problems surrounding pre-emption, yet it could in a future edition help provide a solution to them. The *Manual*, the Committee noted, was 'currently silent on pre-emption' (paragraph 79). The report objected to the statement in paragraph 3.31 of the *Manual* that ministers could 'exercise "any of the legal powers of an individual"', not being accompanied by 'reference to the fact that, whereas private individuals are free to exercise their powers irrationally (for example), ministers are not'. Texts such as *The Cabinet Manual* should, when describing common law authorities, emphasise that they were constrained by 'public law and constitutional principle' (paragraph 65). The Committee concluded that a definitive account of the rules to which pre-emption was subject should be included within the *Manual*. The Government agreed to this recommendation, and added that it would make the text of *Managing Public Money* clearer on this point.

An underlying concern for the Committee involved the Treasury view of its function. In evidence to the inquiry, the Treasury asserted the existence of 'an ancient convention that the Treasury should strive to look after Parliament's interest in Whitehall'; and the Treasury Officer of Accounts referred to the Treasury as functioning 'as the guardian of Parliament' (paragraph 19). The Committee had problems with this outlook. Its apprehension seems to have been that the Treasury might regard itself as acting on behalf of Parliament, and therefore as possessing

[19] House of Lords Select Committee on the Constitution, *The pre-emption of Parliament* (HL 2012–13, 165).

an authorising power that it did not have. Beyond the general constitutional difficulties, there were specific anomalies. The Committee noted that there were times when Treasury ministers themselves might instruct courses of action that challenged the principles of 'regularity and propriety' (paragraph 22). Who in such circumstances would watch the watcher?

It is easy to see how, from the point of view of Parliament, the proposition that the Treasury represented Parliament could contain within it a threat of usurpation rather than assistance. The executive might even in some areas become self-legitimising. The report held:

> The Treasury is responsible to Parliament for the regularity and propriety of Government expenditure; it follows that the Treasury will wish to police these areas within Whitehall. However, it should be recognised that Parliament's interests are primarily guarded by Parliament itself. (paragraph 23)

In its reply, the Government simply recorded that it noted the view of the Committee.

The Committee also recounted that the Treasury Officer of Accounts had told it that 'no documentation exists in support of the convention's ancient origins—she thought that any such documents were "lost in the mists of time"' (paragraph 19). Parliament, the report found, had 'not delegated the protection of its interests to the Treasury', and therefore this function was not 'a constitutional convention in the strict sense'. The Treasury Officer of Accounts explained to the Committee that the term 'convention' in this context meant 'common practice rather than formal agreement'. The Committee concluded that 'the Treasury was not seeking to elevate its internal practices to the status of constitutional conventions', but recommended that the term 'convention' should not be attached to Treasury 'practices' (paragraph 26). The Committee raised a further objection involving the use of the word 'convention'. The Economic Secretary to the Treasury, Sajid Javid MP, had described the practice of allowing expenditure to take place in relation to a bill once it had had a Second Reading in the Commons as 'the second reading convention' (paragraph 27). The Committee preferred the term 'practice'. It stated, 'Parliament is not, and does not regard itself as, bound by the Treasury's guidance. The second reading practice is not a convention, and should no longer be described as such' (paragraph 29). The Government agreed in its response, which came in October 2013, to cease using the word 'convention' in this area. Yet a subsequent—July 2014—edition of the *Guide to Making Legislation*, as we have seen in section II. above, still contained the phrase 'Second Reading Convention' (as did the July 2015 version on p 134). It was probably an accident rather than a deliberate contradiction: the document in question was a Cabinet Office publication, and perhaps there had not been sufficient communication with the Treasury. Lastly, beyond the terminology, the Committee stressed that while having achieved a Second Reading in the Commons could be 'a useful indicator of a bill's prospects of becoming law', it was 'not sufficient to justify pre-empting the legislative process' (paragraph 34).

V. CONCLUSION

Parliament remains a central focus for the UK constitution. It is a point at which a variety of different interests and forces meet. They include the Government, the political parties, individual politicians, the various localities of the UK and the electorate. It is also an arena within which a number of constitutional tasks are performed. Among them are the carrying on of government business, scrutiny and accountability of those same executive activities, the production of legislation, public debate of important issues and representation of the country at large. It is unsurprising, given its complexities as a political institution, that the codification trend has spread to Parliament. In some instances, it involves internal regulation, for instance the codes for members of both Houses or the *Core Tasks for Select Committees*. Other cases of codification deal with relations between different parts of Parliament—such as the efforts to distill the 'Salisbury-Addison' rule.

Lastly, there is often another player involved—the executive. *The Cabinet Manual*, for example, offers its perspective on some arrangements internal to Parliament. Other codes, such as the Osmotherly Rules, *Managing Public Money* and the *Guide to Making Legislation*, deal with intersections between the executive and Parliament. In some cases they have presented versions of events that are contested, and have figured in disputes between the executive and Parliament. Yet generally the response to such disagreements is not to back away from codification. Conversely, there has been a tendency to seek to deploy texts as a means of resolving arguments, using them to promote accounts over which it is hoped there can be consensus. Codification encourages more codification.

9

General Elections and the Formation of Governments

DEMOCRACY IS A complex phenomenon. It has many interconnected components, a number of which are discussed in this book, including rights, the rule of law, principles and practices regarding the operation of the governmental system, the division of responsibilities between different territorial levels, and wider social trends. Indeed no single agreed definition of democracy exists.[1] But a point on which many of these different qualities converge, and which is undoubtedly a central—or perhaps *the* central—feature of a representative democracy such as the UK, is that of the connection between elections and the control of public offices. Once, the rules that applied to the operation of these processes at UK level—involving the composition of the elected chamber of Parliament and of Her Majesty's Government—were to a substantial extent absent from any kind of official document. Lately—thanks to a large extent to *The Cabinet Manual*,[2] which appeared in 2011—they are increasingly codified. Indeed it was the desire to create clarity in the possible circumstances of an inconclusive General Election that provided the most powerful motive for the creation of the *Manual*. In the same year that *The Cabinet Manual* appeared in final form, the Fixed-term Parliaments Act 2011 also passed into law. Taken in combination, the *Manual* and the Act amounted to a radical overhaul in the way the process of government selection and formation operates and is formally described. This transformation has not yet received the full attention it merits. I have discussed the constitutional implications of the 2011 Act elsewhere.[3] Though I refer to the Act in this chapter when appropriate, my focus is upon assessing codes that seek to set out the constitutional principles in these areas. The coverage of these texts is incomplete, and they contain within them significant ambiguities, as we shall see. But codification

[1] D Beetham et al, *Assessing the Quality of Democracy: A Practical Guide* (Stockholm, International IDEA, 2008); SP. Huntington, *The Third Wave: Democratization in the Late Twentieth Century* (Norman, Okla, University of Oklahoma Press, 1992); F Fukuyama, *Political Order and Political Decay: From the Industrial Revolution to the Globalization of Democracy* (London, Profile, 2014); J Teorell, *Determinants of Democratization: Explaining Regime Change in the World 1972–2006* (Cambridge, Cambridge University Press, 2010).

[2] Cabinet Office, *The Cabinet Manual: A guide to the laws, conventions and rules on the operation of government*, 1st edn (London, Cabinet Office, 2011).

[3] A Blick, 'Constitutional Implications of the Fixed-term Parliaments Act 2011' (2016) 69 *Parliamentary Affairs* 19.

has once again made it possible to have a discussion, centring on official accounts of the UK constitution and their meaning, that once we would not have been able to conduct.

I. ELECTIONS AND GOVERNMENT BUSINESS

Even before a General Election has taken place, it has an operational impact upon government. A key driver of codification has been to distinguish the partisan interests of politicians who hold ministerial office from the public function of the institutions they lead. The potential for a blurring of these barriers becomes greater as a poll approaches. Given this tendency, *The Cabinet Manual* sets out rules that apply to government 'in the period immediately preceding an election' (see also Chapter 7 section II.B.). The general rule tended to be known colloquially as the 'purdah' principle, an expression that official documents now often avoid. The *Manual* did not invent the concept but did extend it beyond simply the pre-election phase, to cover the period 'immediately afterwards if the result is unclear, and following the loss of a vote of confidence' (paragraph 2.27).

Though it envisages post-General Election constraints, the *Manual* does not make clear when, precisely, they should terminate. The exact end point 'depends on circumstances'. It may occur 'either when a new Prime Minister is appointed … or where a government's ability to command the confidence of the Commons has been tested in the House of Commons' (paragraph 2.30). In its March 2015 Report, *Government formation post-election*, the House of Commons Political and Constitutional Reform Committee (PCRC) held that there should be a clearer distinction in the *Manual* between the phase of restraint that operates before a General Election, regardless of whether or not the Government retains the confidence of the Commons, and the 'caretaker' stage that comes when a government has lost its majority (or perhaps if its ability to construct a majority is in doubt) but a new arrangement has not yet been confirmed.[4]

Under the rules, though government is expected to continue operating, and ministers are still responsible for the departments they head, there is nonetheless a need 'to observe discretion in initiating any new action of a continuing or long-term character' (paragraph 2.27). In other words, there must be a trade-off between the need to avoid a lack of leadership at particular points—'essential business must be allowed to continue', as paragraph 2.29 of the *Manual* puts it—while preventing abuse of this principle, possibly aimed at manipulating democratic processes, or forcing through policies without the legitimate authority to do so, that may bind a successor government. During the phase, civil servants who are Accounting Officers may require directions from ministers as at other times (paragraph 2.32). However, if Parliament is not sitting, it is not possible—in accordance

[4] House of Commons Political and Constitutional Reform Committee, *Government formation post-election* (HC 2014–15, 1023) 13.

with normal practice—for the Committee of Public Accounts to receive notice of any such direction (forwarded via the Comptroller and Auditor General). In these circumstances, the department concerned should publicise 'the direction, together with the reasoning provided by the accounting officer', and lay it 'before both Houses at the first opportunity after Parliament meets' (paragraph 2.33).

The Cabinet Office issues 'guidance' for officials about the observance of these rules in advance of a General Election, and the Prime Minister communicates with ministers to 'similar' effect (paragraph 2.28). A footnote to paragraph 2.29 (footnote 24) notes that in the past an Election Business Committee has played a role in the execution of this work. It is 'customary' for ministers 'to observe discretion in initiating any action of a continuing or long-term character'. This approach entails postponing actions that include 'taking or announcing major policy decisions' and agreeing 'large/contentious procurement contracts or significant long-term commitments'. Ministers should also, the *Manual* recounts, refrain from 'making some senior public appointments and approving Senior Civil Service appointments'. In every case, however, they should not defer taking action if to do so would be 'detrimental to the national interest or wasteful of public money'. When there is an imperative to act, 'temporary arrangements' or 'relevant consultation with the Opposition' are given as options to follow (paragraph 2.29).

As the stipulation relating to Accounting Officers in the *Manual* demonstrates, the role of the Civil Service with respect to elections, and to possible changes in the party composition of government, is delicate. Career officials are required—as we have seen–to support ministers loyally, while maintaining the ability to do the same for politicians who may come to take their place in future, whether of the same or a different party. Paragraph 2.21 of the *Manual* gives an account of a long-established principle involving the role of the Civil Service in the lead-up to a General Election; but also reveals the vagueness surrounding its precise application, and its dependence upon prime-ministerial discretion. The *Manual* states that 'At an appropriate time towards the end of any Parliament', with the coming General Election drawing close, the premier 'writes to the leaders of the main opposition parties to authorise pre-election contacts with the Civil Service'. This stipulation once again emphasises the constitutional role of parties. It also perhaps requires clarification, particularly in a political era characterised by a rise in the number of viable political parties. What are the 'main opposition parties'? Before 2010, and at least from the early 1980s onwards, this term might have meant either the Conservatives or Labour, and the Liberal Democrats. At the time the *Manual* appeared, with the Conservative and Liberal Democrats in coalition, there was arguably only one 'main' opposition party, Labour. But if the UK is moving into a phase in its political history when more parties are able not only to win representation in the Commons, but also to figure in calculations about the construction of parliamentary majorities, it is probably appropriate to make it clear that Civil Service contacts should range more widely. Simply to talk to one, or perhaps two, parties about their plans for government is a less useful exercise if, following an election, a new programme of some kind is negotiated. Before the 2015 General Election, this kind of shift in the distribution of electoral power was widely assumed. It may seem less plausible in the wake of the 2015 Conservative victory that took place, but should not be excluded.

Some observers have questioned whether the process of pre-election contacts—its timing and whether it takes place at all—should be in the gift of the Prime Minister. The precise likely impact of the *Manual* is difficult to discern here. Has it helped make it clear that the Prime Minister is in charge of the procedure, and thereby strengthened the discretion of the premier? Or has the *Manual* made the existence of this process more firm, thereby constraining prime ministers, since—though theoretically in a position of strength—they may wish to avoid being seen as abusing their position and violating established understandings? Furthermore, might the description of pre-election contacts, and the responsibility No 10 has for them, have encouraged reformers to pay closer attention to them and demand that they be made more effective, including through removing the prime-ministerial control that the *Manual* itself iterates? In a footnote to paragraph 2.21 (footnote 18), the *Manual* notes that talks were permitted from 1 January 2005, despite a poll's not strictly being due until July 2006 (though the then Prime Minister, Tony Blair, must have decided it was imminent), and from 1 January 2009 in advance of the May 2010 General Election. In its January 2015 Report, *Revisiting The Cabinet Manual*, PCRC held that, given the introduction of five-year fixed-term parliaments, it should be possible for pre-election contacts to commence automatically a year before the General Election, and that *The Cabinet Manual* should reflect this change of practice.[5]

Firming up the position of the senior Cabinet Office official further, paragraph 2.21 of the *Manual* explains that the Cabinet Secretary has 'overall responsibility for co-ordinating this process', following a 'request' and agreement from the Prime Minister. This paragraph then goes on to give an idea of the form these discussions take. Importantly, they are 'confidential'. Government ministers do not attend, nor are they informed about what takes place. Thus, while the Prime Minister has given permission for these gatherings to occur, officials are operating—out of necessity—beyond the reach of normal accountability mechanisms. The danger here is that civil servants develop a divided loyalty, serving government—as is their constitutional role—and opposition simultaneously. This proposition is obviously problematic from the point of view of ministers, and also for officials if it undermines their relationship of trust with those whom they serve, though some civil servants might find attractive the idea of advance discussions with potential future political leaders. The description the *Manual* provides of the role of civil servants in these contacts is presumably coloured by the desire precisely to avoid such problems.

Paragraph 2.21 stipulates that the purpose of the talks is to make it possible for shadow ministers 'to ask questions about departmental organisation' and notify

[5] House of Commons Political and Constitutional Reform Committee, *Revisiting The Cabinet Manual* (HC 2014–15, 233) 30.

officials regarding plans they may have to bring about 'organisational changes' if they come to office. For their part, 'Senior civil servants' can inquire about 'the implications of opposition parties' policy statements, although they would not normally comment on or give advice about policies'. This restriction seems to be intended to avoid officials' becoming drawn into opposition policy formation, by definition a party political business and therefore a dangerous area. However, with the use of the word 'normally' the *Manual* leaves open the possibility that they might enter into this territory, though it does not explain why, when or how. Beyond the phrase 'Senior civil servants'—perhaps meaning permanent secretaries, their equivalents or those immediately below them—the text does not state who is involved in this process from the Whitehall end, other than the Cabinet Secretary. Another possible gap arises because neither the *Manual*, nor other guidance in this area addresses the possibility of a party that holds office as part of a coalition wishing to discuss policies individually with the Civil Service. For instance, there may be particular programmes it wishes to pursue, but is unable to within the confines of the existing government, that it is committed to following if it can after a General Election, perhaps because it is in government on its own or in a different coalition, or because it has managed to secure from its present partner a different agreement.

Paragraph 2.14 states that in circumstances when cross-party talks are taking place following an inconclusive General Election, and if leaders 'in any negotiations' request it, they can obtain 'the support of the Civil Service', arranged by the Cabinet Secretary, following 'the authorisation of the Prime Minister'. This conditionality is emphasised immediately afterwards with the statement, 'If the Prime Minister authorises any support …'. If this approval is secured, the 'support' will be 'focused and provided on an equal basis to all the parties involved, including the party that was currently in government'. At the same time the Civil Service 'would continue to advise the incumbent government in the usual way'. The *Manual* describes how, in May 2010, the then Prime Minister (Gordon Brown, though not named) had consented to the provision of 'such support to negotiations between political parties' (paragraph 2.15). It notes that the Civil Service had permission to supply 'advice on the constitutional process of government formation; factual information in relation to specific policy proposals; and facilitation of discussions and negotiations (including the provision of facilities such as meeting rooms)' (paragraph 15, footnote 14).

As we have seen in Chapter 4, section II., the early draft of this part of the *Manual*, published before the 2010 General Election, had helped make this activity by the Civil Service possible. The full text of the *Manual* was subsequently able to point to this event as a precedent, something important to the legitimisation of practices and helpful for the establishment of an accepted convention. These arrangements are a firm example of a way in which the *Manual* process has been able to innovate—contrary to the protestations of O'Donnell in the Preface. Moreover, the role it creates is—like some other functions set out in the *Manual*—attached to the Cabinet Secretary, one of the chief instigators of that text. The

Manual extends the potential fabrication of new arrangements further through the stipulation that the support for talks is potentially on offer not only immediately after a General Election with no one overall winner, but also when a government loses a 'no confidence' vote under the terms of section 2 of the Fixed-term Parliaments Act 2011 (paragraph 2.20). In such circumstances there may follow an attempt to construct a coalition that can win a 'confidence' vote, again as set out in section 2 of the 2011 Act, and forestall the General Election that is otherwise triggered after a 14-day period. A comparison between, on the one hand, the already-existing arrangement—to which the *Manual* refers—for pre-election discussions between civil servants and opposition and, on the other hand, the possibility for supporting coalition negotiations, is instructive. The former process cannot directly lead to a major outcome of the sort that the latter can. Discussions about policy plans between would-be ministers and Whitehall officials are not of great significance in themselves, and any relevance they may prove to have is entirely dependent upon the outcome of the General Election that follows. However, negotiations between parties after a poll may lead directly to an important material outcome: the formation of a government. Through engaging in the latter activity, permanent officials become immediately proximate to processes involving the acquisition, maintenance and loss of power. The salience of any propriety and constitutional issues associated with their role is thereby magnified.

The paragraph 2.14 arrangements for Civil Service support for inter-party negotiations suggest a scenario in which career officialdom is, alongside its regular role in assisting existing ministers, involved in servicing an activity that is clearly party political in nature. This position is problematic in itself. Assuming it is desirable for civil servants to retain impartiality, how are we to ensure they do not extend beyond their proper role in this unusual situation, and that they are regarded from outside as maintaining proper standards? This is a general difficulty, the complications of which—depending on the specifics—might multiply. If a party of government—including, presumably, ministers—is taking part in talks, is it necessary to recognise a distinction between it and its leadership in their capacity as, on the one hand, participants in negotiations and, on the other hand, members of a government—and, if so, how? Concerns may become more complex still if there is more than one party of government, and one or more of those parties is negotiating with one or more parties outside of government with a view to jettisoning one or more existing coalition partners and forming a new coalition. Lastly, if a party (in or out of government) is holding parallel talks with two or more parties, sensitivities could arise regarding claims it might make in its dealing with one party about offers it had received from another, and their veracity.

All of these possible instances present potential conflicts of interest for the Civil Service: between impartiality and participation in a clearly party-political process; between government and ministers on the one hand, and parties of government on the other hand; between different parties that make up a coalition; and involving taking part in more than one negotiation at the same time. A further problem involves another core feature of the UK constitution we have already encountered in Chapter 7: that the accountability of civil servants is achieved primarily through their being answerable to ministers, who are in turn responsible to Parliament. The Prime Minister is responsible for authorising Civil Service support for coalition negotiations. But once that support commences, it is unclear to whom and how officials are accountable for their actions, particularly if the talks they are assisting do not involve the governing party; the Prime Minister and other ministers do not and cannot know what is taking place. While those the Civil Service is helping may go on to become ministers if talks are successful, they cannot—under existing constitutional principles—be responsible for the actions of officials.

In this sense, the participation of civil servants in coalition talks is by definition a violation of the constitutional principle of ministerial responsibility, as defined in the *Ministerial Code*[6] and *The Cabinet Manual*, and of the core values of Whitehall as set out in the *Civil Service Code*.[7] It could mean that civil servants, using rules they have drafted (albeit under the authorisation of ministers), take on power of a type that is not proper given the nature of their accountability. The problem is not just theoretical. We have already seen indications of the practical difficulties that might arise. In practice, the role of civil servants in negotiations between the Conservatives and Liberal Democrats was circumscribed. But the arrangement O'Donnell helped create in May 2010 left him exposed to the charge that he had behaved inappropriately. He subsequently told the BBC that he had provided to Conservative and Liberal Democrat negotiators the advice that 'pace was important, but also the more comprehensive the agreement the better', leading to debate about whether he had sought to bring about a lasting coalition.[8] For an impartial official to seek to influence the type of government that should be formed would seem inappropriate.

Another potential source of difficulty involves circumstances in which conflicting accounts emerge of what took place in negotiations. There was controversy over what precisely Labour had offered the Liberal Democrats in relation to electoral reform in post-election talks the two parties held in May 2010. It did not cause problems for the Civil Service on this occasion, given its lack of involvement in the process. But it shows that, were the Civil Service supporting different sets of parallel negotiations, officials taking part in one set of talks might hear claims about a simultaneous process, also witnessed by career staff, that were at least open to different interpretation. In this scenario, outside critics might claim that the Civil Service was collectively party to some kind of deception. My conclusion is that, whatever the good intentions of individuals involved, and although there has been a genuine attempt to foresee and manage the tensions, the Civil Service should not be in the business of supporting party negotiations. They create a danger that the Civil Service will overreach its proper role. Furthermore,

[6] Cabinet Office, *Ministerial Code* (Cabinet Office, London, 2015).

[7] Civil Service, *The Civil Service Code* (London, Civil Service, 2010).

[8] See House of Commons Political and Constitutional Reform Committee, *Lessons from the Process of Government Formation after the 2010 General Election* (HC 2010–11, 528-I) 14–15.

there is an associated danger of the perception of abuse, whether correct or not, something that is hard to counteract. Coalition negotiations are always likely to create grievances of some kind, and those who hold them may well target the civil servants as culprits, depicting them as meddling in matters in which they should not, to malign ends. Individuals may become subject to unfair personal criticism to which it is hard for them to respond. The Civil Service may suffer, incurring reputational damage for its supposed interference, regardless of whether it actually is involved in a power grab. Moreover, if, as a consequence of involvement in negotiations, officialdom becomes linked, fairly or otherwise, to particular parties or individual politicians, its perceived impartiality will suffer. This outcome could lead to an undermining of the position of the career Civil Service. Whether or not the particular bureaucratic model employed in the UK is the correct one, if it is to be abolished or modified, such changes should take place as part of a deliberate, considered action, not as a secondary, unplanned consequence of practices surrounding government formation. Though it is hard to assess exactly when, it is reasonable to assume that post-General Election negotiations will take place again in the future, and it is this very unpredictability that makes clear and satisfactory provision in codes in advance valuable.

II. PRIME MINISTERS AND GOVERNMENT FORMATION

Changes in government, whether following elections or at other times, are closely connected to the replacement of the individual who holds the most important post within the administration: the Prime Minister. Illustrating the complexities involved, a reading of *The Cabinet Manual* suggests that a number of constitutional players can have a part in decisions about the appointment and removal of premiers:

- The monarch, who has the ultimate legal authority, but is—by convention—supposed to avoid direct engagement in party political matters, therefore meaning that decisions should in practice be devolved to others.
- The incumbent Prime Minister, whose advice is not binding as it is in other cases, but whose counsel and actions may influence the outcome.
- Leading politicians from different parties negotiating between themselves.
- Parties and their processes for determining leaders.
- Parliament, and within it the House of Commons. While the Commons cannot directly remove or install a Prime Minister, decisions about the occupancy of the post are supposed to be based in a judgement of the ability to command confidence—or more precisely, construct a government that can command confidence.
- Others, particularly civil servants, may participate in the process, but are not ascribed the same role in the actual decision.

Many people and institutions are involved in decisions about the occupancy of the premiership. But when should departures from it take place? In defining the circumstances in which premiers might resign, the *Manual* provides an example of its tendency to categorise possibilities. It is possible to infer from the text the existence of three different types of prime ministerial resignation. The first involves a changeover of both premier and government. Commonly, it would occur following a General Election in which the government of a premier loses its Commons majority, or perhaps if there is a shift of allegiances midway through a Parliament. In such circumstances there follows the resignation of a Prime Minister, as *The Cabinet Manual* puts it, 'on behalf of the Government', upon which the monarch asks 'the person who appears most likely to be able to command the confidence of the House to serve as Prime Minister and to form a government' (paragraph 2.8). This account is notable partly for what it does not stipulate: that the Prime Minister has to be the leader of a party. The two posts are not formally conjoined. As we have seen, Winston Churchill became Prime Minister in succession to Neville Chamberlain in 1940, who stayed on as leader of the Conservative Party. For a brief period in 1995, John Major stood aside as Conservative leader, seeking re-election to this office in a bid to restore loyalty to the party. But he first came to the post in 1990 because he was successfully elected leader in succession to Thatcher. Might there still be circumstances in which someone could be appointed Prime Minister without being chosen as leader by a party? The *Manual* leaves this question open, probably deliberately on the part of the authors.

A footnote to paragraph 2.8 leaves open the possibility of a second type of resignation. As the *Manual* puts it 'Rarely, a Prime Minister may resign and then be asked to form a new administration.' The *Manual* cites the examples of Ramsay MacDonald, who was head of a Labour Government and then a National Government in 1931; and Winston Churchill, who formed a Conservative Government after his coalition came to an end in 1945 (paragraph 2.8, footnote 10). In the case of MacDonald, no one party had a majority in the Commons. But this second type of resignation (or non-resignation) can take place in other circumstances—Churchill had a Conservative majority in 1945, and the arithmetic did not strictly require the participation of other parties. In the aftermath of the 2015 General Election, however, it seems that a different type of transition took place. The coalition transmuted into a single party government through the resignation of all Liberal Democrat ministers, followed by a reshuffle and filling of their posts by Conservatives.

The third type of resignation suggested in the *Manual* involves a change in the person holding the premiership, but not the party composition of the government. It has occurred on numerous occasions when there has been a single-party majority in the House of Commons: for instance, Churchill to Eden in 1955; Eden to Macmillan in 1957; Macmillan to Home in 1963; Wilson to Callaghan in 1976; Thatcher to Major in 1990; and Blair to Brown in 2007. Few prime ministers leave office entirely willingly, and such changes might involve immense political drama and disruption—as with the unseating of Thatcher in 1990—but if they do, they need not be constitutionally problematic. However, the Conservative transitions of 1957 and 1963 created difficulties because they were contested, yet the Party did not have a transparent method for choosing a leader. Consequently, the opaque means by which the new Prime Minister took office threatened to draw the monarch and her prerogative power of appointment into party political controversy. Subsequently, the Conservative Party introduced an election process. Thereafter, resignations of the third type have involved a party leadership contest (Labour in 1976 and the Conservatives in 1990), or an unchallenged anointing (Labour in 2007).

The way in which this third type of transition takes place means that internal party procedures in practice form a part of the UK constitution, as allowed for in the *Manual*. It states that if a Prime Minister 'chooses to resign' (or possibly in reality is forced to) as head of a government that is secure in its possession of the confidence of the House of Commons, 'it is for the party or parties in government to identify who can be chosen as the successor' (paragraph 2.18). This statement suggests an existence of party incumbency. Indeed, a party could oust a leader against her will, and would in effect be removing a premier. While the *Manual* elsewhere emphasises that the monarch appoints an *individual person* on a basis that that individual is able to command the necessary Commons support, paragraph 2.18 implies that the premiership is the property of a *party*, or even a group of *two or more parties*. This proposition could become complicated in times of coalition. Presumably the larger or largest participant in the coalition, assuming it had provided the previous Prime Minister, would argue that whomever it elected as its leader should take on the post, though other participants in the coalition may dislike the outcome. Historically, coalition premiers have sometimes come from a smaller group or party: as with David Lloyd George from 1916 to 1922 and Ramsay MacDonald from 1931 to 1935. Thus, while each individual party may now have an open means of determining a leader, there is no clear mechanism for a group of parties taking part in a government for determining a new Prime Minister.

The precise point at which a Prime Minister resigns, the *Manual* broadly acknowledges, is a decision for the individual concerned. But '[r]ecent examples', it holds, point to a practice of premiers' not tendering their resignation before it is possible that 'clear advice could be given to the Sovereign on who should be asked to form a government' (paragraph 2.10). In support of this position the *Manual* refers to the Thatcher, Blair and Brown resignations. The first two cases—Thatcher to Major and Blair to Brown—were 'type 3' transitions, where a single party held a majority and could choose a new leader mid-term. On the subject of Brown in 2010, the *Manual* states that he 'resigned on 11 May, by when it was clear that David Cameron should be asked to form a government' (paragraph 2.10, footnote 13). It then cautiously states, '[i]t remains to be seen whether or not these examples will be regarded in future as having established a constitutional convention' (paragraph 2.10). In a footnote[9] the *Manual* records that the PCRC received evidence asserting the view that the Prime Minister was required to continue in

[9] Fnn 12 and 13 to para 2.10 of the *Manual* appear inadvertently to be reversed, and there appears to be a bracket missing three lines from the bottom of fn 12, at the end of the line.

post until a definite successor was apparent; but that the House of Lords Select Committee on the Constitution concluded that such a responsibility did not exist (paragraph 2.10, footnote 12).

III. CONFIDENCE

Confidence is a critical yet amorphous concept at the heart of the system of parliamentary government in the UK.[10] On the surface it might appear that—as a consequence of the Fixed-term Parliaments Act 2011, section 2 of which deals with confidence motions—it is now more firmly defined, and that is no longer part of convention but has a statutory basis. The reality is more complicated, as a consideration of *The Cabinet Manual* suggests. The *Manual* sets out the fundamental rule that should apply. Governments must be able to 'command the confidence of the elected House of Commons'. No statement could be more important to the UK as a democratic polity than the expression of the principle that central governments rest on the support of the elected portion of Parliament. Confidence, the *Manual* goes on, is measured by confidence or no-confidence votes, and is not synonymous with 'having a majority or winning every vote' (paragraph 2.7). The definition of votes of confidence is therefore an important area of consideration.

The 2011 Act appears to set out a new means by which confidence may be withdrawn and, having been withdrawn, conferred once more; while the *Manual* sets certain ground-rules for the period following the initial loss of confidence. The *Manual* notes in paragraph 2.19 that under the Act, following the Commons' passing a 'no confidence' motion in accordance with the wording it sets out ('this House has no confidence in Her Majesty's Government'), a time-limited period of 14 days begins. If by the close of this two-week window the Commons has not passed a confidence vote in a government ('this House has confidence in Her Majesty's Government'), an early General Election will take place. The only other way in which a poll can take place in advance of the regular five-year term limit that section 1 of the Act creates, is through MPs amounting to at least two-thirds of the total number of seats in Parliament voting specifically for 'an early parliamentary general election' (see section 2 of the Act). Paragraph 2.19 of the *Manual* emphasises that 'Other decisions of the House of Commons which have previously been regarded as expressing "no confidence" in the government no longer enable or require the Prime Minister to hold a general election.' This wording seems to leave open the possibility that these 'Other decisions' could still be interpreted as statements of a lack of confidence, but that while they once might have led to a General Election, they can no longer do so as clearly.

While the Act itself does not seek to prescribe what precisely should happen during the 14-day period that a 'no confidence' vote triggers, the *Manual* does

[10] D Howarth, *The Formation of Governments in the UK: Law, Procedure, Conventions and Politics* (London, The Constitution Society, 2015).

offer guidance. It iterates that, as at other times, a premier is 'expected to resign where it is clear that he or she does not have the confidence of the House of Commons and that an alternative does have the confidence' (paragraph 2.19). This statement is confusing. It seems to imply that the Prime Minister in a government against which a 'no confidence' vote has passed has not necessarily lost the confidence of the Commons. There is, it seems, some other means of discerning the final disappearance of this form of support, but the *Manual* does not specify what it is. Paragraph 2.31 then states that 'a government' that has lost a 'no confidence' vote in the terms of the Act 'will remain in office during the government formation period of up to 14 days, until a government has secured the confidence of the House of Commons, or no government has secured such confidence', after which a date will be set for the early General Election, with Parliament dissolving 17 working days in advance. The *Manual* suggests, then, that a government can potentially stay on to seek to reverse the 'no confidence' vote; or that a different administration may form to attempt to achieve this outcome.

The procedures set out in the Fixed-term Parliaments Act 2011 for 'no confidence' and 'confidence' would be better described simply as an early General Election procedure. The initial 'no confidence' vote should not be seen as dealing directly with 'confidence' but as a decision to hold a poll before the usual term limit (though a government that lost such a vote might well also have lost confidence). This variety of early General Election includes a safeguard mechanism in the form of a 14-day cooling-off period, during which the Commons can reverse its decision through using a specific form of words included in the 2011 Act. The Act is silent on the meaning of these motions for a government as such; and as we have seen, the *Manual*, in particular paragraph 2.31 of the text, allows for an administration to continue in office after losing a 'no confidence' vote.

Confidence remains a freestanding concept, separate from the provisions of the 2011 Act.[11] In paragraph 2.12 the *Manual* iterates that a sitting government, following a poll that does not deliver a single-party majority, 'is entitled to wait until the new Parliament has met to see if it can command the confidence of the House of Commons'. This passage does not specify how this confidence is expressed, nor what would happen if it were not forthcoming. Indeed, in its January 2015 Report, *Revisiting The Cabinet Manual*, PCRC recommended that the Government provide greater clarity than contained in the *Manual* regarding 'the continuance in office or otherwise of administrations following a general election'.[12] Nonetheless, in this particular account of the need for confidence, the *Manual* does allow for it to exist other than in the form provided for under 2011 Act, albeit without a direct link to a possible early General Election. At other times too, a government might decide that it had lost the confidence of the Commons, irrespective of the wording prescribed in the statute. How it acted upon this conclusion is another matter,

[11] For a discussion of confidence in its different manifestations, see House of Lords Select Committee on the Constitution, *Fixed-term Parliaments Bill* (HL 2010–11, 69) 28–30.

[12] House of Commons Political and Constitutional Reform Committee, above n 5, 30.

and the Prime Minister could not request a dissolution from the monarch, as once would have been possible. As the Lords Select Committee on the Constitution put it when considering the 2011 Act when in Bill form, '[b]roadly speaking, we understand the current convention is that it is for the government to determine what constitutes a vote of confidence'.[13] There is no reason to suppose that the 2011 Act has ended this principle, and the *Manual* does not claim that it has.

IV. PARLIAMENTS WITH NO OVERALL MAJORITY IN THE HOUSE OF COMMONS

As previously discussed, an important motive for the creation of *The Cabinet Manual* was the judgement—which proved well-founded—that the General Election due to take place in 2010 might not deliver a clear victor. (The prospect of a similar outcome in 2015 helped sustain the perceived relevance of the text, though this expectation was false.) A crucial component of the *Manual* was therefore its handling of the interconnected issues this eventuality would make more salient: how one government might come to an end and another be formed; the nature of prime-ministerial resignations; what roles, responsibilities and limitations should attach to the different players such as party politicians, officials and the monarch; and where Parliament fitted into the picture. Similar concerns can apply in relation to any General Election or change of premier, but they become more potent when combined with a Commons lacking a single-party majority.

There is some tension and arguably confusion in the description of post-election arrangements contained in the section of the *Manual* entitled 'Parliaments with no overall majority in the House of Commons' (paragraphs 2.12–2.17). Paragraph 2.12 tells us that a government is 'entitled' to wait until Parliament has met, but is also 'expected to resign if it becomes clear' that it will not secure 'confidence and there is a clear alternative'. If its being 'expected' to resign amounts to a constitutional requirement, then perhaps the description of its being 'entitled' to wait is not appropriate if its right to do so is contingent on other circumstances set out in the paragraph. Furthermore, it is not clear whether being 'expected' to stand down at this particular point overrides the reference in paragraph 2.10 to its being 'a matter for the Prime Minister … to judge the appropriate time at which to resign'. Another difficulty is the reference in paragraph 2.12 to 'the incumbent government' staying until the Prime Minister resigns. What should happen, for instance, if a two-party coalition is in power, and then following a General Election that does not yield a single party victor, the smaller parliamentary party—from which the Prime Minister is not drawn—pulls out. Can the Government be said still to be in existence? Should the Prime Minister resign at this point, and if necessary seek reappointment as the head of a new government, whether comprising a single

[13] House of Lords Select Committee on the Constitution, above n 11, 29.

party or a different coalition? What if it is not clear that this new administration would be able to secure confidence, but neither is it clear that another government is possible? Paragraph 2.13 then introduces the idea that, in a Parliament in which 'a range of different administrations could potentially be formed, political parties may wish to hold discussions to establish who is best able to command the confidence of the House of Commons and should form the next government'. One purpose of this formulation is to place on leading politicians the need to resolve the matter between them, and not draw in the monarch.

Providing an example of its tendency to delineate courses of action available to politicians in defined circumstances, the *Manual* asserts in paragraph 2.17 that when the Commons lacks an 'overall majority', there are 'three broad types of government' possible. The first is 'single party, minority government'. This approach, the *Manual* states, can—but does not have to—rest on 'a series of ad hoc agreements based on common interests'. Second is a 'formal inter-party agreement'—that is a parliamentary but not government coalition. A relatively recent case of the employment of this model came with the deal between Labour and the Liberals in 1977–78. The third approach, the one in use at the time the first edition of the *Manual* was published, is that of 'formal coalition government', normally involving the appointment of 'ministers from more than one political party' and 'a majority in the House of Commons'. The *Manual* does not note that full coalitions have occurred in circumstances when, though one party possessed a majority on its own, it was nonetheless in coalition with other parties. Arguably, then, the 'formal coalition government' model could divide into coalitions of arithmetical necessity and those founded for other reasons. There is no reference in the *Manual* to the possibility of pre-election pacts, either through tactical agreements over which seats to contest, or indications by particular parties of their preferred coalition partner in advance of a poll—perhaps because no such arrangements existed prior to the General Election of 2010. Nor is there any discussion of the consequence of coalitions and coalition agreements for mandates, a concept that is referred to elsewhere in the *Manual*.[14]

V. THE MONARCHY AND ELECTIONS

Another force on the electoral and government-forming landscape is the head of state. *The Cabinet Manual* offers a flat description of the role of the monarch—or 'Sovereign', the term the *Manual* employs—in a number of areas of key importance. It notes that the head of state 'opens each new Session of Parliament, and brings the session to an end, proroguing Parliament if necessary by Order in Council'. In circumstances in which, under the terms of the Fixed-term

[14] T Quinn, *Mandates, Manifestos and Coalitions: UK party politics after 2010* (London, The Constitution Society, 2014).

Parliaments Act 2011, an election is triggered before the standard five-year point, the monarch 'fixes the date of the election by Proclamation on the recommendation of the Prime Minister'. Lastly, she 'fixes by Proclamation the date for the next meeting of Parliament' (paragraph 1.1). This issuing of a day for the convening of a newly elected Parliament takes place, the *Manual* tells us, 'on the advice of the Prime Minister'. It notes that it had become practice for this meeting to take place on the first Wednesday after the General Election, but that following a 2007 recommendation from the Select Committee on the Modernisation of the House of Commons, there was in 2010 a reversion to an approach that had prevailed previously, entailing a wait of 12 days (paragraph 2.4). No guidance as to what the position should be now, or the underlying principles, is on offer.

The *Manual* also fails fully to rule out the possibility of radical political intervention in government formation processes drawing on monarchical authority. Paragraph 2.9, part of a section on 'The principles of government formation', states, 'Historically, the Sovereign has made use of reserve powers to dismiss a Prime Minister or to make a personal choice of successor.' The last such deployment of this authority, it notes, took place in 1834, when William IV removed Lord Melbourne without the Government of the latter having lost the confidence of the Commons. This incident, the *Manual* judges, 'was regarded as having undermined the Sovereign'. But it does not clearly state that it could not or should not be repeated. The equivocation continues, '[i]n modern times the convention has been that the Sovereign should not be drawn into party politics'. This sentence is not the firmest possible exclusion of the outcome to which it refers.

In reference to a House of Commons without a single-party majority, paragraph 2.9 then holds that it is the task of 'those involved in the political process, and in particular the parties represented in Parliament', to discern the individual who is most able 'to command the confidence of the House of Commons', and to pass this information on to the monarch. At the centre of this process is the sitting Prime Minister, who is the 'principal adviser' to the monarch. The monarch 'may'—but by implication presumably may not—ask an outgoing premier about who the successor should be (paragraph 2.9). The emphasis in this passage, then, is upon party politicians helping the monarch to avoid becoming embroiled in events; there is no mention of a need for restraint on the part of the head of state. Surely protecting the democratic system from the monarch is the primary concern, not protecting the monarch from the democratic system? If this thought was in the minds of the authors of the *Manual*, they were too deferential to express it. Vagaries continue in the account of the role of the monarch during inter-party talks aimed at forming a government following an inconclusive General Election. The *Manual* tells us, '[t]he Sovereign would not expect to become involved in any negotiations'. Nonetheless, participants should 'keep the Palace informed'. Either 'political parties or the Cabinet Secretary' could do so, and the Principal Private Secretary to the Prime Minister can play a part as well, in such activities as 'communicating with the Palace' (paragraph 2.13).

VI. CONCLUSION

Codification of procedures around elections and government formation was the most important single purpose lying behind *The Cabinet Manual*. Yet in pursuing this objective, a text that was a unilateral output of the executive sought to define and in practice—whether intentionally or otherwise—change arrangements that extended beyond Whitehall. Establishing administrations is a task that engages multiple players, especially the electorate, the House of Commons and the monarchy. It is not a process that can be owned by the executive. Indeed, there are grounds for questioning whether, as a party directly interested in rules determining how one government can succeed another, the Cabinet should be involved in codification in this area at all. Furthermore, the task is not as straightforward as it might initially seem. The accounts provided in the *Manual* are open to dispute in a number of areas.

Nonetheless, for all their problems, this branch of the codification project certainly deals with matters that are central to the UK as a democracy, and have opened up important areas of discussion in new ways. They include questions that are central to any constitution. How is government constituted? From where and by what means does it derive legitimacy? Who is responsible for decisions about the conferral of office? Of particular significance in a democratic system, how do transitions from one administration to another take place? What rules are appropriate in such circumstances? What happens when mechanisms in place do not deliver as clear an outcome as some might wish? These issues are of transcendent importance. Given that concerted official attempts to express in public documents rules that have taken centuries to develop have begun only recently, perhaps we should not be surprised that there are problems with the texts. There is hope that a future edition of *The Cabinet Manual*, for instance, might clarify the nature of confidence in a non-statutory sense more clearly. Perhaps, however, features of the system are so illogical as to defy satisfactory elucidation. It may be that an outcome of codification is not only to explain, but to expose.

10

Devolved and Local Government

I. *THE CABINET MANUAL* AND TERRITORIAL GOVERNANCE

THE UK MAY have appeared historically to have been a unitary state. But the reality has always been more complicated. Generally the label 'unitary' is set out in counterpoint to the description 'federal'. The unitary system accords primacy to the central institutions of governance. Regional and local tiers can exist beneath them, but lack entrenched autonomy. Under the federal model, there is a constitutionally protected sharing of authorities between the 'federal' organs at the centre, and the territorially dispersed 'states'. The principle of supremacy for the UK Parliament at Westminster encouraged a view that the UK, given this legal dominance from the centre, was unitary. But in fact the UK has throughout its existence been characterised by a conflict between a supposedly all-powerful Parliament on the one hand, and pronounced territorial diversity on the other hand. Some believe the UK is best seen as a 'union' rather than 'unitary' state, because it was formed out of a series of combinations of nations, each with their own diverse traditions and identities, some of which have been given legal and institutional expression within the UK.[1] Differences of religion, language, legal and educational systems, and local government have received formal recognition. Moreover, this provision for variation has taken place in an uneven fashion—for instance, with the existence of Secretaries of State for Wales, Scotland and Northern Ireland, but not for England.

In the era of devolution beginning from the late 1990s (though Northern Ireland had a devolved parliament and executive from 1921–72), the UK has moved further still from the unitary model and increasingly taken on a federal quality, with the devolved territories resembling the 'states' found within a federal system. However, the UK is not fully federal. Devolution has not been extended to most of England, where the large majority of the UK population resides: federalisation is only limited. Furthermore, there is no written federal constitution to which all other institutions are subject. Parliament has retained—in theory at least—its legal supremacy, though as we shall see, this principle is in practice under strain as a consequence of devolution (and other factors). Nonetheless, the

[1] S Rokkan and DW Urwin, *Economy, Territory, Identity: the politics of West European peripheries* (London, Sage, 1983) 187; E Wicks, *The Evolution of a Constitution: Eight Key Moments in British Constitutional History* (Oxford, Hart Publishing, 2006) 167–68.

persistence of the centralising dimension to the UK constitution is observable in the status of local as opposed to devolved government. The tier closest to the public, it has at least since the 1930s suffered from progressive removal of control over policy and finance. On a rhetorical level there is a broad political consensus that local authorities ought to possess more power than they do. However, this theoretical commitment has not yet amounted to a comprehensive reversal of the denuding of democratic political autonomy from the localities.[2]

The tensions between these different tendencies relating to the territorial governance of the UK have encouraged the production of codes that attempt to set out the way in which they should be regulated. We saw, for instance, in Chapter 2, section I.A. that the Barnett Formula was introduced to create a viable mechanism for the allocation of funds to the different parts of the UK. Furthermore, the UK Government and the Local Government Association agreed in 2007 a *Central-Local Concordat*, though it made negligible impact (see Chapter 2, section IV.A.). *The Cabinet Manual*[3] attempts to provide a broad overview in its Chapter Eight, entitled 'Relations with the Devolved Administrations and local government'. The text is notable for being more willing to afford constitutional significance to devolved than local government. Its introductory statement remarks that setting up the devolved institutions 'has had a significant impact on the governance of the UK'. It then goes on to state that 'In addition, central government has devolved powers and responsibilities to local authorities which are directly elected and have limited power to tax' (p 62). This account of local government could be misleading if it encouraged the impression that the existence of central government pre-dated local government, and that the former then created the latter. Definite evidence of local government of some kind dates to Anglo-Saxon times.[4] Eventually, and in particular from the 1930s, Parliament—a relative newcomer to the scene dating only to the thirteenth century—began to use its legislative authority to grant more power to UK ministers, at the expense of democratic local government, in such areas as health and education. The reference to local authorities having 'limited power to tax' is telling. It is accurate, especially if 'limited' is treated as the most significant word. Notwithstanding some planned changes, local authorities have an internationally exceptional lack of fiscal autonomy. But they once had more power in this area than they do now, with the 1980s in particular marking the beginning of new controls imposed from Westminster and Whitehall.

The *Manual* makes more of devolution than local government. It notes that 'Government proceeds in accordance with the convention that Parliament would not normally legislate with regard to devolved matters except with the agreement of the devolved legislature' (paragraph 8.5). (The Scotland Bill first introduced

[2] House of Commons Political and Constitutional Reform Committee, *Prospects for codifying the relationship between central and local government*, vol 1 (HC 2012–13, 656-I).

[3] Cabinet Office, *The Cabinet Manual: A guide to the laws, conventions and rules on the operation of government*, 1st edn (London, Cabinet Office, 2011).

[4] A Blick, *Beyond Magna Carta: a constitution for the United Kingdom* (Oxford, Hart Publishing, 2015) 33.

to Parliament in 2015 further complicated the position by seeking to place the rule regarding legislative consent for Scotland on a statutory basis, and declaring the Scottish Parliament and Government to be permanent constitutional fixtures. The Draft Wales Bill then set out a similar plan for Wales.) The word 'normally' is a significant, and vague, qualifier. Moreover, while acknowledging this practical limitation on its legislative power, the *Manual* is careful to iterate that 'Parliament remains sovereign: it expressly retains the power to legislate on any matter, whether or not the devolved legislature could legislate in that area, and to amend the powers of the devolved legislatures' (paragraph 8.1). It then repeats the point, stating that 'Parliament remains sovereign and retains authority to legislate on any issue, whether devolved or not. It is ultimately for Parliament to decide what use to make of that power' (paragraph 8.5). This insistence reflects but also elaborates upon stipulations inserted in the different devolution statutes, such as section 28(7) of the Scotland Act 1998, which provides that the establishment of a Scottish Parliament able to issue Acts does 'not affect the power of the Parliament of the United Kingdom to make laws for Scotland'. There are some important differences between the Acts and the *Manual*. First, the latter uses the word 'sovereign', but it is not included in legislation. Secondly, the *Manual* expressly refers to the right of Parliament to 'amend the powers of the devolved legislatures', while the legislation does not. Is this statement compatible with the declaration included in the present Scotland Bill (and projected for Wales) that the Scottish Parliament (alongside the Scottish Government) is recognised as a 'permanent' part of the constitutional arrangements of the UK?

The *Manual* makes no specific reference to the possibility that the UK Parliament might abolish the devolved institutions altogether, though its wording leaves open the possibility that it could (though again this possibility raises questions about the purpose of the Scotland Bill). Furthermore, it is silent on the role that referendums might play in future decisions. All the devolved systems were established following affirmative popular votes in the areas concerned, and some would argue that it would be inappropriate for them to be undone without further such consent. The *Manual* does not consider this issue. However, the Government conceded this principle through an amendment to the Scotland Bill, and a future edition of the *Manual* would need to recognise it. While the text mentions the initiating referendums in Wales and Scotland (and the second referendum in Wales of 2011, which authorised the expansion of the legislative role of the Assembly), when it refers to the 'Belfast Multi-Party Agreement', it does not state that referendums were held and won on this deal both in Northern Ireland and in the Republic. Nor does it mention the occasions on which the UK Government has suspended devolution in Northern Ireland during difficulties with the peace process. It does not note the provision in the Belfast Agreement, incorporated into UK law by the Northern Ireland Act 1998, that provides for Northern Ireland to leave the UK and join with the Republic.

The *Manual* refers to the *Memorandum of Understanding* and the *Devolution Guidance Notes* that elaborate on it, but stresses that these documents 'are not legally binding' and are merely intended 'to set out principles to which all officials can adhere' (see section II. below for analysis of the *Memorandum*). Much could rest here on what is defined as legally binding, since it is conceivable that the agreements could be regarded as creating a legitimate expectation of certain forms of behaviour by the UK executive, which might figure in judicial review.[5] The *Manual* also notes the existence of individual agreements between departments in Whitehall and devolved administrations (paragraph 8.17). It stresses the importance of 'mutual respect and recognition of the responsibilities' accorded to each party in their relationship (paragraph 8.18).

Presumably because it is a devolved matter in other parts of the UK, the *Manual* deals with local government only in England. It begins in paragraph 8.27 by stating that 'local authorities are statutory bodies created by Acts of Parliament'. We have already considered the potentially misleading nature of this statement. While it exists under statute today, local government as a form of political organisation, as discussed above, pre-dates Parliament. Furthermore, it has surely been an integral part of the UK constitutional system, and has a status as being something more than merely dependent on the will of Parliament. However, from the point of view of Whitehall and Westminster, the conception of local government as a core component of governance may not be as obvious. In footnote 16 to paragraph 8.27, the *Manual* records that '[h]istorically, boroughs were created by Royal Charter', with statutory intervention following later. The *Manual* then goes on in paragraph 8.27 to note that local authorities 'are not accountable to Parliament, as they are directly elected by their local communities'. Yet having acknowledged this self-contained democratic legitimacy, the document then states that 'ministers can direct local government to adhere to national policy frameworks where legislation permits'. The *Manual* does not specifically discuss what, if any, the proper limits are on encroachment on local government from the centre. It does, however, assert that present practices and arrangements in England adhere to the European Charter of Local Self-Government. As previously discussed, it is difficult to sustain this claim with any credence (see Chapter 2, section IV.A.). The *Manual* makes no reference to adherence or otherwise to the Charter in the devolved territories.

II. DEVOLUTION AND THE *MEMORANDUM OF UNDERSTANDING*

Though the account it provides is revealing, devolution and local government are only two of a number of issues addressed by *The Cabinet Manual*. The need to deal with these subjects was not a primary reason that the text came into being. Other codes, however, are specifically focused on territorial governance of the UK. The tectonic shifts that have occurred within the UK constitution with the advent of devolution since the late 1990s have necessitated further codification, exemplified

[5] R Rawlings, 'Concordats of the Constitution' (2000) 116 *LQR* 257.

by the *Memorandum of Understanding*, the most recent version of which used here is dated October 2013, supplanting the earlier version from December 2001.[6]

The *Memorandum*, totalling 60 pages, is an example of how codification can be a response to major structural constitutional change that has been effected through statute, in this instance the various Acts of Parliament giving expression to devolution. While being reactive in its introduction, the *Memorandum* was also creative in intent. Rather than describing pre-existing practices, it sought publicly to announce new arrangements. The *Memorandum* was the product of, in the words of its 'Explanatory Note', 'a series of agreements between the UK Government and the devolved administrations in Scotland, Wales and Northern Ireland'. It set out 'the principles which underlie relations between them'. In the time before the late 1990s (with the exception of the period when devolved government operated in Northern Ireland) there was no such set of relationships to consider. But now the UK constitution had changed significantly. Viewed from one perspective, the UK was moving in the direction of, but not all the way towards, a federal system, within which the UK level was in some ways equivalent to the 'federal' tier, with the devolved areas resembling 'states'. Responsibilities such as foreign affairs, defence and security, and macroeconomic policy were retained at UK level; while policies such as education and health were devolved—a division analogous to that employed in federal countries.

A key difference between the UK and conventional federal constitutions is that within the former, devolution has not extended to much of England (perhaps with the exception of Greater London), where most of the UK population lives (though more regional devolution is being devised and implemented for England at the time of writing). Another distinction is that the UK does not have a single text clearly labelled as its constitution, protected from casual alteration through amendment procedures and judicially enforceable. 'Written' constitutions exist in a variety of systems, federal and otherwise, but such a text would, in a federal system, apportion powers to the federal and state levels of governance, all the organs of which would be subject to the constitution. In the UK, the Westminster Parliament retains a law-making power that is not limited by a 'written constitution', with the devolved institutions subordinate to its legal authority. The constraints upon the supposedly 'sovereign' Parliament, at least in orthodox accounts, are almost wholly practical and political. Furthermore, it would be likely that a 'federal' legislature would include within it, probably in an upper house, a territorial component, to ensure that the states could play a part in federal decision making. The UK does not have any such 'states' chamber' in its Parliament. Despite recent developments, then, there are important distinctions between the UK and a fully federal country. It is notable, however, that the *Memorandum of Understanding*

[6] *Memorandum of Understanding and Supplementary Agreements Between the United Kingdom Government, the Scottish Ministers, the Welsh Ministers, and the Northern Ireland Executive Committee*, Presented to Parliament by Command of Her Majesty and presented to the Scottish Parliament and the Northern Ireland Assembly and laid before the National Assembly for Wales, October 2013.

considered below provides, in a manner that deliberately lacks hard legal force, for some of the features that might otherwise exist under a federal 'written constitution', including provision for consultation with the devolved administrations over matters that, strictly speaking, are legally within the remit of the UK tier of governance alone.

In explaining that it is a product of 'agreements' between different administrations, the *Memorandum* 'Explanatory Note' serves to raise an important point. Generally the texts considered in this book are issued by one institution on its own initiative, perhaps subject to some non-binding consultation. The *Memorandum of Understanding*, however, is the outcome of concurrence between different bodies, affording it a different status—and arguably greater force. However, the 'Explanatory Note' enters the familiar caveat that 'It is not intended that these agreements should be legally binding.' Part I of the text is the *Memorandum of Understanding* itself. It notes that it describes the 'understanding' of the parties to it 'of the principles that will underlie relations between them'. It begins with an account of the ministerial representation of the territories of the UK. The Government of the UK is responsible for policy areas that are not devolved. However, UK departments and ministers accept that the UK Secretaries of State for Northern Ireland, Scotland and Wales have a part to play in 'ensuring that the interests of those parts of the UK' are provided for in the conduct of non-devolved policy. They appear in this account as lobbyists for their respective territories. But who represents England? There is no Secretary of State for England, and the Memorandum notes that '[o]ther UK Ministers and their departments represent the interests of England in all matters' (paragraph 1). The Memorandum does not discuss whether there is a tension inherent in the arrangement whereby UK ministers and departments with policy rather than territorial briefs are, at the same time, representatives of one part of the UK. Paragraph 2 iterates that the *Memorandum* is 'a statement of political intent' and is not intended to be 'a binding agreement. It does not create legal obligations'.

While the *Memorandum* is the central agreement between the UK and devolved administrations, as paragraph 3 notes, there is a variety of further sub-agreements dealing with various matters. A core feature of the agreed relationship is 'Communication and Consultation'. The four participants in the agreement 'are committed to the principle of good communication' between themselves, in particular in circumstances where the activities of one has implications for the sphere of operation of another (paragraph 4). The *Memorandum* therefore states that the administrations will endeavour to give advance notice of 'relevant developments', will take into account responses they receive and will 'establish where appropriate' mechanisms that facilitate cooperation over the devising of policy in areas of overlap (paragraph 5). The *Memorandum* recognises limits to these principles of information sharing, drawing specific attention to national security and the (UK) Budget as areas in which its application will be circumscribed (paragraph 6). Paragraph 7 yet again emphasises the desire to avoid the engagement of the courts, stating that the text 'does not create any ... legal right to be consulted'. Yet whatever this text may insist, ultimately, whether there is a reasonable expectation of consultation over a particular decision, and the part that a document such as the *Memorandum* might play in reaching a conclusion over this question, would be matters for a court to resolve.

The next section, 'Co-operation', opens with the statement that 'All four administrations want to work together … on matters of mutual interest' and that they 'recognise the importance of cooperation across a range of areas'. It goes on to note that the different administrations might choose to 'undertake activities on each other's behalf' (paragraph 8). It is notable, in the light of this commitment, that each of the three devolved administrations that are included within the *Memorandum* have at some point included within them a party that is committed in some way to national independence and the end of the UK as currently composed, even if only as a longer-term goal. Perhaps the concept of 'mutual interest' is, for the purposes of the *Memorandum*, exceptionally flexible; or perhaps there is something of a disconnect between the underlying goals of certain political parties and the capacity of their leaders to engage in ongoing governmental business in a more practical sense, cooperating with others as necessary, regardless of more fundamental incongruities that may exist. Devolution seems to promote collaboration between different camps, even if it has been less successful at encouraging a shared commitment to the union. To facilitate these intra-UK relations, certain ground rules are necessary, such as 'Confidentiality', explained in paragraph 12. One of the principles involved is that 'it is for the administration providing the information to state what, if any, restrictions there should be upon its usage'.

The *Memorandum* then moves, in a section headed 'Parliamentary Business', to matters that might in another country be the subject of a written constitution: the respective powers of the different tiers of governance within the UK. Paragraph 14 is an important statement of constitutional principle, which seeks to assert once again the notion of the supremacy of the UK Parliament, but also to suggest the existence of practical limitations upon its legal authority, rendering it more acceptable from the perspective of sub-UK autonomy. It reads as follows:

> The United Kingdom Parliament retains ultimate authority to legislate on any issue, whether devolved or not. It is ultimately for Parliament to decide what use to make of that power. However, the UK Government will proceed in accordance with the convention that the UK Parliament would not normally legislate with regard to devolved matters except with the agreement of the devolved legislature. The devolved administrations will be responsible for seeking such agreement as may be required for this purpose on an approach from the UK Government.

The last sentence could be read as implying that a devolved administration is committed to trying to pass through its legislature whatever the UK Government wants to do. But the position in practice is that there is a need for some kind of discussion and, as necessary, negotiation to ensure that both sides are happy before progress can be made. Paragraph 15 further asserts that the UK Parliament 'retains the absolute right' not only to legislate as it sees fit, but to discuss, investigate or issue opinions relating to policy areas that are devolved. Once again, the

UK Government commits that it will 'encourage' the Parliament in Westminster to restrain itself, and to take into account 'the primary responsibility of devolved legislatures and administrations' in certain spheres, and 'that it is a consequence of Parliament's decision to devolve certain matters that Parliament itself will in future be more restricted in its field of operation'. In paragraph 16, the devolved administrations agree to reciprocate, encouraging their legislatures to recognise the reserved role of the UK Parliament in some fields. But while the devolved assemblies can in theory debate whatever they choose, their law-making powers are circumscribed in ways that those of the UK Parliament are not. Consequently there is not the same need for the devolved executives to urge self-control in these areas. Paragraphs 14–16 demonstrate that while the *Memorandum* is an agreement between executives, it deals with wider issues, in particular the activities of elected legislatures.

Having set out a requirement for mutual respect of spheres of operation, the *Memorandum* then seeks to establish means by which devolved administrations might have an input into policy areas that, while lying outside their legal area of responsibility, are clearly of direct importance to them. It records 'that the devolved administrations will have an interest in international and European policy making in relation to devolved matters', particularly in cases when they will be responsible for 'implementing action' that arises (paragraph 18). This statement does not amount to an acknowledgement that the devolved systems should have a right, as parts of the whole, to a role in major decisions that the UK takes for itself—as they might under a federal system, possibly to be achieved through their presence in the upper chamber of a federal legislature (if the German model were followed). But it does at least recognise that it is proper for them to have some kind of influence extending beyond their legally delineated authority. It is particularly important that the devolved administrations should have an input into European Union policy, since though not devolved itself, it makes up such a large component of those policies that are devolved. Through the *Memorandum*, the UK Government pledges to 'involve the devolved administrations as fully as possible in discussions' regarding the development of UK stances inside the European Union and in international affairs, where they 'touch on devolved matters' (paragraph 20). Alongside an informal sharing of influence, the *Memorandum* seeks to allocate responsibility for failure. If financial consequences arise from shortcomings in the upholding of European law, they become the responsibility of whichever executive it fell to in the particular instance (paragraph 21).

The text then introduces an institutional mechanism intended to facilitate the arrangements set out in the *Memorandum*: 'The Joint Ministerial Committee'. The document notes that the preferred approach of all parties to the agreement is one of 'bilateral or multilateral' engagement 'on a day-to-day basis' between the particular departments involved in a given matter. However, 'some central co-ordination of the overall relationship is needed'. Hence the *Memorandum* notes the willingness of all the executives to take part in a Joint Ministerial Committee (JMC) comprising their respective ministers (paragraph 23). The business of the

JMC is, first, 'to consider' issues that are not devolved that impact upon those that are devolved, and vice versa; secondly, if devolved and UK administrations wish to do so, to assess how particular aspects of devolved business are handled across the UK; thirdly, to handle disagreements between the executives (paragraph 24). Presumably to seek to prevent the JMC from becoming a perpetual forum for arguments, paragraphs 25 and 26 commit the parties to the *Memorandum* to attempting to deal with disputes by more ordinary means before referral to the JMC. If a disagreement cannot be settled by these means, there are other ways of resolving it, set out in statute and loaded in favour of the UK tier. Under devolution legislation, as the *Memorandum* recalls, UK ministers have the authority to carry out direct intervention in devolved business; and it is also possible for the Law Officers to call on the UK Supreme Court to decide whether an action is within the legal authority provided at devolved level. The UK Government maintains in the *Memorandum* that it 'is prepared to use these powers if necessary', though regarding them 'very much as a matter of last resort'. Consequently, when a devolved administration and the UK Government are engaged in a dispute, they will seek to settle it 'through discussion so as to avoid any action or omission by the devolved administration having an adverse impact on non-devolved matters' (paragraph 27).

Part II of the *Memorandum* comprises a set of 'Supplementary Agreements', providing more detail regarding the arrangements provided for in Part I. They deal with the JMC; a 'Concordat on Co-ordination of European Union Policy Issues'; a 'Concordat on Financial Assistance to Industry'; and a 'Concordat on International Relations', including a sub-agreement with each individual devolved territory, and a collective agreement. Various departments have published bilateral agreements not included in the *Memorandum*. Overall responsibility for the text at UK level was given, during the coalition era, by the Prime Minister to the Deputy Prime Minister. The Foreign Secretary and the Business Secretary also took a lead on certain matters; and the Secretaries of State for the nations had a role in promoting good working relations. At the devolved end, the respective First Ministers had the pre-eminent role in handling the *Memorandum* and associated texts (Explanatory Note).

III. CONCLUSION

This chapter has demonstrated once again that codification involves not only the executive, or the internal arrangements of any one institution, but also the relations between different constitutional entities. In this instance, all of those bodies involved are components of governmental systems able to claim their own distinct democratic mandates (albeit derived indirectly via elections to legislatures). Reflecting the authority of the different parties to it, the *Memorandum of Understanding* is jointly owned, and unlike some texts is not the product of a unilateral initiative. Codification of the kind considered here reveals that it has a spatial, territorial dimension, as well as being simply organisational. The texts dealing with devolution extrapolate some of the constitutional ambiguities inherent in the UK as a union state that have become more pronounced since devolution. Parliamentary 'sovereignty' is asserted in tandem with an acknowledgement of the importance of sources of political legitimacy beyond Westminster—a combination that can seem uncomfortable. Codification in this area is both a reactive phenomenon, arising from the need to respond to the advent of devolution, and creative, in that it seeks to establish new working practices and principles. The arrangements and rules described amount to a substantial practical constraint upon parliamentary supremacy as traditionally conceived, though theoretically subject to an override. The establishment of these precepts is now proving to be part of a process that leads on to legislative enactment, as is taking place with the Scotland Bill already at the time of writing. Codes also depict institutional paraphernalia, without statutory basis, designed to operate in the constitutional environment of devolution.

Yet we should not imagine all the arrangements set out are effective in practice. A 2015 Report by the Institute for Government, for instance, recorded doubts about the efficacy of the JMC, and made recommendations for its improvement.[7] Moreover, descriptions of the position of local government reveal, perhaps unintentionally, the unfortunate circumstances in which this democratic tier has found itself. The way in which it is presented suggests a status clearly inferior to that of the devolved institutions, and of course the UK tier. Moreover, in describing the system of devolved government, though they may promote the need to respect the devolved sphere of interest, codes are careful at present to reserve the ultimate authority of the UK Parliament. They insist that the Westminster legislature still holds the final trump card, even if it might be reluctant to play it.

The potential for a clash between parliamentary supremacy and other values is a theme that continues in Chapter 11.

[7] A Paun and R Munro, *Governing in an Ever Looser Union: How the four governments of the UK cooperate, negotiate and compete* (London, Institute for Government, 2015) 84.

11

Codification and the Rule of Law

THE RULE OF law is a concept fundamental to the UK system of government.[1] It entails the existence of a set of legal norms to which all within society, both governors and those they govern, are subordinate. To be meaningful, it entails more than a simple requirement for formal legality. A rejection of excessively narrow versions of the rule of law means that it is not acceptable for a governing group to claim that it can legitimise oppressive, arbitrary or grossly discriminatory activity through providing for it in legislation. For this reason, law-making processes should be robust and inclusive. The law must be possible to know and understand, it must provide a degree of protection for all and it must be accessible to all. An independent judiciary should be responsible for the consistent, universal application of the law. Though the rise of the rule of law as a concept pre-dates democracy in the UK, the connections between the two are strong. Only a widely participative political system can imbue the law with sufficient legitimacy, and protect against excessive manipulation. Equally, democracy becomes devalued if abuse of the majoritarian principle leads to the denial of basic entitlements. Consequently, a set of rights including freedom of expression, association and assembly, and the right to due process and to participate in free elections, is often seen as intrinsic both to democracy and the rule of law.

In many states the relationship between democracy and the rule of law is managed principally through written constitutions, which provide for popular input into law-making while seeking to ensure that a democratic mandate cannot provide a basis for the undoing of 'thick' conceptions of legality and even democracy itself. In the UK, with no written constitution, guarantees must come from elsewhere. As we have seen, according to more conventional understandings, the Westminster Parliament is supreme or 'sovereign'. According to this theory, ultimately it can legislate largely as it chooses, even in ways that contravene core principles of the rule of law. Another view, not mainstream but held by some eminent advocates, is that the courts could, in extreme circumstances, refuse to recognise an Act of Parliament that seriously contravened fundamental constitutional tenets. Even if this view is valid, it is not yet tested.[2] Consequently, under UK arrangements,

[1] T Bingham, *The Rule of Law* (London, Penguin, 2011).

[2] See, eg, J Goldsworthy, *Parliamentary Sovereignty: Contemporary Debates* (Cambridge, Cambridge University Press, 2010) 14–56.

we depend to an unusual extent upon understandings, practices and conventions to uphold the rule of law. Even if an Act of Parliament, such as the Act of Settlement 1701, the Human Rights Act 1998, the Constitutional Reform Act 2005 or the Equality Act 2010, protects aspects of the rule of law, Parliament could in theory simply repeal it if it wished to do so, unless it felt restrained for some practical or moral reason. Consequently, the contents of codes are an important source in this area. In what ways do they engage with the concept of the rule of law? Do they depict arrangements accurately? Lastly, do codes make a contribution to the upholding—or undermining—of the rule of law in any way?

I. THE JUDICIAL PERSPECTIVE

In its 38 pages, the *Guide to Judicial Conduct* gives the point of view of the judiciary.[3] The text applies to both serving and retired judges. It contains a Foreword by Lord Judge who was, at the time of publication of the most recent edition in 2013, the Lord Chief Justice of England and Wales. There follow 'Acknowledgements', an account of the 'Standing Committee on Guide to Judicial Conduct' and an introduction (Chapter one). The succeeding chapters deal with judicial independence, impartiality, integrity, propriety, competence and diligence, personal relationships and perceived bias, activities outside court and post-retirement conduct. There is then an account of the 'Office for Judicial Complaints', followed by five appendices dealing with a 'Dignity at Work statement', the Equality Act 2010, a 'Letter to all judiciary', blogging by those who hold judicial posts, and amendments to the *Guide*.

The *Guide to Judicial Conduct* describes judicial independence as 'a cornerstone of our system of government in a democratic society and a safeguard of the freedom and rights of the citizen under the rule of law' (paragraph 2.1). This statement is important, because it connects the rule of law with democracy, rather than depicting the two concepts as in tension, with populist urges colliding with legal principles. The *Guide* then cites the text of the judicial oath, which reads, 'I will do right to all manner of people after the laws and usages of this Realm, without fear or favour, affection or ill-will.' The text depicts these words as confirming that a judge 'is primarily accountable to the law which he or she must administer' (paragraph 2.2). One manifestation of this duty is a necessity to avoid both overt and less obvious efforts to 'curry favour'. Another involves 'publicity'. Outside views should not impact upon the judiciary, though there remains a need to appreciate the important consequences that can arise from the work of the courts (paragraph 2.3). While this principle is broadly sound, in practice it is surely unrealistic—and perhaps wrong—to expect courts to exclude external currents of opinion completely and at all times.

[3] *Jackson and others (appellants) v Her Majesty's Attorney General (Respondent)* [2005] UKHL 56; Judiciary of England and Wales, *Guide to Judicial Conduct* (London, Judiciary of England and Wales, 2013).

Another key quality the *Guide* identifies is impartiality. Judges, it holds, should seek to avoid engagement in outside actions that might make it necessary for them to decline to take part in a particular proceeding (paragraph 3.2). They must not engage in party-political activity, and they must take into account the impact that personal connections to certain causes might have (paragraph 3.3). If judges or their families stand to gain or lose financially from a case, they should not take part in it (paragraph 3.8). Being known to have firm opinions on a given subject matter might also be grounds for exclusion (paragraph 3.10).

Next the *Guide to Judicial Conduct* identifies integrity as a crucial characteristic. It entails 'exercising equality and fairness of treatment' within and also beyond the courtroom (paragraph 4.3). The *Guide* then deals with propriety, involving in particular the reality or perception of abuse of office. A further principle concerns competence and diligence. There is also a need to avoid the appearance of bias arising from personal relationships.

The idea of a separation of powers has always been difficult to reconcile with the UK constitutional system. Traditionally, executive, judiciary and legislature were all fused within Parliament. There has lately been something of a distancing of the last two branches from each other, through changes such as the creation of a separate UK Supreme Court under the Constitutional Reform Act 2005 (becoming operative in 2009). But in some ways it has made the points of contact between them more overt when they occur. An important development in recent years has been a rise in the number of occasions on which members of the judiciary give evidence to select committees. In recognition of this pattern, the Judicial Executive Board has issued an eight-page text, *Guidance to Judges on Appearances before Select Committees*, the current edition of which is dated October 2012.[4] It performs a role similar to that of the Osmotherly Rules for civil servants (see Chapter 2, section I.C. and Chapter 8, section III.). The document opens by noting that '[f]or the most part', Parliament operates without the participation of the judiciary, and that the occasion of a judge's giving oral evidence to a select committee 'should be regarded as exceptional'. Before the final 25 years of the twentieth century, it notes, 'there were virtually no' such occasions (paragraph 1). The implication, though the text does not make this point expressly, is that they subsequently became more common.

When a select committee requests that a judge appear before it, the inquiry is handled by the Private Office of the Lord Chief Justice (paragraph 2). If a judge does make this appearance, the guidance notes certain 'longstanding constitutional conventions' that it holds apply in such circumstances. They are 'likely to prevent judges from commenting on' certain issues (paragraph 3). These issues are, first, '[t]he merits of individual cases', regardless of whether the given judge was involved in them, or whether they were due to commence, taking place or finished (paragraph 3 I). This 'convention' serves, among other things, to promote

[4] Judicial Executive Board, *Guidance to Judges on Appearances before Select Committees* (2012).

judicial independence (paragraph 4). The second forbidden area involves comment on the 'personalities or merits of serving judges, politicians, or other public figures, or more generally on the quality of appointments' (paragraph 3 II). This rule is intended to safeguard 'the dignity and status of the judicial office' (paragraph 8). The third restriction is on commenting on '[t]he merits, meaning or likely effect' of planned legislation, or on government policy measures (paragraph 3 III). One purpose of this convention is to protect judges from finding themselves in a position where they are required to interpret a legal provision on which they have previously passed comment, threatening their perceived impartiality (paragraph 10). Fourth is matters on which the Government was consulting, and on which the judiciary planned to submit a view (paragraph 4 IV). The text then explains these rules in greater detail, including the exceptions to them. It holds, for instance, that the Lord Chief Justice and Heads of Division are not necessarily subject to the prohibition on commenting on 'the quality of judicial appointments', since this subject falls within their specific responsibilities (paragraph 9). Furthermore, a judge may 'comment on the merit of a Bill or policy' if it 'affects the independence of the judiciary' (paragraph 13). The guidance notes that retired as well as serving judges are subject to it (paragraph 19), as they are to the *Guide to Judicial Conduct*.

II. THE RULE OF LAW AND THE EXECUTIVE

The documents discussed in section I. above focus on the judiciary and the principles it applies to itself, whether in going about its regular business or interacting with parliamentary committees. But maintenance of the rule of law is dependent on other constitutional players too, prominent among which is the executive. An important requirement is that ministers are limited in their scope for action, and that their potential to behave in an arbitrary fashion is constrained. Paragraph 3.24 of *The Cabinet Manual*[5] explains that the 'powers' that ministers possess have three sources. The first is Parliament, 'which grants powers through legislation'. As the *Manual* notes, statute can both give ministers the ability to act, and require them to do so. It refers to '[n]ormal practice' as being that 'powers and duties involved in exercising continuing functions of ministers'—especially when they involve commitments to spending money that stretch 'beyond a given year'—'should be identified in legislation' (paragraph 3.25). This statement implies the existence of a norm that, in some circumstances at least, it is better to define the authorities and obligations of ministers in statute, presumably to ensure active parliamentary approval for their existence. We have already encountered this idea, and the controversy surrounding its precise application, when considering the pre-emption of Parliament (see Chapter 8, section IV.).

[5] Cabinet Office, *The Cabinet Manual: A guide to the laws, conventions and rules on the operation of government*, 1st edn (London, Cabinet Office, 2011).

While noting this preference for statutory definition, the *Manual* does not suggest whether any principles should condition the statutory attribution of responsibilities to ministers, such as the limits and controls to which they should be subject. Instead, at this point it draws attention to the ability to break with more usual fetters. As the *Manual* states, '[s]tatute also provides ministers with emergency powers, in particular that emergency regulations could be made by Order in Council or by ministers as a last resort where existing legislation is insufficient to respond in the most effective way' (paragraph 3.25). In footnote 16 to that paragraph it refers to sections 19–31 of the relevant Act of Parliament, the Civil Contingencies Act 2004. Again, there is no mention of underlying principles that should apply to those who deploy emergency powers, which are a necessary component of a resilient democracy but also carry with them the potential for abuse. Moreover, the *Manual* omits from this paragraph a point it raises later: that beyond the provision under the Civil Contingencies Act, there remains emergency power under the Royal Prerogative.

The second source of ministerial authority identified in paragraph 3.25 of *The Cabinet Manual* is the 'common law'. In a section entitled 'Inherent or "common law" powers', the *Manual* states that ministers possess powers beyond those contained in statute. Acting as 'an agent of the Crown', a minister can, according to the *Manual*, 'exercise any powers which the Crown may exercise', unless statute prevents her from doing so and as limited by the requirement that the funds to facilitate any action must be authorised by Parliament. The *Manual* then refers to this account as 'a summary of what is known as the Ram doctrine' (paragraph 3.31). We have already considered Ram, and the criticism it has generated (see Chapter 1, section V.). Paragraph 3.32 provides an indicative list of the actions that ministers may carry out under this authority, which—it holds—amount to 'any of the legal powers of an individual'. They include the ability to 'enter into contracts, convey property or make extra-statutory payments'. It notes that the common law or 'inherent powers' have contracted over time as the functions of ministers have tended to receive more statutory definition. The *Manual* proposes no principles that should condition the exercise of these authorities.

The third and final source of ministerial legal authority recorded in *The Cabinet Manual* is that of 'prerogative powers of the Crown'. While the powers in this category technically belong to the monarch, many of them 'are exercised by, or on the advice of, ministers' (paragraph 3.24). Paragraph 3.34 divides the prerogative powers into two groups:

1. *Constitutional or personal prerogatives.* The monarch uses these authorities 'personally or on the advice of the Government'. In this category come the prorogation of Parliament, the appointment and removal of ministers, and the providing of Royal Assent to bills that have passed through the necessary stages in the House of Commons and House of Lords.
2. *Prerogative executive powers.* Ministers wield these authorities in the name of the monarch. Among the activities for which they provide are the granting of

> mercy, the conduct of diplomacy and controlling the disposition of the armed forces. Some prerogative powers, the *Manual* records, have been transferred to ministers at devolved level.

The *Manual* states that the 'scope of the prerogative is affected both by the common law … and by statutes'. It has, the text records, 'accordingly … changed over time' (paragraph 3.35). Footnote 20 to paragraph 3.35 cites the 1610 *Case of Proclamations* and the judicial statement that '[t]he King hath no prerogative, but that which the law of the land allows him'. The *Manual* goes on to describe how the courts are responsible for 'determining the existence and extent of the prerogative from time to time', and that this function 'can be a significant control on the prerogative' (paragraph 3.36). It would have been better to state clearly that the judiciary provides a definitive limit on the prerogative. The *Manual* does recognise the existence of the legal principle that it is not possible for the courts to invent new prerogative powers. However, as the text notes, the courts can discern the existence of a prerogative authority that some might have regarded as not existing; and that they can 'adapt old prerogatives to modern circumstances'. In this sense the courts can do more than simply identify, and in practice they can generate new prerogative powers, though they do not present themselves as doing so. The *Manual* refers to a decision from 1989 that the Secretary of State had the ability to seek through action under the prerogative to preserve law and order, even in circumstances when no public emergency was taking place. This kind of decision is helpful from the point of view of the executive, and is perhaps an example of the *Manual*'s highlighting a rule that serves the perceived interests of its authors.

In accounting for the relationship between statute and the prerogative, the *Manual* could be seen as underplaying the principle that the latter is supposed to be decisively subordinate to the latter. It states that '[o]ver time legislation has … clarified and limited the extent of the prerogative, including in some cases abolishing it' (paragraph 3.37). In footnote 23 it cites just one instance of this kind of curb, dating to 1689, namely the Bill of Rights prohibition on tax-raising under the prerogative. The *Manual* then describes how an Act of Parliament can impact upon the prerogative, even if to do so is not its primary purpose. As an example, it refers to the Civil Contingencies Act 2004, which placed emergency powers on a statutory basis. The *Manual* is careful to note that this Act deals with the 'majority' of emergency circumstances in which it might previously have been possible, under the prerogative, to take urgent action. In other words, some potential for such extra-statutory action remains, but the *Manual* does not specify what, or how it should be deployed (paragraph 3.37). Paragraph 3.38 refers to officials in departments as providing advice on prerogative powers, and the possibility of seeking the views of the Law Officers when complex issues arise, demonstrating the importance of these individuals to the upholding of the rule of law.

The Cabinet Manual notes that all three types of ministerial authority—statutory, common law and prerogative—are 'subject to limits and constraints', and that their 'use may be challenged in the courts' (paragraph 3.24). In paragraph 3.39

it elaborates on this point. Noting that 'courts scrutinise the manner in which powers are exercised', it describes the principal means of carrying out this practice as 'the mechanism of judicial review'. It sets out the main means of questioning the actions of ministers through this route. First is that the power to carry out a particular action did not exist, including because it violated human rights. Second is that a power was deployed in a manner that was not reasonable. Third is that there was a failure to follow proper procedure. The *Manual* does not discuss the possibility that a government might seek to bring about a parliamentary enactment limiting the ability of the courts to carry out review of ministerial actions, nor whether such legislation would be appropriate and, if so, what principles should apply to it.

The *Manual* then describes the legal precept known as the '*Carltona* principle', under which officials and junior ministers 'may exercise powers of the minister in charge of the departments' (paragraph 3.40, also paragraphs 3.41–3.42 and footnote 24 to paragraph 3.41). The court case that gave this doctrine its name was *Carltona Ltd v Commissioners of Works*, from 1943.[6] The *Manual* also notes that Part 2 of the Deregulation and Contracting Out Act 1994 allows for ministers to 'authorise any person'—even if not an official—to carry out their responsibilities, if derived from an Act of Parliament and if it would be possible for a civil servant to carry them out. The text stresses that 'Ministers remain accountable to Parliament for the decisions made under their powers' (paragraph 3.45). Much rests on the effectiveness of parliamentary accountability.

How does the executive view the specific concept of the rule of law itself? The introductory statement to Chapter Six of *The Cabinet Manual*, headed 'The Executive and the Law', states that 'Ministers are under an overarching duty to comply with the law' (p 48), citing paragraph 1.2 of the *Ministerial Code*,[7] a passage that—as discussed earlier—has been altered since the *Manual* was published. The *Manual* explains that the central role of the Law Officers—that is the Attorney-General, the Solicitor-General and the Advocate-General for Scotland—is 'to advise on legal matters, helping ministers to act lawfully and in accordance with the rule of law' (paragraph 6.4). A definition of the rule of law is absent from the *Manual*, as it is from the Constitutional Reform Act 2005. Nonetheless, the wording here seems to imply that there are autonomous standards with which the executive should comply. In referring to the need to act 'lawfully' *and* 'in accordance of the rule of law' the *Manual* seemingly indicates that adherence to the rule of law involves something more or other than simply being lawful. The account suggests that the Law Officers cannot compel ministers to act in a certain way, but through their counsel can assist them to remain within the realms of proper conduct. Paragraph 6.6 proposes a wide range of areas over which '[i]t has normally considered been appropriate' to seek their advice. They encompass circumstances in which a contemplated action would have significant legal consequences in the

[6] *Carltona Ltd v Commissioners of Works* [1943] 2 All ER 560 (CA).

[7] Cabinet Office, *Ministerial Code* (Cabinet Office, London, 2010) was the edition in force at the time.

domestic, European Union or foreign spheres. Another circumstance the *Manual* describes, in which it is 'has normally been considered appropriate' to seek the views of the Law Officers, is one in which the in-house legal adviser of a particular department is not certain about 'the legality or constitutional propriety of proposed primary or subordinate legislation which the Government proposes to introduce'. The idea that *subordinate* legislation could prove not to be legal and be quashed in judicial review is widely accepted. But this statement could be read as suggesting the possibility that *primary* legislation could also potentially not be legal. Under the doctrine of parliamentary sovereignty, endorsed in the *Manual*, surely any—or nearly any—Act of Parliament (which is the form most primary legislation takes) is by definition legal, since the law-making power of Parliament is legally unlimited? Perhaps the *Manual* alludes to implied clashes with European law, or with the European Convention on Human Rights (ECHR), which could lead to a court's respectively disapplying the offending provisions in the Act, or issuing a declaration of incompatibility.

The phrase 'constitutional propriety' implies that primary or subordinate legislation could be legal but nonetheless inappropriate on constitutional grounds. Are we to read from this statement that the Law Officers are required to advise on the constitutionality of legislation as a category in its own right distinct from legality, and that if they deem a proposed action to be unconstitutional, it could be correct for the Government not to pursue it, even if it is 'legal'? There is a double problem here. How are we to define the constitution when no such category of law clearly exists in the UK?[8] Furthermore, how are we to distinguish between (i) law that impacts upon the constitution in a fashion that is appropriate, and (ii) a manner that is improper? Does it involve the substance of the change involved—in other words, are certain principles inviolable? And does it also involve the manner in which change comes about, for instance involving endorsement by referendum? The main clue the *Manual* offers comes in the next paragraph (6.7). It reiterates that the Law Officers play a part

> in ensuring the lawfulness and constitutional propriety of legislation. In particular, the Law Officers' consent is required for legislative provisions that have a retrospective effect or where it is proposed that legislation is commenced with two months of Royal Assent.

While these matters are important, they suggest a narrow conception of legality and constitutionality. Furthermore, the idea of 'consent' could imply slightly more than an advisory function for the Law Officers, that is, that they play an authorising role. If they withhold 'consent', is a particular legislative plan necessarily halted? And does this presentation of the Law Officers create the impression that their approval is, in legal terms, something more than simply an opinion, and possibly amounts to a definitive and final confirmation of the propriety of a

[8] But see *Thoburn v Sunderland City Council* [2002] EWHC 195 (Admin) [102].

particular contemplated course of action? Such a view, if taken, would be inaccurate, since it is for the courts to decide upon matters of law.[9]

Other areas of doubt on which, according to paragraph 6.6 of the *Manual*, the Law Officers might be called to advise include 'the powers necessary to make proposed subordinate legislation' and whether or not a particular administrative act is legal, especially if judicial review could occur. A further reason proposed in the *Manual* for seeking the views of the Law Officers can be that there is a prospect that 'legal considerations' will be discussed at a meeting of a Cabinet Committee or of the Cabinet itself. A specific 'legal difficulty'—perhaps involving 'litigation'—raising 'sensitive policy issues' can necessitate calling on the services of the Law Officers. Lastly, they may be needed if there is a dispute between departments over a legal matter.

Further descriptions of the position of the Law Officers come in the *Ministerial Code*. A passage entitled 'The Law Officers' begins by stating that '[t]he Law Officers must be consulted in good time before the Government is committed to critical decisions involving legal considerations' (paragraph 2.10). It describes a 'convention' that the 'written of opinions of the Law Officers'—in contrast to other official papers—are provided to subsequent governments (paragraph 2.11). The Code provides that the advice of the Law Officers can be produced in abridged form when ministers write to each other, or in Cabinet or Cabinet Committee papers. However, in such circumstances the full advice should be included as well (paragraph 2.12). Only if the Law Officers agree can information about whether or not they have given advice, and what that advice is, be made public (paragraph 2.13). This rule creates potential for two types of controversy. One is that there may be a leak of the opinion of a Law Officer, perhaps to serve the interests of an individual or faction within government at a time of controversy.[10] Another is that there may be demands from outside for the advice of a Law Officer to be made public in relation to a particular policy the legality of which is disputed, as happened over the Iraq intervention of 2003.

Another Cabinet Office document, *Guide to Making Legislation*, provides insight into the role of the Law Officers in the government process of devising legislation.[11] It notes that, when preparing legislation, a department must 'obtain law officers' consent to any retrospective provisions or early commencement of provisions' (paragraph 3.11). The *Guide* refers to a 'convention'—described above—that an Act can begin to come into force less than two months after the granting of Royal Assent only with the agreement of the Law Officers (paragraph 10.67). It also describes the Law Officers as 'the ultimate source of legal advice within government, on human rights questions as on other matters' (paragraph 11.100). Consequently, it is made clear that the Law Officers should have sufficient

[9] See D Howarth and S Wilson Stark, 'The Reality of the British Constitution: H.L.A. Hart and What "Officials" Really Think', *Legal Studies Research Paper Series*, University of Cambridge, Paper No. 53/2014, September 2014.

[10] J Campbell, *Margaret Thatcher*, vol 2: *The Iron Lady* (London, Pimlico, 2004) 487–96.

[11] Cabinet Office, *Guide to Making Legislation* (London, Cabinet Office, 2014).

time to consider the human rights implications of a proposed bill at an early stage, through commenting on a memorandum dealing with its compatibility with the ECHR (paragraph 11.102).

As these provisions in the *Guide* suggest, compliance with the ECHR—which is incorporated into UK law through the Human Rights Act 1998—is an important concern for those engaged in legislative business within government. The 1998 Act sought to preserve the concept of parliamentary 'sovereignty'. It does not allow for courts to disapply primary legislation on grounds of failure to comply with the Convention. However, there are clear practical and political restraints in operation regarding how the executive might seek to induce Parliament to deploy its legislative supremacy. Hence there are definite procedures, set out in the *Guide*, intended to monitor the Convention-compatibility of bills from the outset. The *Guide to Making Legislation* states, 'Consideration of the impact of legislation on Convention rights is an integral part of the policy-making process, not a last-minute compliance exercise … Early discussion with departmental legal advisers is essential.' The *Guide* also refers to the Joint Committee on Human Rights, a parliamentary body, and that it will exercise robust oversight of bills and their compatibility or otherwise with the ECHR (p 98). If we regard human rights as an important component of the rule of law then the procedures and institutional mechanisms connected to the Human Rights Act, as described in the *Guide*, are significant contributors to the maintenance of this principle.

Whatever processes—codified or otherwise—are followed within government, the true test of legality comes not from within the executive, but from the courts. The Law Officers are legal advisers, not conferrers of full legal legitimacy. In the section headed 'Litigation involving ministers', *The Cabinet Manual* acknowledges this point in paragraph 6.10. It states that 'Ministers' decisions, and the process by which they exercise (or fail to exercise) their powers, can be reviewed by the High Court'. But the paragraph then immediately qualifies this statement in a way that emphasises executive discretion, remarking that 'the courts will usually hesitate to intervene in cases where they accept that, because of the subject matter … the decision-maker is better qualified than the courts to make a judgment'.

Paragraphs 5.27 to 5.30 of the *Manual* deal with the issue of Acts of Parliament that 'delegate to ministers powers to make more detailed legal provision' (paragraph 5.27). In some cases, Acts vest this authority in 'persons other than ministers', such as the Commissioners of Her Majesty's Revenue and Customs, to regulatory bodies or to bodies with a role in administrative justice. These powers are potentially controversial. There is no clear limitation on the type or extent of authority Parliament can delegate to ministers. It has in the past conferred sweeping entitlements, such as the ability to detain individuals without charge or trial, that the Government has then heavily deployed.[12] In recent years, controversy has centred on attempts by the Government to introduce legislation aimed at enabling

[12] AWB Simpson, *In the highest degree odious: detention without trial in wartime Britain* (Oxford, Clarendon Press, 1992).

ministers to eliminate supposedly undesirable economic regulations. The favoured method has been to create delegated authorities that would enable the alteration of Acts of Parliament, known as 'Henry VIII' powers. The central objection to Henry VIII provisions is that they create a potential for abuse. The underlying fear is that, in the search for flexibility, the executive can acquire powers that enable it to behave in an arbitrary manner, acting subject to minimal restraint from either Parliament or the courts.[13] *The Cabinet Manual* to some extent concedes that there is a debate in this area. It states in paragraph 5.30:

> A power in an Act which enables primary legislation to be amended or repealed by secondary legislation (with or without further Parliamentary scrutiny) is often described as a 'Henry VIII power'. Questions as to whether it is appropriate for Parliament to confer particular Henry VIII powers, and questions as to the Parliamentary procedure made in the exercise of such powers, often arise during the passage of a bill. Such questions are a particular concern of the House of Lords Delegated Powers and Regulatory Reform Committee and Constitution Committee.

The *Manual* thereby acknowledges that some may identify a problem with proposed delegated powers. Yet it places responsibility for dealing with the issue on Parliament, and in particular two committees within the House it has already identified as of lesser authority, the Lords. It does not refer specifically to any considerations of principle that the executive should take into account when devising such powers for ministers and others to wield, or even acknowledge expressly that such concerns as exist might be valid and, if so, what the proper limits might be. Chapter 15 of the *Guide to Making Legislation* supplies a more detailed account of how the executive should interact with Parliament when bringing forward a bill containing within it provision for delegated power. However, it focuses primarily on the need to supply relevant information to the Lords Delegated Powers and Regulatory Reform Committee, including a justification of the need to create the power and of the form of parliamentary scrutiny of its exercise that is proposed (paragraph 15.9). This part of the *Guide* is concerned with procedure and does not consider the substantive constitutional appropriateness of such powers. A further text, *Statutory Instrument Practice*, provides more procedural detail still about these committees.[14] It is notable, in the light of recent controversy about the role of the Lords in relation to statutory instruments, that government documentation should afford such prominence to committees in the second chamber. To attach to the Lords a substantial part in examining the creation of these delegated powers, yet to claim that its role in overseeing their exercise once they have been included in an Act of Parliament should be heavily circumscribed by convention, could be perceived as perverse.

[13] New Politics Network, *The Legislative and Regulatory Reform Bill 2006* (London, New Politics Network, 2006); Joint Committee on Human Rights, *Scrutiny of Bills: Sixth Progress Report* (2003–04, HL 102, HC 640) 7–35.

[14] Office of Public Sector Information, *Statutory Instrument Practice* (London, Stationery Office, 2006) 79–92.

III. THE PARLIAMENTARY PERSPECTIVE

As in other areas, such as the relationship between Parliament and executive with respect to the authorisation of public expenditure, the codification of arrangements touching upon the rule of law has provided a focus for constitutional discussions and efforts to assert particular interpretations. In 2014, the House of Lords Select Committee on the Constitution issued a Report entitled *The office of Lord Chancellor*.[15] In the decade leading up to the Committee inquiry, the post of Lord Chancellor had passed through major changes, beginning with the Constitutional Reform Act 2005. This law meant that the Lord Chancellor ceased to be the Speaker of the House of Lords and head of the judiciary. Furthermore, in 2007, the office was joined with the post of Justice Secretary. It was vital, the Committee felt, that holders of this post, despite these reorientations, continued to perform their traditional function of promoting the rule of law. The Report described this principle as 'a fundamental tenet of the United Kingdom constitution'. Entailing, '[i]n the context of Government … more than simple compliance with the letter of the law', it required a practice of 'governing in accordance with constitutional principles'. The Lord Chancellor needed both to promote this respect and to protect judicial independence (p 4).

The Committee, then, advocated more than a strict legalistic approach to the rule of law, subscribing to higher principles other than simple adherence to existing legislation. As the Report put it, '[t]he rule of law goes beyond judicial independence and compliance with extant law' (paragraph 19). The Committee was 'reluctant to attempt to define the rule of law' itself. However, it acknowledged that an account provided by the late Lord Bingham of Cornhill was 'a useful articulation of core constitutional principles' (paragraph 25). The eight 'Bingham principles' are:

> Accessibility of the Law … Law not Discretion … Equality before the Law … The Exercise of Power [by ministers and public officers in an appropriate fashion] … Human Rights … Dispute Resolution [that is, the existence of effective procedures for dealing with civil disputes] … A Fair Trial … The Rule of Law in the International Legal Order … (paragraph 21)

When appearing before the Committee, the then Lord Chancellor, Chris Grayling, provided a definition of the rule of law that emphasised judicial independence (paragraph 18). His outlook did not directly contradict the interpretations of the Committee and various other experts, but it was certainly narrower than they were. Grayling also tended to downplay the importance of the Lord Chancellor specifically in maintaining the rule of law, arguing that it was a duty for every government member, and all within Parliament. In the course of questioning, he referred to the *Ministerial Code* as entailing that 'it is absolutely fundamental on

[15] House of Lords Select Committee on the Constitution, *The office of Lord Chancellor* (HL 2014–15, 75).

any one of Her Majesty's Ministers to uphold the rule of law' (paragraph 34). Grayling did not, however, specify which part of the *Ministerial Code* created this requirement. When Committee members challenged him on this point, the legal adviser accompanying Grayling eventually clarified by citing the reference in the Code to the need 'to comply with the law, including international law and treaty obligations, and to uphold the administration of justice'. This provision did not use the specific phrase 'rule of law'. Moreover, as we have seen, the references to international law, treaty obligations and the administration of justice were subsequently removed from the Code in 2015 (see Introduction).

The Select Committee on the Constitution saw the Lord Chancellor as having a crucial role in ensuring the maintenance of the rule of law. It was concerned to ensure that this duty was clearly understood and re-enforced. It found existing codes wanting in this respect; but also saw them, if suitably revised, as a means of helping attain its objectives. The Committee noted that the *Ministerial Code* contained a requirement that ministers engage with the Law Officers 'in good time' over policy deliberations with a legal aspect, a stipulation that was not provided for in legislation. In this sense, a code was filling a gap, though whether it was the best means of fulfilling this purpose is another question. Moreover, *The Cabinet Manual* also outlined a general function for the Law Officers in supporting the rule of law within government, again a requirement that did not exist in legislation (paragraph 71). However, the Committee found it 'regrettable' that in their accounts of the functions of the Lord Chancellor in relation to the rule of law, neither the *Ministerial Code* nor *The Cabinet Manual* went beyond the issue of the independence of the judiciary. In the *Ministerial Code* the only reference to the Lord Chancellor involved appointing members of the judiciary, and staff to inquiries and Royal Commissions. While *The Cabinet Manual*, the Committee noted, described the Law Officers as 'helping ministers to act lawfully and in accordance with the rule of law', there was no reference to the Lord Chancellor's having a similar function (paragraph 49). The Committee therefore recommended that the two codes in future iterate that the Lord Chancellor had a 'duty to respect the rule of law' that 'extends beyond the policy remit of his or her department; it requires him or her to seek to ensure that the rule of law is upheld within Cabinet and across Government' (paragraph 50). In his response to the Committee report, Grayling stressed that

> the Ministerial Code, Cabinet Manual and Oath of Office already accurately reflect ministerial responsibilities in relations to the rule of law. In particular, both the Ministerial Code and the Cabinet Manual note the role of the Law Officers in 'helping ministers to act lawfully and in accordance with the rule of law'. The Government does not agree that there should be specific requirement on the Lord Chancellor in this respect, nor that the Code, Manual or Oath require amendment.[16]

[16] 'The Office of Lord Chancellor', The Right Hon Chris Grayling MP to The Right Hon the Lord Lang of Monckton DL, 26 February 2015.

IV. CONCLUSION

The rule of law is another concept that is vital to the constitution yet difficult precisely to define. It involves the intersection between major institutions: Parliament, the executive and the courts. Each of them has produced or sought to comment upon codes addressing issues in this area. Often their perspectives are different; and at times there can be conflict between their views. Once again the way in which codification clarifies has proved to be perverse. At times it can make clear only that there is a lack of certainty about how a particular principle works, or it can highlight disagreements—and possibly in the process heighten the controversy that surrounds them. Yet a solution proposed to such difficulties can be better or more codification, suggesting that this process, whatever problems it brings with it, is self-perpetuating.

However, while codification might potentially help clarify and solidify the rule of law, its operation in this area suggests that it brings with it potential threats. First, codes that contain unsatisfactory or incomplete accounts of important concepts are clearly a problem. A second observation arises from the line Grayling attempted to take with the House of Lords Select Committee on the Constitution, downplaying his special responsibility as Lord Chancellor to the rule of law by referring to what he believed to be the contents of the *Ministerial Code*. It could be that one impact of codification is that a minister can use it to deflect attempts to probe his position. In this instance, Grayling seems to have misremembered or misrepresented the contents of the Code. But even had he been correct, might it be that, rather than promoting standards, the document could have been providing camouflage, acting as a proxy for genuine maintenance of core principles, and perhaps undermining standards through removing a sense that further action is needed? Codification has potential benefits, but we must also bear in mind the possible negative outcomes. The Conclusion to this book weighs these different impacts.

Conclusion

CODIFICATION MATTERS. WORKING primarily through influence upon perception, it can play a significant part in the deployment of political power. Documents shape understandings within and without the institutions to which they apply. They cause those who draft them and read them to think about important features of the UK constitution, what it is, why it is what it is, and what it should be. It might be difficult to establish how events might have played out in a particular circumstance to which a text was relevant had that document not existed. But the difference made to perception and discourse, both crucial to human and institutional interactions, is beyond question. In the field of codification it is possible for them to contribute to alterations in the substance of the constitution. The change may be noticeable immediately, as when the Civil Service was able to provide (admittedly limited) support to coalition formation in 2010. But even if an immediate innovation of this sort is not detectable, such systemic changes are comparable to modifications in a path of travel. Though they may seem only slight when first effected, their cumulative impact can become substantial in time. We cannot predict where they will lead us, but it will be somewhere other than where we would otherwise have been.

Codification is a means of defining how the political system is supposed to operate. It enables those who draft and promulgate texts to choose which rules and understandings to promote, with a view to attaining adherence to them. Codification can also help encourage a perception that proper standards are being enforced, both within and without the environments in which a given text applies. It may also enable those who engage in production of these documents to some extent to create and alter prevailing norms. But codification does not solely serve the objectives of those who codify, and it can work against them. Codes are generally self-enforced. That is to say, clear means of independent adjudication and binding enforcement are lacking. Yet it is possible for negative consequences to follow failure to abide by the rules set out in texts. There may be complaints from inside the relevant institutions. Moreover, external observers, if they have access to the texts in question, can make judgements about conduct through measuring it against the arrangements set out in these documents.

Codification has two principal dimensions to it. The first involves the operation of institutions. Foremost amongst them is the UK executive, but other entities that have become involved include Parliament and the judiciary. A variety of needs drive this aspect of codification, including efficiency, propriety, consistency of practice, and relationships with other institutions and groups. These requirements were the main motivators of the process in its early phase, and continue to be important. They arose in particular from the growing institutionalisation of the Civil Service and of Cabinet from the First World War period onwards. The second facet, which has become increasingly prominent over time, involves the development of these texts as public documents. There has been a rising expectation that government should be more open about its practices and internal regulations. These two strands of codification must be considered in combination with each other. Between them they mean that it can empower those who engage in the production of texts, but also that they are in practice subject to an increasingly complex set of expectations, standards and rules. The position rarely straightforwardly favours one player or group over others. Moreover, the two strands of codification, the internal and the outward facing, are in some senses in conflict with each another. Individuals within institutions may be uncomfortable with the idea of documents pertaining to their operational rules and practices finding their way into the open. Yet external scrutiny can promote adherence to codes. Moreover, constitutional branches can regard publication as a useful way of enhancing the legitimacy of the provisions they contain.

The deluge of documentation surveyed in this book should always be considered with some important qualifications in mind. However many of these texts we may know about, there are others of which we are not aware, that may contain within them some important constitutional insights. It may be that they are simply neglected, available but unseen on an obscure part of an official website. There are other documents that are deliberately concealed, because their content is deemed too sensitive. A further observation connected to the quantity of these codes is that for those documents that are publicly disseminated, the readership outside government is not vast. It presumably does not extend far beyond some parliamentary staff, journalists and academics—few of whom would read more than one or two texts, and then not in their entirety. Indeed, each new code that appears makes it more difficult properly to appreciate the full body of work in existence. Volume is also relevant to the internal use of these documents by those to whom they are supposed to apply. Officials who wanted to spend the time necessary to familiarise themselves with the content of all the codes that were relevant to them, and then seek to apply them thoroughly in their day-to-day professional lives, might find they had little time left to perform their jobs in practice. Undoubtedly these texts are referred to and relied upon by practitioners and observers. But this usage probably takes place more for specific purposes—for instance Civil Service recruitment, induction, training, appraisal and promotion, or when some kind of problem has appeared—than on a daily basis.

I. CLASSIFYING CODIFICATION

The following set of typologies encompasses different features of the codes themselves.

A. Content

In terms of its content, codification may comprise some combination of the following:

a) the compilation of existing written statements of principle into a larger whole (for instance, the *Precedent Book* or *Estacode*);
b) accounts in its own words, or summaries of, those pre-existing documents (for instance, in the *Directory of Civil Service Guidance*);
c) more original work, though potentially describing well-established arrangements (for instance, the *Armstrong Memorandum*), or otherwise setting out new practices, avowedly or otherwise (for instance, the devolution *Memorandum of Understanding* when first issued, or some of the arrangements around elections in *The Cabinet Manual*).

Codes may describe:

a) conventions (for instance, the numerous references to conventions in the *Guide to Making Legislation*);
b) practices and customs (they may not always be easy to distinguish from conventions). An example of practices comes with the references in *The Cabinet Manual* to when and where Cabinet meets. To change the day on which Cabinet meets might attract some attention, but it would not amount to the clear violation of a rule. To appoint a UK minister who sat in neither House of Parliament and had no intention of doing so, though strictly within the law, might well be a violation of a rule;
c) procedures (more systematic than practices and customs), for instance the different guidance that has been issued on consultation and its references to the practical approach that government departments should take when holding consultations, some of the operational descriptions in *Responding to Emergencies* and significant portions of the *Guide to Making Legislation*;
d) constitutional principles (such as the opening passages of *The Cabinet Manual* describing the key features of the UK constitution, including parliamentary sovereignty, constitutional monarchy and parliamentary democracy);
e) ethical standards (they may sometimes be difficult to disentangle from other items in this list, but take in the efforts in texts such as the *Civil Service Management Code* and the *Ministerial Code* to separate the private interests of office holders from their public roles); and
f) statutory provisions and common law.

B. Process

The process leading to the appearance of a code may involve:

a) an in-house operation carried out by a single institution, subject to varying degrees of secrecy or openness (such as *Responding to Emergencies* or, at the more transparent end of the scale, the *Guide to Judicial Conduct*);
b) an in-house operation with consultation, for instance with the public or parliamentary committees. There is possibly a distinction here between the producing institution's actively seeking views on a draft text (as with *The Cabinet Manual*) and bodies such as select committees choosing to comment on existing documents with a view to securing changes in a future edition (as with the *Ministerial Code*);
c) discussion and agreement between two or more groups (for instance, the devolution *Memorandum of Understanding*, or *The Compact* between central government and representatives of civil society).

C. Availability

The circulation of the document may be:

a) internal to the institution involved and possibly classified, or at least considered confidential, with its very existence as well as content potentially concealed (as was *Questions of Procedure for Ministers* until 1992). A document may possibly be only selectively available within an institution, as was the *Precedent Book*;
b) publicly available (as with numerous documents since the 1990s). The extent to which the availability of a document is actually promoted by its authors or by the media, or simply on offer to those who find out about it and seek a copy, varies. (Texts such as *The Cabinet Manual* and the *Ministerial Code* secured significant attention; many others, such as *Responding to Emergencies*, are more obscure, though could swiftly gain in public salience in certain circumstances.) Technological advances have changed the parameters here. It is generally far easier, both for outsiders and officials, to learn about the existence of and gain access to a document posted online than it was to obtain a copy if it was theoretically published but only available in a location such as the House of Commons Library.

D. Audience

This distinction can be closely connected both to the intended audience and the purpose of the text. The former may be:

a) people working within the institutions concerned with the given document, such as officials or ministers (the primary purpose of texts such as the *Guide to Making Legislation*);

b) people outside these institutions, including opinion formers and commentators, and the wider public (reaching these groups was part of the intention lying behind *The Cabinet Manual*).

E. Purpose

The purposes of a text can include:

a) the internal management of given institutions (as with the *Civil Service Management Code*);
b) the promotion of overarching ethical standards (as with *The seven principles of public life*);
c) the promotion of key constitutional principles (as with the *Civil Service Code*);
d) the handling of relations between different institutions (as with the Osmotherly Rules and the devolution *Memorandum of Understanding*)—or wider still, in the case of *The Compact*, between the UK executive and 'civil society';
e) the promotion of public confidence in institutions and the political system (as with the *Ministerial Code*);
f) to anticipate and prevent difficulties before they arise (as with portions of *Questions of Procedure for Ministers* in the past and the initial draft of *The Cabinet Manual* with respect to the possibility of an inconclusive General Election in 2010);
g) to respond to specific problems that have occurred (as with various alterations to the rules applying to special advisers);
h) clarification to remove uncertainty (such as the *Armstrong Memorandum*, intended to make clear the constitutional position of civil servants);
i) the acknowledgement of uncertainty (as with some of the account of the circumstances in which a Prime Minister resigns in *The Cabinet Manual*);
j) to expand upon or transpose existing arrangements, avowedly or otherwise (as with *The Cabinet Manual's* extension of pre-election rules to the post-election period);
k) to manage the consequences of major constitutional changes (as with the devolution *Memorandum of Understanding*);
l) to create entirely new arrangements, avowedly or otherwise (as with the early draft of *The Cabinet Manual* creating a specific possibility for Civil Service support for coalition negotiations).

At times it may possibly be difficult to distinguish purposes j), k) and l) from one another).

F. Issuing Power

The legal basis for the issuance of codes may be:

a) non-statutory, that is the Royal Prerogative (as with most of the codes considered here);
b) statutory. It is arguable that a code with a statutory basis is something qualitatively different from the other types of code considered here. However, it is notable that certain codes, in particular those applying to civil servants and special advisers, did not initially possess a statutory footing, which they then acquired through the Constitutional Reform and Governance Act 2010; and that this transition may be a new phase in the broader codification trend that is the subject of this work.

II. THE HISTORIC EMERGENCE OF CODIFICATION

Any attempt to identify a precise start point to the codification process is difficult. It is convenient to identify the introduction of minuted (War) Cabinet meetings late in 1916 as an important initiating point. This change brought with it both new practices and staff, and an institution in the nascent Cabinet Office. All of them created momentum for the production of systemic texts, to which the unification of the Civil Service under Treasury control shortly after the First World War added. By the early 1950s—with *Eastacode, Questions of Procedure for Ministers* and the *Precedent Book* all in existence and in use in Whitehall—the first full stage of codification had taken hold. The second began to come clearly into effect in the 1980s with the publication of such documents as the *Armstrong Memorandum*. Increasingly, codes became publicly available, and were sometimes designed specifically with a wider audience in mind. By the first decade of the twenty-first century codification had spread firmly to constitutional branches other than the UK executive, including Parliament and the judiciary.

Without being planned in this way, a process the initial impetus for which originated largely inside the UK executive blossomed into a public, pan-constitutional phenomenon. Interests external to Whitehall—the media, think tanks, pressure groups, parliamentary committees, the Committee on Standards in Public Life and so on—all contributed to it. Various branches of the constitution—judicial, legislative, devolved—joined the process, creating their own texts. Through *The Compact*, even civil society supposedly became a party to a code. In many ways these developments attest to the health of UK democracy as a pluralist, open environment. The efforts of the executive to retain secrecy proved unsustainable, and eventually it embraced the idea of publication (in some but not all cases). Moreover, there was a political infrastructure spread across places such as Parliament and other official institutions, and in civil society, necessary to maintaining a discourse about the texts, and prompting alterations to them, or even the production of new documents.

But the use of the term 'public' should be qualified. First, as already suggested, among the general population, levels of interest in or knowledge of these codes have been limited. Relevant passages from the *Ministerial Code* have managed to attain relatively wide recurring attention at times of scandal. The draft of *The Cabinet Manual* filtered into discussion around the time of the inconclusive General Election of 2010.[1] But even these uses of documents do not equate to full popular awareness of them, or even what they are called. The code that has probably attained the greatest degree of public consciousness and name recognition, though it is slightly different from the others, is the Barnett Formula. Few would or could truthfully purport to understand it completely (and I share in this lack of comprehension). But it achieves traction partly because of the darker instincts with which it is connected, such as envy, greed, resentment and national rivalry. In as far as it has achieved notoriety through this route, the Formula raises an important feature of public codification. Codes often receive attention for negative reasons, because of problematic incidents or disagreements. Any efforts to promote them in a more positive sense, or as important statements in their own right, have achieved less impact than have these contentious associations. Positive dissemination is limited anyway. The texts are neither displayed on public buildings nor taught in schools. Indeed, it is difficult to identify passages within them that would be suited to such purposes—resonant proclamations of self-evident truths and universal norms are conspicuously lacking. Perhaps *The seven principles of public life* comes closest to attaining this quality, and is probably the most widely reproduced of these documents, though mainly in other codes.

A second reservation regarding the idea of these texts as 'public' is that the means by which they are produced generally remains exclusive. Their production is often formally reserved to one particular institution, albeit potentially subject to outside influence. The public are now entitled to read texts (though some remain secret) and comment on them, perhaps by way of official consultation. But it would be misleading to claim that codification is fully public-owned. The subject matter these documents address—and can impact upon—is vital to the UK democratic system, but they do not rest on as wide a consensual footing as they might. The idea of unilateral statements of conventions, when they apply to more than one constitutional player, is particularly problematic, especially when those conventions are disputed. That codification falls short in this respect is a shortcoming in particular need of correction.

III. THE DEVELOPMENT OF CODIFICATION

As an historic process codification is connected to wider developments of the times in which it occurred. It was clearly associated with the rise of formalised

[1] I used it, for instance, in background briefing to the mainstream *One Show* on BBC 1 television, before appearing on it in May 2010 to talk about the Election.

administration supported by a permanent Civil Service. Texts served the needs of this system of governance. They might also have helped to manage changes in the way it operated, including when potential challenges to its principles arose, such as the use of special advisers. Codification, especially from its second phase onwards, was also linked to constitutional tensions within the UK. A heightened tendency for critical public scrutiny of governmental institutions created a perceived need not only for the existence of effective regulation, but for the relevant documents to be published for all to see. It is tempting to conclude that, more than allaying concerns, this form of openness created frameworks that formed a basis for more challenging of official conduct, and created an expectation for more codification still. Technological trends—most notably the spread of the Internet—have made the dissemination of such texts far easier and probably more likely to take place (though the actual audience is in practice limited), as well as perhaps adding to the general impression that the public are entitled to access them. Another area of constitutional stress reflected in codification is horizontal as opposed to vertical in nature. That is to say, rather than involving a tension between governors and governed, it engages the relationship between different parts of the constitution. The *Osmotherly Rules*, for instance, were an effort by the UK executive to regulate its engagement with Parliament. The devolution *Memorandum of Understanding* represented an attempt to ensure smooth dealings between the UK and devolved administrations. Codification could in a sense be seen as a proxy for a decline in more informal methods of operating, and as amounting to a recognition that there was less trust between individuals and groups in their relations with each other. Another way of viewing it would be as the product of a healthy desire to establish clarity and transparency in important constitutional interactions. More broadly still, codification could be seen as the outgrowth of a general social trend for the formalisation and routinisation of relationships and working objectives that can be found across public and private sectors alike.

The devolution *Memorandum of Understanding* was also a manifestation of a further connection between codification and underlying dynamics in the UK constitution. In the period since the 1950s, many interconnected systemic upheavals have taken place. They have included participation in European integration, the rise of judicial review, freedom of information and reform of the House of Lords. Devolution, one of the most important reforms of all, necessitated the *Memorandum of Understanding*. Other such changes have also triggered instances of codification. The *Osmotherly Rules*, though a successor to an earlier document, were drafted and became public following the establishment from 1979 of the new House of Commons select committee system. Alterations to the role of the Lord Chancellor and other judicial reforms prompted the Concordat of 2004, soon largely provided with a statutory basis under the Constitutional Reform Act 2005. *The Cabinet Manual* included an attempt to provide for scenarios that could develop under the Fixed-term Parliaments Act 2011. But—whether or not the authors of the documents involved admit to it—codification can contribute to as well as respond to change. The *Manual* did so in relation to the rules around election periods and government formation; and the *Ministerial Code* during the coalition period (along with other coalition documentation) sought obliquely to make it apparent that the convention of collective responsibility was likely to be subject to suspension during that particular government. Recently, the *Code of Conduct for Special Advisers* altered the rules around parliamentary candidature.

Another sense in which codification is part of a wider tendency is that it is part of an increase in the publication of official texts of a constitutional nature. A parallel manifestation of this trend is the growth in statutes that can reasonably regarded as constitutional, even if no such legal category clearly exists in the UK. Acts of Parliament providing for the various reforms discussed above fit this definition. Yet though the UK constitution tends increasingly to be set out in official documents, it is not yet fully a 'written' or 'codified' constitution.[2] As paragraph 4 of *The Cabinet Manual*—a text that Gordon Brown intended as a possible step towards a written constitution—puts it:

> The UK does not have a codified constitution. There is no single document that describes, establishes or regulates the structures of the state and the way in which these relate to the people. Instead, the constitutional order has evolved over time and continues to do so. It consists of various institutions, statutes, judicial decisions, principles and practices that are commonly understood as 'constitutional'. The UK does not have a constitutional court to rule on the implications of a codified constitution, and the sovereignty of Parliament is therefore unrestrained by such a court.

The Brown project was not successful, and the UK constitution remains 'unwritten'. But as this book has shown, in describing crucial features of the political system, documents such as *The Cabinet Manual* are performing some of the functions that might otherwise fall to a written constitution. It is notable that the country that provided some of the inspiration—and the name—for the *Manual*, New Zealand, is another one of the small number of states that do not have a written constitution. Moreover, the increased use of codes in the UK might even be interpreted as representative of a breakdown in the traditional UK constitutional system in which tacit assumptions were regarded as of exceptional value. In this sense, there are three different, though not necessarily mutually exclusive, interpretations we can place upon codification. It might represent progress towards a written constitution. It could be a surrogate for a written constitution. Or it could be a stage in the failure of the unwritten constitution. However, we can also find similar documents in countries that do have written constitutions, such as Australia and Canada. Peter H Russell identifies deep social trends across all these countries that have prompted codification.[3] They include changes in ethnic composition, and more fundamentally the shift towards mass electorates that did not exist in the

[2] For my examination of this subject, see A Blick, *Beyond Magna Carta: a constitution for the United Kingdom* (Oxford, Hart Publishing, 2015).

[3] PH Russell, 'Codifying conventions' in B Galligan and S Brenton (eds), *Constitutional Conventions in Westminster Systems: Controversies, Changes and Challenges* (Cambridge, Cambridge University Press, 2015) 233–47.

nineteenth century, when the classic accounts of Westminster model conventions were produced. Texts are needed, he holds, because 'To believe that the citizens of today's parliamentary democracies carry around in their heads a knowledge of the conventions of parliamentary and cabinet government is to believe in fairy tales.'[4] Codification of the kind discussed in this book is likely to remain with us in some form regardless of other developments. If the UK adopts a written constitution (an outcome I advocate), the documents considered here may have played a part in that transition. At the same time, they are likely still to be used, and perhaps provided for under the new constitutional text. On the other hand, if the UK continues its 'unwritten' system, then codes will also still be needed. Nonetheless, codes are probably relatively more important as systemic tools under current arrangements in the UK than they would be if it introduced a written constitution.

Two potential future developments require attention. The first involves the possibility that more constitutional codes will acquire a statutory basis, rather than resting in the Royal Prerogative. In 2015 the House of Commons Political and Constitutional Reform Committee (PCRC) considered a proposal I submitted to it that it might be appropriate for *The Cabinet Manual* to receive 'Statutory underpinning'. The Committee concluded that while the option might seem desirable on the surface, it would prove an inapt 'halfway house to full codification of the constitution'.[5] This response might suggest that the idea at present is unlikely to make political headway. Yet we already have an example of codes that previously lacked statutory grounding being provided with it, through the Constitutional Reform and Governance Act 2010, and in particular sections 5–9 in Part 1, with respect to various Civil Service codes.

The merit of this development is that it facilitates the public ownership identified above as desirable. It makes codification more inclusive, formally involving Parliament in a process that was previously under the control of the executive alone. It provides codes with derivation from primary legislation, but without their being set out in full on the face of an Act of Parliament—an important distinction. Following the model of the 2010 Act, statutes of this variety can either authorise or actively require the issuing of codes by the executive (or potentially another constitutional branch), and they can specify certain basic provisions for compulsory inclusion in the text, and for its dissemination. Future such statutes could make express parliamentary (or Commons) approval for the whole document necessary, by committee or in plenary, if deemed desirable. But drafting and redrafting of the text would not require the full legislative process involved in altering primary legislation, and flexibility could be retained, but in a more accountable form.

In the past some within Parliament have shown reluctance to take on responsibility for documents such as the *Ministerial Code* that they feel pertain to the

[4] ibid, 236.

[5] House of Commons Political and Constitutional Reform Committee, *Revisiting the Cabinet Manual* (HC 2014–15, 233) 28.

internal regulation of an external entity—in the case of the *Code*, the executive. However, this book has shown repeatedly that some of the issues dealt with in the texts under consideration spread well beyond the confines of any one institution, engaging as they do relations between different constitutional branches and vital facets of the democratic system. It is these aspects of codification that any attempt at fuller collective ownership should address, rather than more parochial matters. Another sensitivity for Parliament is that it might, through endorsing certain procedural principles, compromise its control over its own business—known as its 'exclusive cognisance', a central plank of Parliamentary Privilege. But parliamentarians should ask themselves whether they lose more by not imposing firmer rules, in particular with regard to executive accountability.

IV. POSSIBLE OUTCOMES OF CODIFICATION

Some object to the idea of hard legal enforcement of these documents. But a statutory basis for texts need not lead in this direction. As the *Guide to Making Legislation* states, the contents of codes of practice provided for by an Act of Parliament 'are not directly enforceable by legal proceedings'. However, the *Guide* goes on, they can 'have significant legal effects' (p 312). It seems that 'significant legal effects' are a plausible outcome of codification, even if it does not reach the statutory stage. In its consideration of *The Cabinet Manual*, PCRC expressed doubt over whether this text would ever come to 'feature extensively in court proceedings'. But noting that the equivalent document in New Zealand had been used by courts in that country, the Committee concluded that the *Manual* could become 'part of the UK's accepted constitutional arrangements'. As a consequence, it concluded, the *Manual* 'could acquire a legal status more significant than that originally intended'. In the view of PCRC, a court might decide for itself that *The Cabinet Manual* was part of 'constitutional law'. Such a change ought to take place only after a 'process of public deliberation and debate'. The Committee held, furthermore, that should a court try to use the *Manual* in this way, the Government 'must be prepared to intervene … to set out its view of the Manual's constitutional position'.[6]

What is true for *The Cabinet Manual* could apply just as well to other texts that have not yet been deployed by the courts. As this book has shown, there is a large number to choose from—a code for any occasion, perhaps. Parliamentary committees, protective of their territory, tend to evince concern about this kind of development, their members often seeing it as an inappropriate expansion of the remit of the courts, a rival constitutional authority to their own. But in my view a growing use of these documents in court cases could well be a positive development, providing a firmer basis for important constitutional principles. This practice would likely involve documents being taken into account as part of a judicial review proceeding, for instance to discern whether a legitimate procedural

[6] ibid.

expectation had been met by a public authority in its decision-taking. If it were found that a rule had been violated, it might be possible, for instance, to quash a particular action and re-run the decision-making process.

For those concerned about a judicial power grab, it is worth pointing out that courts already make these kinds of decisions, and the increased use of codes could in some senses reduce their discretion, since they would be using a pre-existing text produced by others, rather than relying more on judicially-divined standards. Moreover, courts would be unlikely to involve themselves in disputes over whether conventions specific to parliamentary procedures had been adhered to, since they tend to approach such territory with great caution. However, where they were employed in judicial review, codes could not only help ensure adherence to important principles, they could also promote greater clarity about what the constitutional rules were for parties such as the courts themselves, the institutions and appellants involved, and the wider public. Indeed, bodies that issued these texts might refer to them in support of their own legal arguments. As we have seen, the Government used this approach in relation to the Crossman case in 1975. This relatively gentle incorporation of a clearer, independent form of appeal regarding constitutional rules is attractive, and preferable to the creation of pseudo-independent oversight mechanisms, such as that attached to the *Ministerial Code*, that in reality lack autonomy. It would help complete the necessary transition of codification from a partially public to a publicly-owned phenomenon. A more dramatic outcome would be a refusal by a court to recognise as law a provision in an Act of Parliament deemed to violate a fundamental constitutional principle as set out in a code. This latter form of action would, under our current constitutional system, possibly amount to democratic overreach by the judiciary. But at present it seems unlikely to occur.

Yet though the utilisation of codes by the courts could have merits, PCRC was correct to argue that such a judicial development should be preceded by a 'process of public deliberation and debate'. Strengthening the necessary public-ownership principle, an exercise as suggested by PCRC could provide a wider base of consent to the codes themselves, and afford close attention to their contents, improving their accuracy, quality and acceptability. This process, if it were to be effective, would ideally consider wide a range of the existing body of codes, across different branches of the constitution. A possible approach to the task would involve taking into account the following positive and negative features of codification as it has developed to date:

1. *Desirable features or outcomes of codes*:

— The creation of greater clarity about important principles, rules and practices, both within the institutions to which they apply, and among outside observers.
— The promotion of adherence to important rules and principles.
— The facilitation of the smooth running of the system on a basis of genuinely shared assumptions.

- That they facilitate change which is open and consensual.
- That they anticipate possible difficulties; and respond to the creation of new procedures and systems (such as devolution) in ways that make it possible for them to function more satisfactorily.
- That they are produced on an inclusive basis, seeking to attain agreement to the stipulations contained within them from all those to whom they apply.

2. *Qualities and outcomes to be avoided*:

- The creation of confusion about the arrangements they seek to describe.
- The promotion of particular disputed accounts of the constitution, especially those that serve the interests of the issuing institution.
- That they are deployed as a means of altering important arrangements without acknowledging expressly that they are doing so.
- That they are obscure and overlooked, both by outsiders and possibly those within the issuing institutions themselves.
- That they contain empty rhetorical statements, or unnecessary references to current policy initiatives, alongside more essential and lasting principles.

To be fully effective, this process could strive towards the adoption of a 'code of codes'—a distillation of the most important provisions currently spread across disparate documents, with the agreement of all the institutions that were relevant to their operation. It could seek to clarify matters such as the nature of the 'confidence' of the House of Commons, distinct from the use of the term in the Fixed-term Parliaments Act 2011; and the pre-emption of Parliament by the executive, particularly with respect to the spending of public money. The finished products could have a basis in an Act of Parliament (and perhaps one day a written constitution), specifying minimum content, periodic revision and the form of approval required for future editions. Each section could be consulted as a freestanding item, but would be bound together by this overall statute, and could be compiled as a single text. An important section would be a statement, agreed by the different constitutional branches, of the meaning of the rule of law. It could take the account promoted by Lord (Tom) Bingham as its basis, and might in his honour become another 'name code', as the 'Bingham Principles'.[7] Those engaged in the process should also give attention to the language utilised, and the desirability of addressing the broadest audience possible. They should aim, while honestly representing the text and retaining precision of expression, to include some passages capable of capturing wider attention, to assist in the dissemination of this vital constitutional document. This overall project would amount to a new phase for the codification project, in which the immense effort that has taken place to date would be fused into a single project and given a new, consensual foundation. Based in a firm principle of public ownership, it would represent a compilation, renewal and legitimisation of the codes of the constitution.

[7] For the work of the Bingham Centre for the Rule of Law, see <http://binghamcentre.biicl.org/>.

Appendix

LIST OF TEXTS

The following texts referred to in this book are UK in origin unless otherwise stated:

Accountable Government: A Guide for Ministers and Ministers of State (Canadian text)

The Armstrong Memorandum

The Barnett Formula

CabGuide (New Zealand)

Cabinet Handbook (Australian text)

The Cabinet Manual

The Cabinet Manual (New Zealand text)

The Civil Service Code

Civil Service Competency Framework

Civil Service Management Code

Coalition agreement for stability and reform

Code of Conduct for Special Advisers

The Central-Local Concordat

Code of Conduct for Ministers of the Crown (New South Wales, Australia)

Code of Practice on Consultation

The Compact

Consultation Principles

Core Tasks for Select Committees

Corporate governance in central government departments: Code of good practice

Directory of Civil Service Guidance

Estacode

Extended ministerial offices: guidance for departments

Federal Executive Council Handbook (Australian text)

General Election Guidance

A Guide on Key Elements of Ministerial Responsibility (Australian text)

Guidance on the collective agreement process

Guidance to Judges on Appearances before Select Committees

Guide to Cabinet and Cabinet Committees

Guide to Judicial Conduct

Guide to Making Legislation

Guide to Working with the Parliamentary Counsel Office (New Zealand)

House of Lords Code of Conduct

Instructions to the Secretary

The Legislation Advisory Committee Guidelines: Guidelines on Process and Content of Legislation (New Zealand)

Legislation and House Procedure Handbook (New Zealand)

House of Commons Code of Conduct

The Lord Chancellor's judiciary-related functions: Proposals

Machinery of Government Changes: best practice handbook

Managing Public Money

Memorandum of Understanding and Supplementary Agreements Between the United Kingdom Government, the Scottish Ministers, the Welsh Ministers, and the Northern Ireland Executive Committee

Ministerial Code

Ministerial Code (Northern Ireland)

Notes on War Cabinet Procedure

The Osmotherly Rules

PAC Concordat of 1932

The Precedent Book

Questions of Procedure for Ministers

Responding to Emergencies: The UK Central Government Response, Concept of Operations

Rules of Procedure

Scottish Ministerial Code

Senate Ethics Manual (US text)

Senate Code of Official Conduct (US text)

The seven principles of public life

Standards of Ministerial Ethics (Australian text)

Statutory Instrument Practice

Welsh Ministerial Code

Index

www.ingramcontent.com/pod-product-compliance
Ingram Content Group UK Ltd.
Pitfield, Milton Keynes, MK11 3LW, UK
UKHW020137290926
15471UKWH00003B/536